The Horseman's English/Spanish Dictionary

The Horseman's English/Spanish Dictionary

el diccionario equino en inglés/español

Maria Belknap

Breakthrough
Publications

For information address:

Breakthrough Publications, Inc.
www.booksonhorses.com

Library of Congress Catalog Card Number: 96-079132

ISBN: 0-914327-68-2

Book design and typesetting by Peggy Hurley
Cover design by Tricia Tanassy
Decorative line drawings by M. Theresa Brown
Computer-generated illustrations by Maria Belknap

Printed in the United States of America

Acknowledgments

This translation dictionary is the result of the efforts of many, many people. People who believed in the book and people who believed in me. They gave of themselves and their time freely, without expectation, and for that I shall always remain thankful. Of these, there are a few special souls I will mention: Madelyn Larsen, my editor at Howell Bookhouse, who believed in my vision enough to publish the dictionary the first time, and Lisa Mooney of Breakthrough Publications, for taking it to a second edition; Dr. Walter de la Brosse for his friendship and help with the difficult translations; John Hall for the countless hours he spent proofreading the Spanish text; Michelle Perez, who so willingly, and for so long, picked up the slack with a smile; and Jesse Mendoza, Luis Sanchez Tena, Pablo Rincon Gallando, Dr. Greg Ugarte, Rafael Bourdieu, and D. Wayne Lukas, for their yeoman efforts.

The publisher wishes to thank Sonya Manes and Elizabeth Shaw for their editorial services in both English and Spanish; Theresa Brown for her illustrations; Peggy Hurley for design and typesetting; Tricia Tanassy for jacket art and design; and Boris Zambrano for his advice on Spanish regionalisms.

*To Glen,
for having made a young girl's
dream of horses a reality.*

Contents

List of Illustrations xiii
Foreword xv
Guide to Spanish Pronunciation xix
Introduction xxix

1. The Horse

Horse and Pony Breeds 1
Classifications of Horses 4
Points of the Horse 5
Conformation of the Horse 9
Colors of the Horse 16
Markings of the Horse 18
Measuring the Horse 19
Blemishes of the Horse 20
Identifying the Horse 21
Vices of the Horse 22
Temperament of the Horse 23
Breeding the Horse 24
Ailments and Diseases of the Horse 28
Veterinary Equipment 39
Veterinary Treatments 39
Veterinary Medications 42
Feeding 43
Types of Feed 45
Shoeing 48

2. The Horse and Rider

Grooming the Horse 51
Clipping and Trimming the Horse 54
Tacking up the Horse 56
Training the Horse 58
Gaits and Movements of the Horse 60
Reactions of the Ridden Horse 63
Riding Technique 68
Dressage 73
Eventing 75
Hunting 76
Jumping 77
Polo 81
Racing 84
Western 89
Transporting the Horse 90
Showing the Horse 91
Riding Habit 94
Tack 98
Equine Personnel 108
Equine Words and Expressions 110

3. Equine Facility Management

The Equine Facility 113
Facility Maintenance and Equipment 116
Staff Management 119
Payroll Management 121

4. Conversation Basics

Colors 123
Communication 123

Expressions of Time 125
Expressions of the Weather 127
Measures 128
Numbers 129
Salutations 130

5. Illustrations

Points of the Horse 134
Primary Veins of the Horse 136
Bone Structure of the Horse 138
Muscles of the Horse 140
Sites of Lameness of the Horse 142
Set of the Legs 144
Parts of the English Saddle 148
Parts of the Stock Saddle 150

6. 5,000 Everyday Words

English/Spanish 153
Spanish/English 207

Contenido

Lista de Ilustraciones xiii
Prefacio xv
Introducción xxix

1. El Caballo

Razas de Caballos y Poneys 1
Clasificaciones de Caballos 4
Puntos del Caballo 5
Conformación del Caballo 9
Colores del Caballo 16
Marcas del Caballo 18
Midiendo el Caballo 19
Defectos del Caballo 20
Identificación del Caballo 21
Vicios del Caballo 22
Temperamento del Caballo 23
Crianza del Caballo 24
Enfermedades del Caballo 28
Equipo del Veterinario 39
Tratamientos del Veterinario 39
Medicaciones Veterinarias 42
Alimentando 43
Tipos de Comidas 45
Herrando 48

2. El Caballo y el Jinete

Aseando el Caballo 51
Rasurando y Recortando el Caballo 54
Ensillando el Caballo 56
Entrenando el Caballo 58
Aires y Movimientos del Caballo 60
Reacciones del Caballo Montado 63
Técnica de Montar 68
Adiestramiento 73
Prueba Militar 75
Cazando 76
Saltando 77
Polo 81
Carreras 84
Vaquero 89
Transportando el Caballo 90
Concursando el Caballo 91
Traje de Montar 94
Equipo 98
Personal Ecuestre 108
Palabras y Expresiones Equinas 110

3. Administración de Instalaciones Ecuestres

La Instalación Equina 113
Mantenimiento de la Instalación y Equipo 116
Administración de Personal 119
Administración de Pagos 121

4. Conversación Básica

Colores 123
Comunicación 123
Expresiones de Tiempo 125
Expresiones del Clima 127
Medidas 128
Números 129
Saludos 130

5. Ilustraciónes

puntos del caballo 134
venas primarias del caballo 136
esqueleto del caballo 138
músculos del caballo 140
puntos cojos del caballo 142
aplomas 144
partes de la silla inglesa 148
partes de la silla vaquera.............................. 150

6. 5,000 palabras de cada día

Inglés/Español 153
Español/Inglés 207

List of Illustrations
Lista de Ilustraciones

Points of the Horse 134
Puntos del Caballo

Primary Veins of the Horse 136
Venas Primarias del Caballo

Bone Structure of the Horse 138
Esqueleto del Caballo

Muscles of the Horse 140
Músculos del Caballo

Sites of Lameness of the Horse 142
Puntos Cojos del Caballo

Set of the Legs 144
Aplomas

Parts of the English Saddle 148
Partes de la Silla Inglesa

Parts of the Stock Saddle 150
Partes de la Silla Vaquera

Foreword
prefacio

The history of the horse—his strength, his endurance, and his contributions to humankind—is as magnificent as the horse himself. In fact, the history of the horse spans more than 55 million years. Humans first domesticated the horse a mere 5,000 years ago, and it was only in the 1600s that the Spanish Conquistadores reintroduced him to the American continent.

As old as the story of the horse may seem, it is also—and perhaps surprisingly—a very young one in this respect: It has only been during the last forty years that the worldwide interest in horses for sport has truly exploded. Countless books have been published about breeding, training, and the psychology and the use of the horse, but very little exists that deals with the terms and language unique to the horse world.

Indeed, how can we talk about a subject as diverse and complex as the horse without a common ground upon which to base our understanding? As a trainer, I know that communicating my goals and attitude to my staff is not just part of the winning formula; it's the key. If you work hard and you're lucky, winning can become a habit. But this is not a popular psychology book about motivational success. It's more basic—and possibly more important.

I have training facilities across the country, and more than 75 percent of my staff is Spanish speaking. But I do not speak Spanish. Still, we all work as a team to win. To win you've got to set goals and develop a winning attitude. You've got to preach it. You've got to think it. You've got to feel it. And perhaps most important, you've got to communicate it. Moreover, in the world of horses, you've got to communicate highly specialized information and instruction.

Not until Maria Belknap compiled this dictionary did such a comprehensive communication resource become available to English- and Spanish-speaking horsemen. This dictionary not only provides equivalent Spanish words and phrases for the terminology and jargon of those who ride, train, and show, but it also gives some of the common regional idiomatic expressions found in the Spanish language. Bilingual, labeled illustrations of the anatomy of the horse are a further bonus.

It is not enough to say that this book is the first of its kind. It must be acknowledged as an important and necessary reference for horsemen everywhere. For me, it will become an invaluable and inseparable part of my work, which is my life.

La historia del caballo, su fuerza, su resistencia y su contribución a la humanidad es tan magnífica como el mismo caballo. De hecho, la historia de este se extiende a más de 55 millones de años. El hombre lo domesticó por primera vez sólo 5,000 años atrás, y fue sólo en el siglo XVII que los conquistadores españoles lo reintrodujeron al continente americano.

Aunque la historia del caballo le parezca tan vieja es también, sorprendentemente, muy joven en este respecto: es sólo durante los últimos cuarenta años que ha nacido el interés mundial por el caballo como deporte. Numerosos libros han sido publicados sobre la crianza, el entrenamiento, la sicología y los usos del caballo, pero muy poco existe que trata con los términos y el lenguaje único en el mundo del caballo.

En efecto, ¿cómo podemos hablar sobre un tema tan diverso y complejo como el caballo sin tener terreno común en el cual basar nuestro entendimiento? Como entrenador, sé que comunicarles mis objetivos y mis actitudes a mis empleados no sólo es parte de la fórmula ganadora, es la clave. Si usted trabaja duro, y tiene suerte, el ganar puede hacerse un hábito. Pero este no es un libro de sicología popular para motivar el éxito. Su propósito es básico y posiblemente más importante.

Tengo centros de entrenamiento hípicos por todo los Estados Unidos, y más del 75 por ciento de mis empleados son de habla hispana. Pero yo no hablo español. Sin embargo, todos trabajamos como un equipo para ganar. Para conseguir esto tenemos que poner metas y desarrollar una actitud triunfadora. Hay que predicarla, pensarla y sentirla. Tal vez más importante, hay que comunicarla. Además, en el mundo del caballo, hay que comunicar información e instrucciones de alta especialidad.

No ha estado disponible un recurso de comunicación tan amplio para el jinete de habla inglesa o hispana, hasta que Maria Belknap recopiló este diccionario. No sólo ofrece palabras y frases en español equivalentes a la terminología y jerga de esos que montan, entrenan y concursan, sino también incluye algunas expresiones y regionales idiomáticas que se encuentran con frecuencia en el idioma español. Ilustraciones con indicaciones bilingües de la anatomía del caballo es otro beneficio.

No es suficiente decir que este libro es el primero en su clase. También debe ser reconocido como una referencia importante y necesaria por jinetes de todos los lugares. Para mí, será una inestimable e insepa- rable parte de mi trabajo, el cual es mi vida.

D. Wayne Lukas

Guide to Spanish Pronunciation

This guide provides an overview of practical rules for pronouncing Spanish words. With an estimated 266 million mother-tongue speakers worldwide,[1] Spanish has a great deal of regional variation in pronunciation of sounds, primarily of the consonants. Although a few variations are given, the focus here is on general Latin American Spanish. English sounds are used as the point of departure; where they don't adequately approximate the target sound, the differences between Spanish and English articulation are explained in terms of the position of the tongue and other articulators. To further assist with pronunciation and writing, this guide covers syllable stress. Throughout the descriptions, *italic* type is used for Spanish words and Spanish and English letters, **boldface** is used for English words, and "quotation marks" enclose sounds.

Consonants and Vowels

Spanish and English share the same basic alphabet except that Spanish has three additional

---

[1] Grimes, Barbara F. 1992, *Ethnologue: Languages of the World*, 12th ed. (Dallas: Summer Institute of Linguistics, Inc.), p. 485.

letters — *ch, ll,* and *ñ* — and does not traditionally contain a *w.* Though it does not begin any
words, the written combination *rr* represents a dis-
crete sound in Spanish and is never divided when
a word is broken into syllables. All the sounds represented by the letters differ between English and
Spanish, some starkly, others by varying degrees
of subtlety; this guide addresses major distinc-
tions. Two general features, which apply to several
of the vowels and consonants, merit introduction
(and are referred to in several locations throughout
the alphabet list):

1. The Spanish vowels represented by *e, i, o,*
and *u* can be compared to the English vowel sounds
contained in **wait, fleet, goat,** and **boot,** respec-
tively, but the Spanish sounds are held for a shorter
duration. Also, Spanish articulation of the vowels
e, i, o, and *u,* once started, involves little movement
of the tongue and lips. The English counterparts of
these vowels, in contrast, tend to involve movement
of the tongue or lips during articulation and are
diphthongized (a diphthong is a speech sound in
which the tongue glides from one vowel position to
another).

2. Spanish consonants *p, t,* and hard *c* (as in
the word **cape**) are not aspirated (aspirated sounds
end with a puff of air), whereas their English counterparts are, except when preceded by a consonant (**pin** vs. **spin**). For the English speaker, this
lack of aspiration sometimes makes the sounds of
Spanish *p, t,* and hard *c* seem quite similar to those
of *b, d,* and hard *g* and occasionally leads to com-
prehension difficulties.

Each entry in the following list contains the letter of the alphabet (including *rr* and *w*), the Spanish name for that letter of the alphabet (in parentheses), and a description of the sound(s) represented by that letter.

a (*a*) Similar to the "a" in **father**; e.g., *caballo, agua, rápido.*

b (*be*) In the initial position, nearly identical to the "b" in **book**; e.g., *botas, brida, bolsa.* Between two vowels or followed by *l* or *r*, the sound represented by the Spanish *b* is, like the English *v,* a *spirant,* a speech sound produced when the moving together of two articulators partially obstructs air from leaving the mouth and causes friction. In English, top teeth and bottom lip form the spirants represented by *f* and *v,* but for the Spanish spirant represented by *b,* the lips press together instead; e.g., *labio, hablar, sobre.*

c (*ce*) Before *a, o,* or *u,* similar to the "c" in **cape**, but not aspirated (see 2. preceding this list); e.g., *caballo, descanso, curso.* Before *e* or *i,* similar to the "c" in **cell**; e.g., *cepillo, circo, separación.* Two *c*s together are similar to the "ks" sound in **planks**; e.g., *lección, inspección, acceso.*

ch (*che*) Similar to the "ch" in **each**; e.g., *mucho, rancho, cheque.*

d (*de*) At the beginning of a word, before an *n,* or after an *l,* similar to the "d" in **door**, but with the tongue against the back of the top teeth instead of against the alveolar ridge (the part of the hard pal-

ate just above the teeth, site of the English "d");
e.g., *defecto, rebeldo, drogas*. Between two vowels, preceded by an *r* and followed by a vowel, or at
the end of a word, similar to the "th" in **there**; e.g.,
criador, cardón, penalidad.

e (e) At the end of a syllable, similar to the "ai"
in **wait**, but tenser, shorter, and without the
diphthongization (see 1. preceding this list) present
in English (e.g., an English speaker might pronounce it somewhat like "ai-ee"); e.g., *freno, vena,
equipo*. Followed by a consonant in the same syllable, similar to the "e" in **bet**; e.g., *cerca, vengo,
perla*.

f (efe) Similar to the "f" in **food**; e.g., *fusta, fuete,
forrado*.

g (ge) Before *a, o,* or *u,* similar to the "g" in
good; e.g., *galope, golpe, gusano*. That sound also
occurs when the *g* precedes *ui* and *ue,* the *u* being
silent; e.g., *erguido, guerra*. Before *e* or *i,* similar to
the "h" in **hat**; e.g., *general, gimnástico, alergia*.
Before *e* or *i,* the combination *güi* is similar to "gw"
in **guava**; e.g., *lingüística, averigüé, güiro*.

h (hache) Silent in all positions, like "h" in **herb**
(unless part of the *ch* combination); e.g., *hípico,
hecho, almohada*.

i (i) Similar to the "ee" in **fleet**, but tenser,
shorter, and with no diphthongization (see 1. preceding this list); e.g., *índice, quitar, cepillar*.

j (jota) Similar to the "h" of **home**, but with strong aspiration; in some dialects like the "ch" of **Bach**; e.g., *jinete, jugar, traje.*

k (ka) Like the hard Spanish "c" (the sound that precedes *a, o,* or *u*); e.g., *kilo, kimono, keroseno.*

l (ele) Similar to the "l" in **look**, but with a difference: for both English "l" and Spanish "l," the tip of the tongue touches the alveolar ridge (see entry for the letter *d*), but for the Spanish "l" the back of the tongue is arched high in the mouth; for the English "l" the back of the tongue is low (listening to native speakers may be the best way to capture this); e.g., *limpiar, calificar, piel.*

ll (elle) In many dialects of Spanish, the *ll* and *y* are pronounced alike, sometimes similar to the "y" in **yes**, sometimes to the English "j" of **joyce**, sometimes to the "zh" in **measure**; in dialects where merging of "ll" and "y" hasn't occurred, similar to the "ly" in **million**; e.g., *caballo, lleno, silla.*

m (eme) Similar to the "m" in **mother**; e.g., *montura, hermano, máquina.*

n (ene) Similar to the "n" in **nice**; e.g., *nariz, punto, equitación.*

ñ (eñe) Similar to the "ny" in **canyon**; e.g., *dueño, bañar, ñame.*

o (o) Similar to the "o" in **goat**, but tenser, shorter, and without diphthongization (see 1. preceding this list; unlike the English *o*, which the speaker starts with lips apart and ends with lips rounded, the Spanish *o* starts and ends with the lips rounded); e.g., *otro, síntoma, estribo.*

p (pe) Similar to the "p" in **park**, but not aspirated (see 2. preceding this list); e.g., *potro, para, espuma.*

q (cu) Like the Spanish hard "c" (the sound that precedes *a, o, u*) but always followed by *ue* or *ui*, the *u* being silent; e.g., *que, equino, esqueleto.*

r (ere) In the initial position, pronounced like Spanish *rr* (see next entry); e.g., *rienda, rodilla, ropa.* Within a word, slightly similar to the "r" in **right**, but instead of the tongue curling back behind the alveolar ridge (see entry for the letter *d*) the tip of the tongue taps the alveolar ridge; e.g., *pero, cara, pasear.*

rr (erre) Slightly similar to the "r" in **right**, but instead of the tongue curling back behind the alveolar ridge (see entry for the letter *d*) the tip of the tongue trills (vibrates) against the alveolar ridge; e.g., *amarrar, aserrín, recorrido.*

s (ese) Similar to the "s" in **sock**; e.g., *salto, pista, más.* A common variant is to voice the "s" (change it to a sound produced with the same movements of the mouth but with the vocal cords vibrating) to a "z" as in **zebra** when the letter *s* precedes one of the voiced consonants: *b, d, g, m, n*; e.g., *mismo, rasgar, desde.*

t (te) Similar to the "t" in **toy**, but not aspirated (see 2. preceding this list) and articulated with tongue against the back of the teeth (see entry for the letter *d*); e.g., *tiempo, rastrillo, reglamento.*

u (u) Similar to the "oo" in **boot**, but tenser, shorter, and without diphthongization (see 1. preceding this list; the English "oo" starts with the lips apart and ends with the lips rounded, whereas the Spanish sound starts and ends with the lips rounded); e.g., *usted, luces, sucio.*

v (ve, ve corta, or uve) Like the Spanish *b.* Initial position: *vaquero, vendar, vuelta*; between two vowels: *averiguar, aliviado, evasión.*

w (doble ve or doble uve) (Used only for words of non-Spanish origin.) Traditionally like Spanish *b*; now sometimes like *gu* of Spanish *gua* for more English-like pronunciation; e.g., *waterproof, winch, windsurf.*

x (equis) In some cases, similar to the "x" in **extra**; e.g., *flexible, exilio.* In some cases, similar to the "h" in **heart** (or the Spanish j) e.g., *San Xavier, México.* In some cases, similar to the "s" in **sock**; e.g., *xenofilia, xilografía.*

y (i griega or ye) Similar to the "y" in **yes** (see description for *ll*); e.g., *yegua, enyesado, yo.* The conjunction *y* is pronounced like the Spanish letter *i.*

z (zeta) Like Spanish soft "c" (that appears before *e* or *i*) in all positions; e.g., *cabeza, zanja, zorro.*

Diphthongs and Vowel Combinations

Diphthongs are a complex topic, and what constitutes a Spanish diphthong is subject to controversy, but one common interpretation defines the diphthong as a weak vowel — *i* (or *y*) or *u* — combined with another weak vowel or with a strong vowel — *a, e,* or *o* — to form a single syllable. The *i* (or *y*) approximates the English "y" (as in **yes**) sound; the *u* approximates the English "w" (as in **word**) sound. In the case of *iu* and *ui*, either the first or second sound takes precedence (the *ui* can sound like English "w" + Spanish "i" or Spanish "u" + English "y").

ai, ay: hay	*au: auto*
ei, ey: veinte	*eu: deuda*
oi, oy: voy	*iu: ciudad*
ui, uy: cuidar	Use of *ou* is rare.
ia: emergencia	*ua: cuarto*
ie: cubierto	*ue: bueno*
io: ejercicio	*uo: cuota*

Spanish vowels are not only combined within words. The language abounds with words that begin or end with vowels, and when a word ending with a vowel is followed by a word starting with a vowel, two transformations can occur:

(1) If the ending vowel and the beginning vowel (or the second vowel if the word begins with *h*) are the same, the vowel is only pronounced once; e.g., *a* + *hacer* is pronounced as *hacer*.

(2) If the ending vowel and beginning vowel are different, they are often run together: *la* +

imaginación is pronounced like *laimaginación,* a unit of five syllables, joined by the combination *ai.*

Stress

Familiarity with a few rules makes determining what syllable of a written Spanish word receives the primary stress quite straightforward (stressed syllables are shown in italics):

(1) If a word ends in a letter other than *n, s,* or a vowel and does not have a written accent mark, the last syllable receives the stress: e.g., *usted* (us•*ted*), *trabajar* (tra•ba•*jar*).

(2) If a word ends in *n, s,* or a vowel and does not have an accent mark, the next-to-last syllable receives the stress: e.g., *caballo* (ca•*ba*•llo), *dice* (*di*•ce).

(3) If a word has an accent mark, the accented syllable carries the stress: e.g., *está* (es•*tá*), *fósforo* (*fós*•fo•ro), *kilómetro* (ki•*ló*•me•tro).

(4) A handful of words have a redundant accent mark, which serves the purpose of differentiating several homonyms (*de/dé; el/él; mas/más; mi/mí; se/sé; si/sí; solo/sólo; te/té;* and *tu/tú*); certain words from their corresponding question words (e.g., *donde/¿dónde?*); and demonstrative adjectives from their corresponding demonstrative pronouns (e.g., *este/éste*).

Beyond this introduction to word pronunciation, one enters the realm of combining words at the sentence level, at which point pronunciation is inextricably linked to syntax and meaning. Inspired second-language learners will find that conversation and listening practice with native speakers, exposure to Spanish through video and audio media, and consultation with the countless written references available will enable them to speak with increasing precision and fluency.

References

Bowen, Donald J., and Stockwell, Robert P. 1960. *Patterns of Spanish Pronunciation: A Drillbook.* Chicago: University of Chicago Press.

Candela, Salvador. 1951. *Diptongos castellanos.* Montevideo.

Fromkin, Victoria, and Rodman, Robert. 1983. *An Introduction to Language.* 3d ed. New York: Holt, Rinehart, and Winston.

Simon and Schuster's International Dictionary. 1973. New York: Simon and Schuster; *New Revised Velázquez Spanish and English Dictionary.* 1985. Piscataway, N.J.: The New Century Publishers, Inc.; and other standard dictionaries.

Spinelli, Emily, García, Carmen, and Galvin, Carol E. 1990. *Interacciones.* Fort Worth: Holt, Rinehart, and Winston; and other standard textbooks.

Sonya Manes
Tucson, Arizona

Introduction
Introducción

"The difference between the right word and almost the right word is the difference between lightning and the lightning bug."

—Mark Twain

Although human interest in the horse is universal, the languages spoken by horse people are not. Despite shrinking international boundaries, significant language barriers still exist. These barriers are quite apparent in the management, training, and showing of horses by the Spanish- and English-speaking horse people around the world.

It is said that necessity is the mother of invention. Many times over the past ten years, I have been asked to translate "horse talk" between Spanish- and English-speaking owners, trainers, riders, and caretakers. Eventually I realized there was a compelling need for a clear, correct, and precise communication tool.

Ineffective or nonexistent communication can be very frustrating. Worse, when it comes to equestrian activities, it can be hazardous. I have often witnessed situations where poor communication has jeopardized the safety of the horse, the rider, and those around them.

Hence, I have written *The Horseman's English/ Spanish Dictionary*. The second edition of this translation dictionary contains more than 40,000 words, terms, and expressions. For clarity, it has been reorganized and is divided into four chapters—"The Horse," "The Horse and Rider," "Equine Facility Management," and "Conversation Basics"— with multiple subsections in each. The entries within each subsection are listed alphabetically. Subentries are listed alphabetically under the original entry (e.g., the entry "breeding" is followed by four subentries: "cross breeding," "horse breeding," "inbreeding," and "incestuous breeding.") I have also included some regional variations in the Spanish translations, the origins of which are identified parenthetically following the entry: Argentina—Arg., Brazil—Br., Chile—Ch., Mexico—Mex., Spain—Sp., Uruguay—Ur., and Venezuela—Ven. As an added feature, the second edition includes a guide to Spanish pronunciation and an additional 5,000 everyday words.

It is my sincere hope that the *Horseman's English/Spanish Dictionary* will facilitate effective communication between English- and Spanish-speaking horse people. Such communication will ultimately transcend the world of horses and bring us closer together.

Aunque el interés de la humanidad en el caballo es universal, los lenguajes hablados por los jinetes no lo son. A pesar de la disminución internacional de fronteras, todavía existe significantes barreras lingüísticas. En ningún lugar se nota más estas barreras que en el mantenimiento, el entrenamiento y la enseñanza del caballo por la gente caballista de habla inglesa o hispana de todo del mundo.

Es un dicho que la necesidad es la madre de la invención. Durante los últimos diez años, me han pedido con frecuencia que traduzca para los dueños, entrenadores, jinetes y esas gentes de habla hispana quienes mantienen y manejan nuestros caballos e instalaciones. Con el tiempo me di cuenta de la necesidad de un medio de comunicación preciso, claro y correcto.

No poder comunicarse correctamente puede ser algo muy frustrante. Además, he visto que la incapicidad de no poder expresarse adecuadamente puede ser peligroso. He sido testigo de muchas situacciones en donde la escasa comunicación arriesga la seguridad de caballo, el jinete y a todos alrededor.

Por esto, he escrito *El Diccionario Equino en Inglés/Español*. La segunda edición ha sido reorganizada y contiene más de 40,000 palabras, frases y oraciones, para que sea más claro y preciso. Para facilitar su uso, este diccionario está dividido en cuatro capítulos—"El Caballo," "El Caballo y el Jinete," "Administración de Instalaciones Ecuestres" y "Conversación Básica"—con subdivisiones múltiples. Las anotaciones en cada subdivisión están en orden alfabético (según el inglés). Las subentradas están colocadas alfabéticamente bajo la anotación original (por ejemplo: la anotación "crianza" es seguida por cuatro subentradas: "crianza de cruzamiento," "cría de caballos," "procreación en

consanguinidad" y "procreación incestuosa").
También he incluido algunos regionalismos
españoles, el origen de cuales está identificado
en paréntesis después de cada palabra de la
siguiente forma: Argentina—Arg., Brazil—Br.,
Chile—Ch., México—Mex., Spain—Sp., Uruguay—
Ur., y Venezuela—Ven. Para más mérito de esta
segunda edición se incluye una guía para la
pronunciación en español y addicional cinco mil
palabras de cada día.

Es mi esperanza que *El Diccionario Equino en
Inglés/Español* pueda efectuar la comunicación
entre la gente caballista de habla inglesa e hispana.
Esta comunicación últimamente trascenderá el
mundo del caballo y nos permitirá ser más unidos.

1
<u>The Horse</u>
el caballo

Horse and Pony Breeds
razas de caballos y poneys

Akhal-Teké	turkmeno
Alter-Real	alter
American Mustang	mustango americano, mesteño americano
American Saddle Horse	paso americano
Andalusian	andaluz
Appaloosa	appaloosa
Arab	caballo árabe
Ardennais	ardenés, ardenas
Auxois	auxoise
Barb	beréber
Bavarian Warmblood	media sangre bávaro
Beberbeck	beberbeck
Belgian Ardennes	ardenés Bélgica
Belgian Draft Horse, Brabant	caballo de tiro belga, brabanzón
Boulonnais	bullones
Breton	bretón
burro	burro
Charollais	charollais
Clydesdale	clydesdale
Cob	jaca
Comtois	comtoise
Connemara	connemara
Creole	criollo
Argentinean Creole	... criollo argentino
Brazilian Creole	... criollo brasileño
Chilean Creole	... criollo chileno
Paraguayan Creole	... criollo paraguayo
Venezuelan Creole	... criollo venezolano
Døle Gundbrandsdal	gundbrandsdal
Døle Trotter	døle
Don	don
Donkey	asno, burro
Dutch Draft Horse	caballo de tiro holandés

Dutch Warmblood	caballo holandés de media sangre
Einsiedler	einsiedler
Exmoor	exmoor
Fell Pony	fell poney
Finnish	finlandesa
Fjord	caballo de los fiordos
Frederiksborg	frederiksborg
Freidberger	freidberger
French Anglo-Arab	angloárabe francés
French Trotter	caballo trotón francés
Frisian	frisón, frisia
Furioso	furioso, furious
Gelderland	caballo de gueldría
Gidran Arabian	gidranés
Groningen	caballo de groninga
Hackney	hackney
Haflinger	raza aveliñesa, haflinger
Hanoverian	hanoverian, hannover, hanoveriano
Highland	poney de highland
Holsteiner/Holstein	caballo de holstein, holsteiner
Irish Draught	caballo de tiro irlandés
Irish Hunter	media sangre irlandés
Italian Heavy Draft	tiro pesado italiano
Jutland	jutlandia
Karabair	karabagh
Karabardin	karabarda
Kazakh	kazakh
Kirghiz	kirguiz
Knabstrup	knabstrup
Latvian	lóton
Limousin	limosino
Lipizzaner	lipizano
Lusitano	lusitana
Maremmana	maremmano
Miniature Horse	caballo miniatura, falabella
Missouri Fox Trotter	caballo trote-zorro de Misuri
Morgan	morgan
Mule	mula, macho
Mustang	mustango, mesteño
New Forest	new forestal
Nonius	nonius
Noriker	norico
North Swedish	caballo sueco del norte
Oldenburg	oldenburg, oldenburgo
Orlov	orloff
Paint	paint, caballo pinto
Palomino	palomino

Paint
paint, caballo pinto

Paso Fino	paso fino
Percheron	percherón
Peruvian Paso	paso peruano, caballo aguililla
Pinto	pinto
Pleven	pleven
Poitevin	poitevin
Pony of the Americas	poney de las Américas
Quarter Horse	cuarto de milla
Rhineland Heavy Draft	tiro pesado renania
Russian Heavy Draft	tiro pesado ruso
Saddlebred	caballo de silla norteamericano
Salerno	salerno
Schleswig	schleswig
Selle Francais	silla francesa
Shagya Arabian	árabe shagya
Shetland Pony	poney de Shetland
Shire	shire
Spanish Barb	beréber español, árabe española, criollo (Arg., Ch., Br.)
Spanish Mustang	mustango español, mesteño, criollo (Arg., Ch., Br.)
Standardbred	caballo de trote
Suffolk	suffolk
Swedish Ardennes	ardénes sueco, ardenas sueco
Swedish Warmblood	caballo sueco de media sangre, caballo sueco de sangre tibia
Tennessee Walking Horse	caballo de paso de Tennessee
Thoroughbred	pura sangre, fino
Trakhener	trakhener, trakhenen
Welsh Pony	poney galense
Westfalian	westfalian
Württemberg	württemberg

Classifications of Horses
clasificaciones de caballos

beginner's horse	caballo de jinete noviciado, caballo de entrenamiento, caballo de novicio
breeding horse	caballo de cría,* caballo de crianza
carriage horse	caballo de coche, caballo de tiro
cart horse	caballo de carro, calesa
coach horse	caballo de coche
coldblood	caballo de sangre fría
colt	potro, potranco
young colt	potrillo
cutting horse	caballo de apartar
docked horse	caballo rabón
draft horse	caballo frisón, caballo de tiro
dressage horse	caballo de adiestramiento, caballo de alta escuela
driving horse	caballo de tiro
endurance horse	caballo de dureza, caballo de resistencia, caballo de aguante
event horse	caballo de prueba completa, caballo de prueba militar
fast horse	caballo lijero, caballo rápido
filly	potra, potranca
young filly	potrilla
hackamore horse	caballo de falsa rienda, caballo de jáquima
halfbred horse	mestizo
heavy horse	caballo pesado
horse	caballo
hot-blooded horse	caballo de sangre caliente
hunter	cazador, caballo de caza
jumper	saltador/a, caballo de salto
jumping horse	caballo de salto
light horse	caballo liviano
mare	yegua
mature horse	caballo maduro
mount (a)	un caballo
bad mount	... mala monta (Mex.)
beginner's mount	... caballo de jinete novicio
good mount	... buena monta (Mex.)
polo mount	... caballo de polo, jaca de polo
poor mount	... mala monta (Mex.)
nag	rocino
worn-out nag	... rocinante

pacing horse	caballo de paso
pack horse	caballo de carga
pedigree horse	caballo de raza
pleasure horse	caballo de paseo, caballo de placer
polo pony	poney de polo, jaca de polo
pony	jaca, caballico/ito, pony, poney
pureblood horse	caballo de pura sangre
race horse	caballo de carrera
registered horse	caballo registrado, caballo inscrito
reining horse	caballo de cala, caballo de riendas, caballo arrendado
riding horse	caballo de silla
roping horse	caballo de lazo
saddle horse	caballo de silla
school horse	caballo de escuela, caballo de lección, caballo de instrucción
show horse	caballo de concurso
small horse	jaca
stallion	semental
stock horse	caballo vaquero
three-gaited horse	caballo de tres pasos
trail horse	caballo huellero
trick horse	caballo de circo, caballo de trucos, caballo de astucia
trotter	caballo trotón, caballo de trote
vaulting horse	caballo de circo, caballo de trucos, caballo de astucia
warmblood	caballo de media sangre, caballo de sangre tibia
western horse	caballo de vaquero
work horse/draft horse	caballo de tiro, caballo frisón

Points of the Horse
puntos del caballo

abdomen	abdomen
ankle	tobillo
anus	ano
arm	brazo
artery	arteria
back, lower	lomo
back, upper	espalda
barrel	costilla
belly	estómago, barriga

body	cuerpo
bone	hueso
breast	pecho
bridge of the nose	puente de la nariz
bridle path	pasaje de freno, nuca
buttock	grupa, nalga
cannon bone	caña
cheek	carrillo, mejilla
chest	pecho
chestnut	ergot, castaña, espejuelo
chin	mentón
chin groove	ranura de mentón
coat	pelo
coffin bone	bolillo
coffin joint	articulación del bolillo
coronet	corona, corona del casco, margen superior del casco
crest	cresta, cresta del cuello
croup	grupa, rabadilla
dock	maslo, maslo de cola
ear	oreja
elbow	codo, codillo
elbow joint	articulación del codo
ergot	especie de espolón en las patas
eye	ojo
eyeball	globo del ojo
face	cara
feathers	cernejas
feet	pies, patas, manos
back feet	patas
front feet	manos
fetlock	cerneja, nudo, nudillo
fetlock joint	articulación de la cerneja, menudillo
flank	flanco
foot	pata, mano
back foot	pata
front foot	mano
forearm	antebrazo, brazuelo, brazo
forehead	frente
foreleg	brazo anterior
forelock	copete, chasca, mechón, tupe
frame	marco, esqueleto
frog	ranilla, horquilla, corazón del casco
front leg	pierna anterior
Galvayne's groove	canal de Galvayne
gaskin	muslo de la pierna, muslo

girth	cinchera, ruedo
groin	ingle
hair	pelo
haunches	ancas
head	cabeza
heel	talón, talón del casco
heel bulb	punta del talón
hind leg	pierna posterior, posterior
hindquarters	cuartos traseros, cuartos
hip	cadera
hip joint	articulación de la cadera
hock	corvejón, garrón, corva, tarso
hocks	corvejos
hoof	casco, pezuña
hoof wall	pared del casco
incisor	incisivo
central incisor	incisivo central, incisivo
corner incisor	incisivo del borde
lateral incisor	incisivo lateral
intestine	intestino
large intestine	intestino grueso
small intestine	intestino delgada
jaw	quijada
jawbone	hueso de quijada
joint	articulación, coyuntura
jugular groove	canal yugular
jugular vein	vena yugular
knee	rodilla
leg	pierna
back leg	pierna trasera, pata trasera
front leg	pierna delantera, pierna anterior, pata delantera
ligament	ligamento
limb	pierna, miembro
lip	labio
lower lip	labio inferior
under lip	labio bajo, mentón
upper lip	labio superior
loins	ijadas, lomos
lung	pulmón
mane	tuse/a, crin, crinera, clin
mane hair	tuse/a, crin, crinera, clin
molar	molar
mouth	boca
muscle	músculo
musculature	musculatura
muzzle	hocico, boca
neck	cuello, pescuezo

nerve	nervio
nipple/teat	teta, pezón
nose	nariz
nostrils	ollaras
organs	órganos
pastern	cuartilla, cuarta
pastern joint	articulación de la cuarta
pelvis	región caudal, pelvis
penis	pene, verga
point of the hip	punta de la cadera
point of the hock	punto del corvejón
point of the shoulder	punto del hombro, punta del pecho
poll	nuca
rib	costilla
rib cage	costillaje, costillar
scrotum	escroto
sheath	vaina
shoulder	hombro
shoulder joint	articulación del hombro
skeleton	esqueleto
skin	piel
sole	suela, planta
spine	columna vertebral, espina
stifle	babilla
fold of the stifle	pliegue de la babilla
stifle joint	articulación de la babilla
stomach	estómago
tail	cola, rabo
tail hair	cerda
teeth	dientes
canine teeth	dientes caninos, caninos
changing teeth	dientes cambiantes, dientes de cambio, incisivos cambiantes
milk teeth	dientes de leche
permanent teeth	dientes permanentes
wolf teeth	dientes de lobo
tendon	tendón
testicles	testes, testículos, huevos
thigh	muslo
lower thigh	muslo inferior
thorax	tórax
throat	garganta
throatlatch	fiador, ahogador
toe	punta de pie, uña del casco, punto
toe of the hoof	punta de pie, uña del casco, dedo, punta, uña

tooth	diente
tooth grinding surface	superficie moledora
trunk	tronco
udder	ubre
vagina	vagina
vein	vena
vertebra	vértebra
vulva	vulva
windpipe	traquea
withers	cruz

Conformation of the Horse
conformación del caballo

back, lower	lomo
back, upper	espalda
hollow back	espalda hueca
long back	espalda larga
roached back	espalda corvada, espalda curcuncha (Ch., Arg.)
round back	espalda redonda
short back	espalda corta
straight back	espalda derecha, espalda recta
strong back	espalda fuerte
sunken back	espalda hueca
sway back	espalda panda, sillón
weak back	espalda débil
belly	estómago, barriga
big belly	barrigudo, barrigón
cow belly	barriga de vaca
narrow belly	barriga de anguila
pot belly	barrigón
body	cuerpo
balanced body	cuerpo balanceado
compact body	cuerpo bien hecho, cuerpo compacto
close-coupled body	cuerpo compacto, cuerpo apretado
proportioned body	cuerpo proporcionado
short-coupled body	cuerpo en junto, cuerpo apretado
stocky body	cuerpo rechoncho, cuerpo robusto
sturdy body	cuerpo fuerte
body build	conformación del cuerpo
body structure	estructura de cuerpo

bowlegged (behind)
piernas arqueadas de atrás

body width	amplitude del cuerpo
bog spavin	corvejo con esparaván falso
bone spavin	corvejo con esparaván oseo
bowlegged (behind)	piernas arqueadas de atrás
bowlegged (in front)	curvada, rodilla arqueada
camped out (behind)	plantado de atrás
camped out (in front)	plantado adelante
camped under (behind)	remitido de atrás, pata de sable
camped under (in front)	remitido adelante
cannon bone	caña
defined cannon bone	caña definida
long cannon bone	caña larga
short cannon bone	caña corta
weak cannon bone	caña débil
wide cannon bone	caña ancha
chest	pecho
narrow chest	pecho angosto
pigeon chest	pecho de pichón
thick chest	pecho grueso
wide chest	pecho ancho
closed (behind)	piernas cerradas de atrás, cerrado de atrás
closed (in front)	cerrado adelante
cow bellied	barriga de vaca
crooked legged	piernas chuecas
croup	grupa, rabadilla
broad croup	grupa espesa, grupa ancha
flat croup	grupa plana
long croup	grupa larga
narrow croup	grupa angosta
oval croup	grupa ovalada
short croup	grupa corta
depth to the body	cuerpo profundo
lacking depth to the body	cuerpo sin profundidad
dish face	hundida
ears	orejas
lop ears	orejas caídas

mule ears	orejas de mula, orejas de macho
elbow	codo
loose elbows	codos sueltos
turned-in elbows	codos hacia adentro
turned-out elbows	codos hacia afuera
eyes	ojos
cloudy eye	nube en el ojo, nublado
pig eyes	ojos puercos
small eyes	ojos pequeños
wall eye	zarco
wide eyed/big eyed	ojón
feet	pies, patas, manos
fetlock lump	hinchazón en la cerneja, hinchazón en el nudo
foot	pata, pie, mano
broken-back foot	pie con inclinación excesiva hacia atrás
broken-forward foot	pie con inclinación excesiva hacia adelante
club foot	pie zopo
clubfooted	de pie zopo
mule foot	pata de mula
forearms	antebrazos, brazuelos
flat forearms	antebrazos planos
long forearms	antebrazos largos
narrow forearms	antebrazos angostos
short forearms	antebrazos cortos
weak forearms	antebrazos débiles
wide forearms	antebrazos anchos
gaskin	muslo de la pierna
defined gaskin	muslo de la pierna definido
long gaskin	muslo de la pierna largo
short gaskin	muslo de la pierna corto
strong gaskin	muslo de la pierna fuerte
tied-in gaskin	muslo de la pierna amarrado
weak gaskin	muslo de la pierna débil
well-muscled gaskin	muslo de la pierna bien definido, muslo de la pierna musculoso
goose rumped	grupa de ganso, grupa de pollo
head	cabeza
big head	cabeza grande
fine head	cabeza fina
heavy head	cabeza corriente, cabeza ordinaria, cabeza pesada
noble head	cabeza noble
poor head	cabeza pobre

small head	cabeza chica
straight head	cabeza recta
heel	talón, talón del casco
no heel	destalonado
herring gut	barriga de pescado
hind legs	piernas posteriores, piernas traseras
long hind legs	piernas largas posteriores
narrow hind legs	piernas angostas de atrás
sloping hind legs	piernas anguladas posteriores
well-muscled hind legs	piernas posteriores bien musculosas
wide-set hind legs	piernas abiertas de atrás
hindquarters	cuartos posteriores, piernas, piernas traseras
weak hindquarters	cuartos posteriores débiles
hip	cadera
pointed hip	cadera punta
prominent hip	cadera saliente, cadera prominente
hocks	corvejos, corvas
bent hocks	patas de sable
bowed hocks	corvejos arqueados
cow hocks	patizambo, corvas de vaca
large hocks	corvejos grandes
lean hocks	corvejos secos, corvejos enjutos
long hocks	corvejos largos
open hocks	corvejos abiertos
sickle hocks	patas de sable
spongy hocks	corvejos esponjosos
straight hocks	corvejos derechos, corvejos erguidos
well-defined hocks	corvejos bien definidos
wide hocks	corvejos anchos
hocks close to the ground	corvejón cerca de la tierra
knees	rodillas

sickle hocks
patas de sable

buck knees	sobre las rodillas, rodillas de pichón
calf knees	rodillas de buey
flat knees	rodillas planas
hollow knees	rodillas trascortas, rodillas huecas
knock kneed	patizambo
large knees	rodillas grandes
lean knees	rodillas flacas
long knees	rodillas largas
open knees	rodillas abiertas
over at the knee	sobre la rodilla
rounded knees	rodillas redondas
sprung knees	rodillas transcortos
well-defined knees	rodillas definidas
wide knees	rodillas anchas
loins	ijadas, lomos
level loins	ijadas planas
long loins	ijadas largas
narrow loins	ijadas angostas
short loins	ijadas cortas
strong loins	ijadas fuertes
sunken loins	ijadas caídas
weak loins	ijadas débiles
wide loins	ijadas anchas
mouth	boca
monkey mouth	boca de mono
mule mouth	boca de mula
parrot mouth (overshot jaw)	boca de loro
sow mouth (undershot jaw)	boca de chancho, boca de arda
neck	cuello, pescuezo
bowed neck	cuello arqueado
bull neck	cuello de toro
elegant neck	cuello elegante
ewe neck	cuello hundido, cuello invertido
heavy neck	cuello grueso
high-set neck	cuello insertado alto

parrot mouth (overshot jaw)
boca de loro

swan neck
cuello de cisne

long neck	cuello largo
low-set neck	cuello insertado bajo
poorly proportioned neck	cuello mal proporcionado
proportioned neck	cuello proporcionado
short neck	cuello corto
straight neck	cuello derecho
swan neck	cuello de cisne
thick neck	cuello grueso
thin neck	cuello delgado
well-developed neck	cuello desarrollado
well-muscled neck	cuello musculoso
well-proportioned neck	cuello bien proporcionado
open behind	piernas abiertas de atrás
open in front	abierto adelante
overshot jaw	boca de loro
pastern	cuartilla
long pastern	cuartilla larga, larga de cuartilla
short pastern	cuarilla corta, corta de cuartilla
sloping pastern	cuartilla angulada
stumpy pastern	corto de cuartilla
too-long pastern	cuartilla muy larga
upright pastern	cuartilla erguida, pie de mula
weak pastern	cuartilla débil
pigeon-toed	pie de paloma
pot belly	barrigón
Roman nose	nariz acarnerada, nariz romana

Roman nose
nariz acarnerada, nariz romana

round lines	cuerpo con líneas redondas
shoulder	hombro
broad shoulder	hombro ancho
long shoulder	hombro largo
narrow shoulder	hombro angosto
pronounced shoulder	hombro pronunciado
short shoulder	hombro corto
sloping shoulder	hombro angulado
straight shoulder	hombro derecho
weak shoulder	hombro débil
stands close	pararse cerrado, se para cerrado
stands wide	pararse abierto, se para abierto
stifle	babilla
large stifle	babilla grande
lean stifle	babilla seca
open stifle	babilla abierta
tail	cola
bang tail	cola de escoba
broken tail	cola quebrada
broom	cola de escoba
deep-set tail	cola insertada profunda
docked tail	cola mochada, cola mocha
full tail	cola llena
high-set tail	cola insertada alta, cola de origen alto
long tail	cola larga
low-set tail	cola insertada baja, cola de origen bajo
rat tail	cola de rata, rabón
thin tail	cola delgada
tail attached too high	cola insertada muy alta
tail attached too low	cola insertada muy baja
toes out	patizambo
topline/profile of a horse	perfil, el perfil de un caballo
trueness to breed	fiel a la raza, estirpe
undershot jaw	boca de chancho, boca de arda
withers	cruz
bony withers	cruz huesuda
flat withers	cruz plana
high withers	cruz alta, cruz definida
long withers	cruz larga
narrow withers	cruz angosta
pronounced withers	cruz pronunciada
short withers	cruz corta
wide withers	cruz ancha

Colors of the Horse
colores del caballo

albino	albino, zarco
bay	bayo, colorado
blood bay	zaino colorado
brown bay	bayo obscuro, zaino negro
chestnut bay	bayo castaño
dapple bay	tordo rodado
dark bay	colorado requemado
light bay	bayo dorado, bayo blanco, pangaré
mealy bay	zaino pangaré
red bay	zaino colorado
red and white flecked bay	bayo rosillo
striped light bay	gateado pangaré
yellow bay	bayo amarillo
bay with black points	bayo cabos negros
black	negro (Arg.), oscuro, tordillo (Mex.)
shiny black	caballo retino
black with white legs and face	picazo
brown	marrón
dark brown	zaino negro, café oscuro
light brown	doradillo, café claro
buckskin	gateado
chestnut	castaño, alazán
dark chestnut	castaño obscuro, tostado
light chestnut	castaño claro
chestnut with black mane and tail	raya de mula, raya cruzada
chestnut with white mane and tail	ruano
cream	crema
cream bay with white mane and tail	bayo ruano
dun	perlino
blue dun	lobuno
chestnut-striped dun	gateado naranjado
red dun	rosado, gateado rosado
red-striped dun	gateado rubio
striped dun	gateado claro
yellow dun	amarillo
flaxen	rubio
gray	gris, tordillo
black gray	tordillo negro
dapple gray	rucio rodado, tordillo rodado
flea-bitten gray	pardo, tordillo mosqueado
flecked gray	tordillo

silver gray	tordillo plateado
smoke gray	tiznado
steel gray	tordillo carbonero
white gray	tordillo blanco
white-striped gray	yaguane
grulla	grulla, barroso
leopard	leopardo
mouse colored	cebruno
overo	overo
bay and white overo	zaino overo
black and white overo	overo negro
chestnut and white overo	alazán overo
dark chestnut and white overo	tostado overo
odd-colored blue dun and white overo	lobuno overo
odd-colored dun and white overo	bayo overo
odd-colored chestnut with white overo	overo rosado
odd-colored mouse and white overo	cebruno overo
odd-colored with blue and white overo	azulejo overo
red and white overo	manchado
palomino	palomino, ruano
piebald	picazo/a, tobiano negro, overo negro
pinto	pinto
red	colorado
common red	colorado corriente
red and white spot	overo
roan	rodado, roano, rosillo
blue roan	rosillo moro, moro
chestnut roan	rosillo rubio
light roan	rosillo blanco
red roan	rosillo colorado
striped roan	rosillo gateado
skewbald	pío, tobiano colorado
silver	plateado
silver tail	rabicano
sorrel	alazán, alazán claro
brown sorrel	alazán tostado
dapple sorrel	alazán rodado
golden sorrel	alazán dorado
tobiano	tobiano
What color is the horse?	¿De qué color es el caballo? ¿Cómo está pintado?
white	caballo blanco

blaze
lista

flea-bitten white	blanco mosqueado
porcelain white	blanco porcelana
red-speckled white	blanco sabino
rose-flecked white	blanco porcelana rosado
silver white	blanco plateado
snow white	tapado, nevado
speckled white	caballo rubicán
white with black eyes	blanco con ojos negros, blancas anteojeras negras

Markings of the Horse
marcas del caballo

ankle marks	tobillo manchado, tobillo marcado, tobillo pintado
bald face	malacara, calbo, pampa
blaze	lista
body marks	marcas del cuerpo
coronet marks	manchas de la corona, cornillas
distal spots	marcas distales
dorsal stripe	marcas de la espina dorsal
face marks	marcas de la cara
leg marks	marcas de las piernas
lip marks	marcas en el labio
natural markings	marcas naturales, señales
pastern marks	pintas de la cuartilla
half-pastern marks	pintas de media cuartilla
points	cabos, puntos
black points	cabos negros, puntos negros
saddle marks	marcas en el lomo, fajados
sock	alba
socks	albas
one (1) white sock	una (1) alba, uno blanco
one (1) white sock in front, one (1) behind	una (1) alba anterior y una (1) alba posterior

two (2) white socks	dos (2) albas, dos (2) blancos
two (2) white socks behind	dos (2) albas de atrás, dos (2) albas posteriores, maneado de atrás
two (2) white socks in front	dos (2) albas adelante, dos (2) albas anteriores, dos (2) blancos adelante, maneado de adelante
three (3) white socks	tres (3) albas, tres (3) blancos
four (4) white socks	cuatro (4) albas, cuatro (4) calzados de blancos, cuatro (4) blancos

snip	mancha, pico blanco
speckled belly	lagarto
spotted	manchado
star	estrella, frontino
large star	lucero
small star	estrella/ita
star and stripe	estrella y cordón
star, stripe, and snip	estrella, cordón y mancha
stripe (on the face)	cara blanca, cordón, lista
striped (body)	atigrado, barcino, cebrado
stocking	calzado
half stocking	medio calzado
stockings	calzados, medidas
horse with black stockings	caballo calzado de negro
horse with white stockings	caballo calzado de blanco
wall eye	ojo azul, zarco
white around the back and cinch	fajado
white hairs on the face	pelo blanco de la cara
white heel	talón blanco
white inside heel	talón blanco adentro
white outside heel	talón blanco afuera
white marks or spots	pintas, manchas, marcas blancas
white on the right back	argel (Arg., Urg., Br.)

Measuring the Horse
midiendo el caballo

bone circumference	ruedo del hueso, circunferencia del hueso
centimeter	centímetro
girth circumference	ruedo de la cincha

hand [four (4) inches/ten point sixteen (10.16) centimeters]	mano [cuatro (4) pulgadas o diez punto dieciséis (10.16) centímetros)
The horse is sixteen (16) hands tall.	El caballo tiene dieciséis (16) manos.
The horse is seventeen (17) hands tall.	El caballo tiene diecisiete (17) manos.
height at the withers	altura a la cruz
How tall is your horse?	¿Cuánto mide su caballo? ¿Cuántos centímetros tiene su caballo? ¿Cuántas manos tiene su caballo? ¿Qué altura tiene su caballo?
measuring stick	metro
tape measure	métrica
weight of the horse	peso del caballo

Blemishes of the Horse
defectos del caballo

blindness	ceguera
moon blindness	ceguera nocturna
bowed tendon	tendinitis, curva en el tendón
bucked shins	periostitis de los huesos metacarpianos, sobre huesos en la caña
capped elbow	capalete (Sp., Arg.), bursitis del codo
capped hock	bursitis corvejón
cataracts	cataratas
crack	rajado
quarter crack	cuarto rajado, fisura de cuarto
toe crack	fisura de la uña
crooked tail	cola chueca, rabo chueco
curb	corva, corvaza
firing marks	puntas de fuego
mouth deformity	boca deformada
ring bone	sobrehueso, sobrehueso de la cuartilla, sobrehueso de la corona
rope burns	quemaduras de lazo, quemaduras de reata
saddle sores	mataduras, pasmudos

scar on the face	cicatriz en la cara
scar on the leg	cicatriz en la pierna
scars	cicatrices
seedy toe	separación del casco, hormiguillo
side bones	endurecimiento de los cartílagos de las patas
skin conditions	condiciones del cuero, condiciones de la piel
spavin	esparaván
bog spavin	... esparaván falso
bone spavin	... esparaván óseo
splints (without lameness)	sobrehuesos
thoroughpin	hinchazón tarsal
wind gall (without arthritis)	inflamación de la bursa, distensiones sinoviales de la cerneja
wire cut	corte de alambre

Identifying the Horse
Identificación del caballo

age of the horse	edad del caballo
blood type	grupo sanguíneo, tipo de sangre
brand (the)	hierro, marca
brand (to)	marcar, herrar
brand (to have a)	tener marca
branded (to be)	estar marcado
branding	marcando
branding iron	hierro de marcar
cold brand (the)	marca fría
cold brand (to)	marcar al frío
electrical implants	injertos eléctricos
finger printing of horse chestnuts	huellas de los espejuelos

brand (to have a)
tener marca

freeze brand (the)	marca a congelación
freeze brand (to)	marcar a congelación
hide brand (the)	marca en la piel
hide brand (to)	marcar en la piel
hot brand (the)	marca a fuego
hot brand (to)	marcar a fuego
How old is the horse?	¿Cuántos años tiene el caballo?
lip tattoo (the)	tatuaje del labio superior
lip tattoo (to)	tatuar el labio superior

Vices of the Horse
vicios del caballo

aggressive (to be)	ser agresivo
bite (to)	morder
bolt food (to)	desbocar comidas
buck (to)	reparar, corcovear
charge (to)	embestir, atacar
chew the feeder (to)	masticar los comederos
chew wood (to)	morder la madera, masticar la madera
chewing the feeder	mordisquero de los comederos
chewing wood	masticador de madera
crib (to)	chupar aire, tragar aire
crowd (to)	amontonar, empujar
eat dirt (to)	comer tierra, ingerir tierra
eat feces (to)	comer las heces, ingerir heces, comer excrementos
eating dirt	comiendo tierra, ingestión de tierra
fight (to)	pelear
hang out the tongue (to)	arrastrar la lengua, sacar la lengua
kick (to)	dar coces, patear
mouthy (to be)	ser mordedor
mouthy horse	mordelón
nasty (to be)	ser necio, de mal temperamento
nipper	mordelón
nipper (to be a)	ser mordedor
nod the head (to)	cabecear
nodding the head	cabeceo
obstinate (to be)	ser obstinado
paw (to)	piafar
pull back (to)	echarse atrás, repropiarse atrás
pull the halter (to)	echarse atrás, repropiarse atrás
rear (to)	empinar
shy (to)	espantarse

rear (to)
empinar

stall walk (to)	caminar
stall walker	caminador en el establo, caminador de establo
strike (to)	tirar una patada, manotear
tail rub (to)	refregar la cola, frotar la cola
tail rubbing	frotado de la cola
weave (to)	zigzaguear
weaving	zigzagueo

Temperament of the Horse
temperamento del caballo

aggressive horse	caballo agresivo
angry horse	caballo enojado
balky horse	caballo repropio
calm horse	caballo calmado, caballo tranquilo
disobedient horse	caballo desobediente
fresh horse	caballo fresco
frisky horse	caballo juguetón
gentle horse	caballo manso, caballo gentil
good-natured horse	caballo de buena disposición
handy horse	caballo suave
high-spirited horse	caballo fogoso, caballo brioso
high-strung horse	caballo difícil, caballo tenso
hot horse	caballo caliente
intelligent horse	caballo inteligente
lazy horse	caballo haragán
mean horse	caballo malo
nasty horse	caballo necio
obedient horse	caballo obediente
obstinate horse	caballo obstinado, caballo terco
quiet horse	caballo tranquilo, caballo calmado
rebellious horse	caballo rebelde

relaxed horse	caballo relajado, caballo tranquilo
scared horse	caballo asustado, caballo asustadizo, caballo espantadizo
skittish horse	caballo espantadizo, caballo medroso
spooky horse	caballo asustado, asustón
stubborn horse	caballo terco
submissive horse	caballo sumiso
tame horse	caballo dócil, caballo manso
tense horse	caballo nervioso
timid horse	caballo tímido, caballo miedoso
weak horse	caballo débil
wild horse	caballo salvaje, caballo feral

Breeding the Horse
crianza del caballo

abortion	aborto
agalactia	agalactia
ancestry	ascendencia, descendencia
artificial insemination	inseminación artificial
at stud	al servicio
barren mare	yegua seca, yegua abierta, yegua infecunda
bloodline	línea de procedencia
What is the bloodline?	¿Cuál es la línea de procedencia?
bloodstock	caballo de pura sangre
breed (the)	raza
breed (to)	reproducir, inseminar, dar servicio
breed classifications	clasificaciones de raza
breed registry	registro de raza
breed stock	animales para reproducción
breeding	cría, crianza
cross breeding	crianza de cruzamiento
horse breeding	cría de caballos
inbreeding	procreación en consanguinidad
incestuous breeding	procreación incestuosa
breeding ailments	enfermedades de crianza
breeding animal	reproductor/a
breeding contract	contrato de servicio
breeding equipment	equipo de cría
breeding farm	rancho de criador, criadero, yeguada
breeding methods	métodos de servicio

breeding period	período de cría
breeding record	registro de cría de caballos
breeding season	tiempo de la reproducción
breeding soundness evaluation	evaluación del potencial reproductor
breeding soundness evaluation of the male	evaluación de las condiciones reproductoras del macho
broodmare	yegua de vientre
castrate (to)	castrar, emascular
colostrum	calostro
colt	potro, potranco
herd of colts	potrada
young colt	potrillo
congenital defect	defecto congénito
cover (to)	inseminar, cubrir
crossbreed (the)	cruzado
crossbreed (to)	cruzar, mestizar
cut (to castrate)	emascular, castrar
cut horse	caballo castrado, caballo capado
cystic mare	yegua enquistada, ovario quístico en la yegua
dam	yegua madre
dry mare	yegua infecunda, yegua seca
embryo transfer	transferencia de embriones
empty mare	yegua infecunda, yegua seca
equine race	raza de equina
fertile	fértil
fertile mare	yegua fértil
fertile stallion	semental fértil
fetus	feto
filly	potranca, potra
young filly	... potrilla
foal (the)	potro/a
foal (to)	parir
foal (to be in)	estar encinta, estar preñada
foal certificate registration	certificado de nacimiento de caballo
geld (to)	capar, castrar, emascular
gelding	caballo capado, caballo castrado, caballo emasculado
gestation	gestación
gestation period	período de gestación
period of gestation	tiempo de gestación
half brother	medio hermano
half sister	media hermana
half-breed	mestizo/a
heat (in)	en calor, en celo
hereditary	hereditario/ria

heredity	herencia
hobble (to)	trabar, manear
hobble strap	tira de la manea, manea
hobbles (the)	trabas, maneas
breeding hobbles	maneas de cría, trabas de cría
horse	caballo
herd of horses	caballada
inborn defect	defecto innato
inbred	procreado en consanguinidad
inbreed (to)	procrear en consanguinidad
infertile	infecundo/a, infértil
infertile mare	yegua seca
infertile stallion	potro vano
infertility	infecundidad, esterilidad
in heat	en calor, en celo
inherit (to)	heredar
in season	en calor, en celo
When is the mare in season?	¿Cuándo está en celo la yegua?
inseminate (to)	inseminar
jump (to)	dar servicio, montar
kicking boots	pateadoras
labor	parto
labor (to be in)	estar en parto
lactate (to)	lactar
lactating mare	yegua lactante
lineage/line	línea
mare	yegua
served mare	yegua servida, yegua inseminada
mare at foot	yegua con potrillo, yegua parida
mare's milk	leche de yegua
mastitis	mastitis
mate (to)	acoplar, aparear, montar
miscarry (to)	abortar
mixed breed	mezcla
mount (to)	dar servicio, montar
The stud mounts the mare.	El semental monta la yegua.
neck guard	manta de cuello, protección, protector
nine-day heat	calor de nueve días, celo de nueve días
nurse/suckle (to)	lactar, mamar
offspring	procedentes, descendientes
out of heat	fuera de calor, fuera de celo
ovulate (to)	ovular
ovulation	ovulación
papered (to be)	tener papeles
papered horse	caballo con papeles
papers	papeles

parturition	parición, parto, parturición
induced parturition	parto inducido
premature parturition	parto prematuro
pedigree	pedigree, pedigrí
What is the pedigree?	¿Cuál es el pedigrí?
pedigree horse	caballo de raza
performance test	prueba de actuación, prueba de habilidad
potency	potencia, fuerza
pregnancy	preñez
pregnant	preñada, encinta
pregnant (to be)	estar preñada, estar encinta
puberty	pubertad
pure blood	caballo pura sangre
pure breed	caballo pura sangre
race	raza
registered horse	caballo registrado
registration	registro, registración
reproduction	reproducción
reproductive	reproductor/ra
reproductive cycle	ciclo de reproducción
reproductive track	sistema reproductivo
rigging	equipo de inseminar, equipo
semen	semen
semen collection	recolección de semen
semen evaluation	evaluación de semen
service (to give)	dar servicio, servir
sire	padre, semental, garañón
grandsire	abuelo
great-grandsire	bisabuelo
This horse had a good sire.	Este caballo tuvo buena línea.
sire (to)	engendrar, producir
stallion	semental
stallion infertility	semental infértil, semental infecundo, vano, infertilidad
sterile	estéril
sterility	esterilidad
stud	semental
stud book	registro genealógico de caballos
stud farm	yeguada
stud fee	precio del servicio, maquila
stud horse	caballo semental, caballo padre, padre
suck (to)	mamar
suckle (to)	mamar
tease (to)	calentar
teaser	calentador
teasing boards/rails	barda de calentamiento, riel de calentamiento

throw (to)	producir
throw back (the)	retroceso
throw back (to)	retroceder
tipped vulva	vulva empuntada
true to type	tira al tipo, tira a la raza, representa a su raza
not true to type	no tira al tipo, no tira la raza, no representa a su raza
twitch	naricera
udder	ubre
wax (to)	producir cera en las tetas
wean a foal (to)	destetar
weanling	potrllo/a, animal recién destetado
young stock	potrillada

Ailments and Diseases of the Horse
enfermedades del caballo

abort (to)	abortar
abortion	aborto
equine abortion	aborto equino
abrasion	abrasión
abscess	absceso
adhesion	adhesión
aerophagia	aerofagia
African horse sickness	enfermedad equina africana
allergy	alergia
dust allergy	alergia de polvo
anemia	anemia
anthrax	ántrax
arthritis	artritis
arthritis of the shoulder joint	artritis en la articulación del hombro
ascarids	ascáridos, parascaris
ataxia	ataxia
atrophy	atrofia
avulsion	avulsión
azoturia	azouria
bacteria	bacteria
bean	esmegma, piedra de esmegma
bee sting	picazón de abeja
birth defect	defecto congénito
bladder infection	infección de la vejiga
bleeder	epistaxis equina, sangrador
bleeding	sangrando
bleeding horse	caballo sangrante

bloody (to be)	estar sangrando, sangriento
bone chip	esquirla, chip, pedacito de hueso
bone spur	espolón, calcificación
bots	gastrófilo
bots infection	infección de gastrófilo
botulism	botulismo
bowed tendon	tendinitis, tendón botado (Arg., Ch., Ven.), tendón arqueado
break (to)	fracturar
break out (to)	sudar
brittle hoofs	cascos quebradizos
broken leg	hueso roto, pierna rota
broken wind	pulmón dañado, corto de resuello
bronchitis	bronquitis
bruise	contusión
stone bruise	contusión de piedra
bruised sole	contusión de la suela, planta contusa
bucked shins	periostitis de los huesos metacarpianos
burn	quemadura
friction burn	quemadura fricción, rozadura
rope burn	quemadura de lazo, quemadura de reata
sunburn	quemadura de sol
bursitis	bursitis
bicipital bursitis	bursitis bicipital
calking	empacamiento
cancer	cáncer
canker	ulceración
capped elbow	capelet (Sp., Arg.), higroma del codo, bursitis del codo
capped hock	higroma del corvejón, bursitis del corvejón
capped knee	carpitis, rodilla dislocada
carcinoma	carcinoma
carpal hygroma	higroma carpiano
carpitis	carpitis, rodilla dislocada
cast	atorado, atroba
cast horse	caballo atorado
cataract	catarata
choke (to)	atragantarse, ahogarse
choking	atragantamiento
chronic	crónico/a
chronic obstructive pulmonary disease	enfermedad pulmonar obstructiva crónica
cold (to have a)	estar resfriado
colic	cólico

sand crack
fisura del casco

obstructive colic	cólico obstructivo
sand colic	cólico de arena
verminous colic	cólico verminoso
colic in foals	cólico en potrillos
colicky	cólico/a
colitis	colitis
coma	coma
concussion	conmoción cerebral
conjunctivitis	conjunctivitis
constipation	estreñimiento, constipación (Arg.)
contracted heels	talones encogidos, talones contraídos (Arg.)
contracted tendon	tendón encogido, tendón contraído (Arg.)
contusion	contusión
corns	callos
cough (to)	toser
cough (to have a)	tener tos
coughing	tosiendo
coxitis	coxitis
crack	rajado, fisura
quarter crack	fisura del cuarto
sand crack	fisura del casco
toe crack	fisura de la uña
cracked heels	talones rajados
cracked hoof	casco rajado, vaso partido, fisura del casco
crib (to)	chupar aire
cryptorchid	cryptorchidio, criptórquido
cryptorchism	cryptorchidismo, criptorquidia
curb	corva, corvaza
cut (the)	herida, incisión, corte
clean cut	herida limpia
torn cut	herida desgarrada
cut (to be)	estar cortado, estar lacerado
cut horse	caballo lacerado
cyst	quiste

cystic mare	ovario quístico en la yegua, yegua equistada
cystitis	cistitis
damaged back	espalda lesionada, espalda dañada
dead (to be)	estar muerto
defect	defecto
dehydrated	deshidratado/a
depraved appetite	mal apetito, apetito depravado
dermatitis	dermatitis, dermitis
diarrhea	diarrea
chronic diarrhea	diarrea crónica
chronic diarrhea in horses	diarrea crónica en los caballos
disease	enfermedad
contagious disease	enfermedad contagiosa
dislocated joint	luxación
dislocation	dislocación
dislocation of the hip	dislocación de la cadera
distemper	moquillo
distended abdomen	abdomen distendido, abdomen hinchado
drool (to)	babear
dropped sole	suela caída
dry-coat	pelo seco
dysentary	disentería
dysphagia	disfagia
dysuria	disuria
dysuric	disúrico
dysuric horse	caballo disúrico
eczema	eccema
edema	edema
emaciation	emaciación, adelgazamiento
embolism	embolia
emphysema	enfisema
chronic aeveolar emphysema	enfisema alveolar crónica
pulmonary emphysema	huélfago, hemiplejía laríngea, enfisema alveolar crónico
empyema	empiema
encephalomyelitis	encefalomielitis
enteric diseases in foals	enfermedades entéricas de los potrillos
enteritis	enteritis
entropion	entropión
epidemic	epidemia
epilepsy	epilepsia
epiphysitis	epífisitis
epistaxis	epistaxis equina
equine infectious anemia	anemia infecciosa equina

equine influenza	gripe, influenza equina
equine piroplasmosis	piroplasmosis del caballo
equine Potomac fever	fiebre equina del Potomac
equine viral arteritis	arteritis viral equina
equine viral rhinopneumonitis	rinoneumonitis equina viral
exercise-induced pulmonary hemorrhage	hemorragia pulmonar inducida por esfuerzo
exotosis	exotosis equina
exudate	exudado
fever (the)	fiebre, calentura
high fever	fiebre alta, fiebre elevada
mud fever	fiebre de lodo
slight fever	poco de fiebre, fiebre moderada
fever (to have)	tener fiebre
fever in the feet	fiebre de los cascos, laminitis
feverish	febril
fistula	fístula
fistular	fistular
fistulus withers	cruz fistulosa, fistulada, mal de cruz (Arg.)
fly	mosca
black fly	mosca negra
deer fly	mosca de ciervo
horse fly	tábano
stable fly	mosca de establo
fly bites	picaduras de mosca
foal septicemia	septicemia, septicemia en los potrillos
founder	aguado, infosurado
grain founder	aguado de grano
foundered horse	caballo aguado, caballo infosurado
fracture (the)	fractura
compound fracture	fractura complicada
pelvic fracture	fractura pélvica
saucer fracture	fractura en platillo
sesamoid fracture	fractura sesamoidea
fracture (to)	fracturar
fracture of the elbow	fractura del codo
fracture of the navicular bone	fractura del hueso navicular
fracture of the pedal bone	fractura del hueso podal
fracture of the shoulder	fractura del hombro
frostbite	congelación
fungus	fungo, fungus
gall	matado, bilis
saddle gall	lastimado por la silla, desolado
galled horse	caballo matado

gangrene	gangrena
gasterophilus	gastrófilo
gasterophilus infection	infección de gastrófilo
gastritis	gastritis
glanders	muermo
glaucoma	glaucoma
goiter	bocio
gonitis	gonitis
granulation	granulación
gravel	arenilla
greasy heel	talón graso
habronema	habronema
habronema infection	infección de habronema
heat cramps	calambres por calor
heat exhaustion	agotamiento por calor
heaves	huélfago, hemiplejía laríngea, enfisema alveolar crónico
heaves (to have)	estar enfisematoso, tener enfisema
hematoma	hematoma
hemophilia	hemofilia
hemorrhage	hemorragia
hepatitis	hepatitis
hernia	hernia
hives	urticaria
horse pox	viruela equina
hunter's bumps	chinchón de cazador
hurt withers	matado en la cruz
hyperlipemia	hiperlipemia
hyperthermia	hipertermia
hypothermia	hipotermia
illness	enfermedad
immobile	inmóvil
impaction	impactación
colon impaction	impactación del colón
intestine impaction	impactación del intestino, impactación de la tripa
infected	infectado/a, infecto/a
infection	infección
infectious	infeccioso/a
inflammation	inflamación
acute inflammation	inflamación grave
chronic inflammation	inflamación crónica
inflammation of the fetlock	inflamación del nudo
inflammation of the hock	inflamación del corvejón
inflammation of the stifle	inflamación de la babilla
injury	daño, herida
jaundice	ictericia
keratoma	queratoma

kidney failure	falla de los riñones
laceration	laceración
lame	cojo/a
lame in the foot	cojo en el pie, cojo en la pata, manco (Arg.)
lame in the leg	cojo en la pierna, rengo (Arg.)
laminitis	laminitis
laryngeal hemiplegia	hemiplejía laríngea
laryngitis	laringitis
lesion	lesión
lethargic horse	caballo letárgico/a, caballo aletargado
lethargy	letargo
lice	piojo
limp (to)	cojear
limping	está cojeando
lipoma	lipoma
lockjaw	trismo
lose the appetite (to)	perder el apetito
lose the hair (to)	perder el pelo
loss of appetite	pérdida de apetito
loss of hair	pérdida de pelo
lymphangitis	linfangitis ulcerante equina
maggots	cresas, gusanos
mange	roña, sarna
mangy	sarnoso/a
meningitis	meningitis
mites	aradores
ear mites	aradores de las orejas
mange mites	aradores de sarnas
moon blindness	ceguera nocturna
mosquito	mosquito
mosquito bites	picaduras de mosquito
motion sickness	mareo, enfermedad de movimiento, enfermedad de moción
muscle spasm	espasmo de músculo
muscle tear	desgarro del músculo
muscle tremor	temblor de músculo
narcosis	narcosis
nasal discharge	moquillo
navicular disease	enfermedad navicular, navicular
obesity	obesidad del caballo, gordura
off (to be)	estar coja
off behind	está coja en el trasero
off in front	está coja en la delantera
off in the left front leg	está coja en la pierna izquierda delantera

off in the left hind leg	está coja en la pierna izquierda trasera
off in the right front leg	está coja en la pierna derecha delantera
off in the right hind leg	está coja en la pierna derecha trasera
osselets	huesecillos, osteítis
osteitis	osteítis
osteomyelitis	osteomielitis
oxyuris	oxiuria
oxyuris infection	infección de oxiuria
pale membranes in the nose and mouth	membranas claras en la nariz y la boca
paralysis	parálisis
parasites, external	parásitos externos
parasites, internal	parásitos internos
parascaris	parascaris
parascaris infection	infección de parascaris
patellar luxation	luxación de la patela
pedal osteitis	osteítis podal
periodic ophthalmia	ceguera nocturna
peritonitis	peritonitis
pleuresy	pleuresía
pneumonia	pulmonía, neumonía
poisoned (to be)	estar envenenado
poisoning	envenenamiento
blood poisoning	envenenamiento de la sangre
chemical poisoning	envenenamiento químico
digestive poisoning	envenenamiento digestivo
lead poisoning	saturnismo
plant poisoning	envenenamiento por plantas
poll evil	úlcera de la nuca
proud flesh	mejido granulado
pumiced hoof	casco pómez
pyramidal disease	enfermedad piramidal
quittor	gabarro
rabies	rabia, hidrofobia
rapid pulse	pulso rápido
rash	sarpullido
rhinopneumonitis	rinoneumonitis equina viral
ring bone	sobrehueso, sobrehueso de la cuartilla, sobrehueso de la corona
ring worm	tiña
roaring	huélfago, roncando
rough coat	pelo seca
rupture	ruptura, hernia

salmonellosis	salmonelosis
scab (the)	costra
scab (to)	costrar
scabies	sarna
scours	diarrea
scratches	rasguños, raspaduras
seedy toe	separación del casco, separación de la punta del casco, hormiguillo, separación de la uña
sesamoiditis	sesamoiditis
sheared heels	asimetría del talón
shock	choque
shoe-boil	capelet (Sp., Arg.), higroma del codo, bursitis del codo
sick	enfermo/a
sick horse	caballo enfermo
side bones	endurecimiento de los cartílagos laterales de las patas
skin condition	dermatitis
skin disease	dermatosis, enfermedad de la piel
snake bite	mordedura de serpiente
sore back	espalda dolorida
sore knee	rodilla adolorida
sore muscles	músculos lastimados, músculos adoloridos
sore shins	tibias doloridas
sores	lastimados, úlceras, heridas
back sores	heridas en la espalda, úlceras
cinch sores	úlceras de cincha
saddle sores	mataduras
summer sores	lastimados de verano, ulceraciones de verano
spavin	esparaván
blood spavin	esparaván venoso
bog spavin	esparaván falso
bone spavin	esparaván óseo
occult spavin	esparaván oculto
splint	sobrehueso
spondylitis	espondilitis
sprain	torcedura, esfuerzo
sprain (to)	torcer
starvation	inanición
starve (to)	hacer hambre
starve to death (to)	hacer morir de hambre
starving to death	haciendo morir de hambre
stiff	anquilosada
stiffen (to)	anquilosar

stifled	desviación de la patela
stock up (to)	hinchar
stocking up	hinchado
stones	cálculos, piedras
strain	esfuerzo
strangles	papera equina
stringhalt	mioclonía de las patas traseras
strongyles	estróngilos
large strongyles	estróngilos grandes
small strongyles	estróngilos pequeños
strongyles, large infection	infección de estróngilos grandes
strongyles, small infection	infeción de estróngilos pequeños
strongyloides	estrongiloides
strongyloides infection	infección de estrongiloides
stunted growth	crecimiento canijo
sunstroke	insolación
sweat (to)	sudar
sweeny	atrofia de los músculos del hombro
swell (to)	hinchar
swelling	hinchazón
swollen	hinchado/a
tapeworm infection	infección de tenias
temperature (the)	temperatura
What is the temperature of the horse?	¿Cuál es la temperatura del caballo? ¿Qué temperatura, tiene el caballo?
temperature (to have)	tener fiebre, tener temperatura, tener calentura
tender (to be)	tener dolorido/a
tenosynovitis	tenosinovitis
tetanus	tétano
tetanus toxoid	tétano toxoide
thoroughpin	hinchazón tarsal
thrush	afta, enfermedad del pie del caballo con descarga fétida
ticks	garrapatas
ear ticks	garrapatas en las orejas
tie up (to)	engarrotar, envarar (Arg.)
torn	desgarrado/a, roto/a
torn ear	oreja abierta, oreja lesionada
torn ligament	ligamiento roto
torn muscle	músculo roto
trichostrongylus	tricostróngilo
trichostrongylus infection	infección por tricostróngilo
tucked-up flanks	flancos chupados, contracción en los flancos

tumor	tumor
benign tumor	tumor benigno
malignant tumor	tumor maligno
sarcoid tumor	tumor epidérmico
twist	torsión
twist (to)	tocer
twisted gut	torsión del intestino
tying up	envaradura, síndrome de paralización
ulcers	úlceras
unsound	insaludable, mal de salud
unthrifty	despilfarrador
vesticular stomatitis	stomatitis vesticular
villonodular synovitis	sinovitis villonodular
viral artheritis	arteritis viral
virus	virus
vomit (to)	vomitar
vomiting	vómito, vomitando
warbles	habronemiasis, reznos
warts	verruga, excrecencia cutánea
weak	débil
weakness	debilidad
weave (to)	zigzaguear
whirlbone lameness	cojera de rótula
whistling	chiflando
wind gall	distensiones sinoviales de la cerneja
wind puffs	bolsas de aire
wind suck	chupar aire
wire cut	corte de alambre
wobbles	portanco/a tambaleante
worm	lombriz
worms	lombrices
lung worms	lombrices del pulmón
pinworms	oxiurias
screw worms	lombrices de heridas abiertas
small stomach worms	tricostróngilos
stomach worms	habronemas
tapeworms	lombrices solitarias, tenias
wound	herida
bruised wound	herida con contusión
infected wound	herida infectada
puncture wound	herida de punción
puncture wound of the foot	herida podal por pinchazo
spur wound	espoleadura

Veterinary Equipment
equipo del veterinario

bucket	cubeta, balde, bote, cubo
catheter	cáteter
first-aid kit	botiquín de urgencia, botiquín de emergencia
hoof tester	pinza de casco, probante del casco
laser	láser
cold laser	láser frío
needles	agujas
rubber gloves	guantes de goma, guantes quirúrgicos
sphygmanometer	esfigmanómetro
stethoscope	estetoscopio
syringe	jeringa
tape	cinta adhesiva, cinta
thermometer	termómetro
tooth rasp	raspadura de dientes, escarpelo de dientes
ultrasound	ultrasonido

Veterinary Treatments
tratamientos del veterinario

accupressure	acupresión
accupuncture	acupuntura
apply a poultice (to)	aplicar un emplasto
aspirate (to)	aspirar
ausculate (to)	auscultar
autopsy (to)	autopsiar
bathe the wound (to)	regar la herida
blister (the)	ampolla, blistera
internal blister	ampolla profunda, blistera profunda (Mex.)
blister (to)	levantar ampollas en la pierna, producir ampollas en la pierna, ampollar
call the vet (to)	llamar al veterinario/a
cast (the)	vendaje enyesada
cast (to)	enyesar
castrate (to)	castrar, emascular

catheterize (to)	cateterizar
cauterize (to)	cauterizar
check (to)	examinar
check the breathing (to)	examinar la respiración
check the respiration (to)	examinar la respiración
chiropractics	quiroprácticos
circulatory system	aparato, circulatorio
clean (to)	limpiar
clean the sheath (to)	limpiar la vaina
clean the wound (to)	limpiar la herida
clip or shave the hair (to)	trasquilar el pelo, rasurar el pelo
cold hose the legs (to)	regar las piernas con agua fría
cut (the)	corte, incisión
cut (to castrate)	castrar, emascular
cut (to open)	cortar
destroy a horse (to)	eliminar al caballo, destruir al caballo
deworm (to)	quitar las lombrices, desparasitar
diagnose (to)	diagnosticar
diagnosis	diagnóstico
disinfect (to)	desinfectar
dress a wound (to)	vendar
drug (to)	drogar
drug test (the)	examen de drogas
drug test (to)	examinar para drogas
dry the wound (to)	secar la herida
enema (to give)	dar una enema
exercise	trabaja
no exercise	no trabaja
exercise (to)	trabajar
examine (to)	examinar
examination	examen
float the teeth (to)	raspar los dientes, igualar los dientes
give a shot (to)	dar inyección
hand walk (to)	pasear a mano
hand walk the horse (to)	pasear el caballo a mano
hand walk the horse for five minutes a day (to)	pasear a mano el caballo por cinco minutos al día
heal (to)	sanar
healing	sanando
The wound is healing.	La herida está sanando.
heat therapy	terapia caliente
immobilize (to)	inmovilizar
incise (to)	cortar
incision	incisión
injection (the)	inyección

intramuscular injection	inyección intramuscular
intravenous injection	inyección intravenosa
subcutaneous injection	inyección subcutánea
injection (to give)	dar inyección, inyectar
inoculate (to)	inocular
inoperable (to be)	ser inoperable, ser impracticable
kill the germs (to)	matar las gérmenes
massage (to)	dar masajes
nerve (to)	obstruir los nervios, cortar los nervios
nerve block (to)	obstruir los nervios
operate (to)	operar
pack (to)	rellenar
pack the hoof (to)	rellenar el casco
palpate (to)	palpitar
percussion	percusión
physical examination	reconocimiento médico
pin-fire (to)	poner puntas de fuego
plaster cast	vendaje enyesado
prepurchase exam	examen antes de compra
prescribe (to)	recetar
pulse (the)	pulso
digital pulse	pulso digital
lateral pulse	pulso lateral
normal pulse	pulso normal
pulse (to take)	tomar el pulso
digital pulse (to take)	tomar el pulso digital
lateral pulse (to take)	tomar el pulso lateral
pulse point	punto del pulso
quarantine	cuarentena
quarantine the horse (to)	poner el caballo en cuarentena
rehabilitate (to)	rehabilitar
rest the horse (to)	descansar el caballo
salve on the wound (to put)	aplicar ungüento a la herida
sanitize (to)	limpiar
shot (the)	inyección
shot (to give a)	dar inyección, inyectar
shot (to receive a)	recibir inyección
soak (to)	remojar
soak the hoof (to)	remojar el casco, remojar la pata
stall rest the horse (to)	descansar el caballo en el establo
sterilization	esterilización
sterilize (to)	esterilizar
stitch (to)	suturar
stop the bleeding (to)	parar la sangre
surgery	cirugía
suture (to)	suturar
sweat the legs (to)	sudar las piernas

temperature (to take the horse's) ..	tomar la temperatura del caballo
test (to)	examinar
therapeutic	terapéutica
therapy	terapia
tourniquet	torniquete
tracheotomy	traqueotomía
traction	tracción
tranquilize (to)	tranquilizar
treat the horse (to)	curar el caballo, tratar el caballo
undress a wound (to)	quitar el vendaje, desvendar
unsanitary	antihigiénico
vaccinate (to)	vacunar
vaccination (to give a)	dar una vacuna
vet check (the)	revisada veterinaria, examen del veterinario
vet check (to)	revisar por veterinario, examinar por veterinario
vet clean (to)	revisar sanamente, pasar el examen del veterinario limpio
vet out (to)	revisar sanamente, pasar el examen del veterinario
The horse did vet out.	El caballo pasó el examen del veterinario.
The horse did not vet out.	El caballo no pasó el examen del veterinario.
veterinary medicine	medicina veterinaria
vital functions (to check)	examinar las funciones vitales
X rays	radiografías
X-ray (to)	examinar con rayos x, radiografiar

Veterinary Medications
medicaciones veterinarias

ace	promazín
adjuvant	auxiliar
analgesic	analgésico
anesthesia	anestesia
local anesthesia	anestesia local
topical anesthesia	anestesia topical
anesthetic	anestésico
anthelmintic	antihelmíntico
antibiotic	antibiótico
antihistamine	antihistamínico
anti-inflammatory drugs	drogas anti-inflamatorias
antiphlogistic drugs	drogas antiflogísticas

antiseptic	antiséptico
antispasmodic	antiespasmódico
antitetnus serum	suero antitetánico
antitoxin	antitoxina
antivenin	antiveneno
antivirus	antivirus
bactericidal	bactericida
brace	linimento
cortisone	cortisona
counterirritant	revulsivo
dimethasulphoxide (DMSO)	dimetilsulfóxido
disinfectant	desinfectante
diuretic	diurético
dose	dosis
regular dose	dosis regular
single dose	dosis singular
drug	medicamento, medicina, droga
laxative	laxante
leg brace	linimento
liniment	linimento
medication	medicación
medicine	medicina
muscle relaxant	relajante de músculos
narcotic	narcótico
ointment	crema
penicillin	penicilina
phenylbutazone (Bute)	butazolidán
pill	píldora, pastilla
poultice	emplasto
salve	ungüento, remedio
sedative	sedativo
serum	suero
steroids	esteroide
stimulant	estimulante
tetanus antitoxin	suero antitetánico
tranquilizer	tranquilizante
turpentine	terpentina
Venice turpentine	terpentina de Venecia
vaccine	vacuna

Feeding
alimentando

bag/sack	saco, bolsa, costal
bale	fardo, paca

bolt food (to)	desbocar comidas
depraved appetite (to have)	tener un mal apetito, tener un apetito depravado
The horse has a depraved appetite.	El caballo tiene un mal apetito. El caballo tiene un apetito depravado.
eating	comiendo
The horse is eating.	El caballo está comiendo.
The horse is not eating.	El caballo no está comiendo.
fat horse	caballo gordo
feed (the)	comida, forraje, alimento
double feed	doble comida
extra feed	más comida, comida extra
half feed	mitad de comida
lack of feed	falta de comida
no feed	no comida
self-feed	autoalimentar
too little feed	muy poca comida
too much feed	mucha comida, demasiada comida
feed (to)	dar de comer, forrajear, alimentar, mantener
cut the feed (to)	reducir la comida
Do not feed the horse.	Favor de no alimentar al caballo.
double the feed (to)	doblar la comida
half feed (to give)	dar media comida
increase the feed (to)	aumentar la comida
reduce the feed (to)	reducir la comida
feed bag	cebadera morral
feed bucket	cubo, balde forrajero, cubeta de comida
feed cubes (to)	alimentar cubos
Do not feed cubes.	Favor de no alimentar cubos.
feeding	alimentación
rate of feeding	ritmo de alimentación
lake/section	sección, escama
flake of hay	sección de heno
fodder/forage	forraje
good keeper	bien tenido
graze (to)	pastar
graze the horse (to)	pastar el caballo
hand graze the horse (to)	pastar el caballo a mano
hay net	red para heno
The horse is sick, do not feed him.	El caballo está enfermo, no alimento por favor.
hungry horse	caballo hambriento
nutritive content of the feed	contenido nutritivo de la comida

overfeed (to)	sobrealimentar, comer demasiado
poor keeper	mal tenido
put the feed away (to)	guardar la comida
ration	ración
daily ration	ración diaria
full ration	todo de ración, ración llena, ración completa
half ration	mitad de ración, semiración
working ration	ración para trabajo, comida para trabajo
skinny horse	caballo flaco
thin horse	caballo delgado
thirsty horse	caballo sediento
turn out to grass (to)	soltar al potrero, soltar al pastizal
water (to)	darle agua
water bucket	balde de agua
water the horses (to)	abrevar los caballos, darle agua a los caballos

Types of Feed
tipos de comidas

acids	ácidos
amino acids	aminoácidos
ascorbic acid	ácido ascórbico
pathothenic acid	ácido pantoténico
alfalfa	alfalfa
alfalfa cubes	cubos de alfalfa
apple	manzana
barley	cebada
cracked barley	cebada quebrada
rolled barley	cebada aplastada
biotin	biotina
bran	salvado afrecho, salvado
wheat bran	salvado de trigo
bran mash (the)	amasijo de salvado
bran mash (to make)	remojar el afrecho, hacer el amasijo de salvado
calcium	calcio
carbohydrates	carbohidratos
carotene	caróteno
carrot	zanahoria
chlorine	cloro
citrus pulp	pulpa cítrica
clover	trébol

cobalt	cobalto
concentrates	concentrados
copper	cobre
corn	maíz
cracked corn	... maíz aplastado
cottonseed meal	harina de semilla de algodón
cubes	cubos
electrolytes	electrólitos
fats	grasas
feed	comidas, alimiento
commercial feed	comida comerical, alimiento comerical
innutritious feed	comida poco nutritiva
mixed feed	granos compuestos, granos
succulent feed	comida suculento
supplementary feed	comida suplementaria
sweet feed	comida dulce, melaza
flax seed	linaza
flourene	flúor, fluoreno
folacin	folacina
forages	hierbas
grains	granos
grass	hierba, pasto
grasses	hierbas
hay	heno, pasto seco, paja
first-cut hay	heno de primer corte
meadow hay	prado, pastizal
oat hay	heno de avena
second-cut hay	heno de segundo corte
seed hay	heno de semilla de pasto
haystack	almiar, pajar
iodine	yodo
iron	hierro
limestone	caliza
linseed	linaza
linseed meal	harina de linaza
magnesium	magnesio
manganese	manganeso
minerals	minerales
molasses	melaza
cane molasses	melaza de caña
molybdenum	molibdeno
niacin	niacina
oats	avena
crimped oats	avena quebrada
rolled oats	avena aplastada
oil	aceite
corn oil	aceite de maíz

linseed oil	aceite de linaza, aceite de lino
soybean oil	aceite de soja
wheatgerm oil	aceite de trigo
pasture	pasto, pastizal
pellets	bolitas
alfalfa pellets	bolitas de alfalfa, cubos de alfalfa
phosphorus	fósforo
potassium	potasio
protein	proteína
high protein	alta proteína
riboflavin	riboflavina
roughage	forraje
salt	sal
mineral salt	sal mineral
rock salt	sal de roca
salt block	bloque de sal
salt lick	lamedura, salegar
selenium	selenio
silage	ensilaje
sodium	sodio
sorghum grain	grano de sorgo
soybean meal	harina de soja
starch	almidón
straw	paja
sugar	azúcar
sugar beet	remolacha, betarraga
sugar cube	cubo de azúcar
have sugar cubes (to)	tener azúcar en cubos, tener cubos de azúcar
sugar-beet pulp	pulpa de betarragas, pulpa de remolachas
sulfur	azufre
supplements	suplementos
thiamine	tiamina
timothy	heno de fleo
urea	urea
vegetables	vegetales
vitamin	vitamina
vitamin A	vitamina A
vitamin B_{12}	vitamina B_{12}
vitamin D	vitamina D
vitamin E	vitamina E
vitamin K	vitamina K
water	agua
clean water	agua limpia
dirty water	agua sucia
fresh water	agua dulce, agua fresca

wheat	trigo
yucca	yuca
zinc	zinc cinc

Shoeing
herrando

barefoot	descalzo/a, sin herradura
borium	borio
calk	ramplón
clenches	remaches
clinch	apretador de clavos
clips	agarraderas
quarter clips	agarraderas de cuartos
toe clips	agarraderas de punta
Does this horse need shoes?	¿Necesita este caballo herraduras?
Do you have the shoe the horse threw?	¿Tiene Ud. la herradura perdió el caballo?
farrier	herrero/a
forge (the)	forja
forge (to)	forjar
hammer	martillo
hoof	casco
hoof dressing (to apply)	aplicar crema para el casco
hoof knife	cuchillo herrero
hoof wall	uña, pared, pared de casco
horseshoe	herradura
horseshoe nail	clavo de herradura
horseshoeing tools	herramientas de herraje
How many horses need shoeing?	¿Cuántos caballos necesitan herraduras?
loose shoe	herradura suelta
This horse has a loose shoe.	Este caballo tiene una herradura suelta.
lose a back shoe (to)	perder una herradura trasera, perder una herradura de una pata
lose a front shoe (to)	perder una herradura delantera, perder una herradura de una mano
lose a shoe (to)	perder una herradura
My farrier is . . .	Mi herrero se llama . . .; Mi herrero es . . .

horseshoe
herradura de caballo

nail	clavo de herradura
pack the foot (to)	rellenar el casco
pads	cojines, protectoras de plantas
pads on the front feet (to put)	poner protectores en los pies delanteros
poultice shoe	herradura con lodo, herradura con emplasto
pricked	pinchado/a
pull the shoes (to)	desherrar, sacar las herraduras
racing plates	herraduras de carrera
rasp	lima, escofino
reset the shoe (to)	reaplicar la herradura
shod	herrado
shoes (the)	herraduras
aluminium shoes	herraduras de aluminio
bar shoes	herraduras de barras
cold shoes	herraduras hechas, herraduras de fábrica
corrective shoes	herraduras correctivas
heart-bar shoes	herraduras de barras de corazón
horseshoes	herraduras de caballo
hot shoes	herraduras calientes
plain shoes	herraduras simples
ready-made shoes	herraduras hechas, herraduras de fábrica
rim shoes	herraduras de reborde, herraduras de canto
steel shoes	herraduras de acero
shoe (to)	herrar
cold shoe (to)	herrar en frío
hot shoe (to)	herrar en caliente
shoe the back feet only (to)	herrar solamente las patas
shoe the front feet only (to)	herrar solamente las manos
shoe the front only (to)	herrar solamente el frente
shoe the horse (to)	herrar el caballo

shoe the horse every . . .
    weeks (to) ....
	herrar al caballo cada . . .
	    semanas

stud kit	equipo para remachar
studs	remaches
screw-in studs	remaches atornillados
take this horse to the farrier (to)	llevar este caballo al herrero
throw a shoe (to)	perder una herradura
The horse threw a shoe.	El caballo perdió una herradura.
training plates	herraduras de entrenamiento
trim the foot (to)	recortar el casco
trim the hoof (to)	recortar el casco

What barn does this horse
    come from? ....
	¿De qué cuadril viene este
	    caballo?

What is the name of this horse?	¿Cómo se llama este caballo?,
	    ¿Cuál es el nombre de este
	    caballo?

Where is the farrier?	¿Dónde está el herrero?
Who owns this horse?	¿Quién es el dueño de este caballo?

2
The Horse and Rider
el caballo y el jinete

Grooming the Horse
aseando el caballo

bath (the)	baño
cold-water bath	baño de agua fría
sponge bath	baño de esponja
warm-water bath	baño de agua tibia
bath (to give a)	dar un baño
sponge bath (to give a)	bañar con esponja
bathe (to)	bañar
bathe the horse (to)	bañar el caballo
bathe with medicated shampoo (to)	bañar con champú medicinal
bathe with shampoo (to)	bañar con champú
bathe with warm water (to)	bañar con agua tibia
bathing	bañando
blanket (to)	cubrir con manta, cobijar, encamisar (Mex.), mantear
blanket the horse every night (to)	cobijar el caballo cada noche
blanketing	cobijado, encamisado, manteando
brush (the)	cepillo
body brush	cepillo de cuerpo
face brush	cepillo de cara
natural-bristle brush	cepillo natural
synthetic-bristle brush	cepillo sintético
water brush	cepillo de agua
brush (to)	almohazar, cepillar
brush the horse (to)	almohazar el caballo
bucket	balde, bote, cube, cubeta
plastic bucket	balde de plástico
rubber bucket	balde de goma
steel bucket	balde de acero
water bucket	balde de agua
check the feet (to)	revisar las patas
clean the feet (to)	limpiar las patas
clipper blade	hoja de rastrillo, navaja de rasurar
clippers	máquina de rasurar, maquinilla

body clippers	máquina de rasurar para el cuerpo
face clippers	máquina de rasurar para la cara, máquina pequeña
comb (the)	peine para la crin, peine
curry comb	almohaza, rasqueta
mane comb	peine para la crin
metal curry comb	almohaza de metal
pulling comb	peine de entresacada, peine para jalar crin
rubber curry comb	almohaza de hule, almohaza de goma
tail comb	peine para la cola
comb (to)	peinar
comb the mane and tail (to)	peinar la crin y la cola
conditioner	condicionante
conditioner (to use)	usar condicionante
Use conditioner on the mane and tail.	Use condicionante en la crin y la cola.
curry (to)	almohazar, rasquetear
Do not stand behind this horse.	No se pare detrás de este caballo.
Do not tie this horse in the wash rack.	No amarre el caballo en el lavadero.
fly spray	espray para moscas, rociador para moscas
groom (to)	asear, cuidar, almohazar, limpiar el caballo
groom the horse (to)	asear el caballo
grooming	almohazado, cuidado
grooming box	caja de útiles de limpieza, caja de aseo
grooming glove	guante de limpieza, guante de aseo
hole punch	sacabocado
hoof dressing	crema para el casco
hoof paint	pintura para el casco
hoof pick	piquete para el casco

hoof pick
piquete para el casco

horse vacuum	aspiradora de caballo
hose off the horse (to)	bañar el caballo, regar el caballo con agua
hose off the legs (to)	bañar las piernas, regar las piernas con agua
oil (the)	aceite
hoof oil	aceite para el casco
oil (to)	aceitar
oil the hooves (to)	aceitar los cascos
paint the hooves (to)	pintar los cascos
pick out the hooves (to)	limpiar los cascos
pocket knife	navaja
put the horse away when he is dry (to)	encerrar el caballo cuando esté seco
put the horse in the cross ties (to)	poner el caballo en los amarraderos
put the horse on the hot walker (to)	poner el caballo en mecánica para pasear, poner el caballo al caminante
rag	trapo
rub	dar masajes, sobar
rub down the horse (to)	dar masajes al caballo, sobar el caballo
rub the legs with liniment (to)	dar masajes a las piernas con linimento
scraper	raspador
sweat scraper	raspador para secar
water scraper	raspador para secar
scissors	tijeras
scrub (to)	limpiar
scrub the face with soap (to)	limpiar la cara con jabón
shampoo	champú
soap	jabón
sponge	esponja
big sponge	esponja grande
small sponge	esponja pequeña
spray bottle	botella de rociar
sweat the neck (to)	sudar el pezuezo, sudar el cogote
tack hook	gancho para el equipo, gancho
tape	cinta, huincha
This horse will not tie.	Este caballo no se puede amarrar.
towel	toalla
twitch	twitch, naricera, torcedura de labio
unblanket (to)	descobijar
unblanket the horse (to)	descobijar el caballo

unblanket the horse every morning (to)	descobijar el caballo cada noche
vacuum the horse (to)	limpiar el caballo con la aspiradora, aspirar el caballo
walk the horse until it is dry (to)	caminar el caballo hasta que se seque, caminar el caballo sudado
wash (to)	lavar
wash the mane and tail with soap (to)	lavar la crin y la cola con jabón
wash the wraps (to)	lavar las vendas
wipe off the horse (to)	limpiar el caballo
wrap (the)	vendar
wrap (to)	vendar
wrap all four legs (to)	vendar las cuatro piernas
wrap the back legs (to)	vendar las piernas traseras
wrap the front legs (to)	vendar las piernas delanteras

Clipping and Trimming the Horse
rasurando y recortando el caballo

braid (the)	trenza
dressage braid	trenza para adiestramiento
hunter braid	trenza para salto, trenza para cacería
stallion braid	trenza para potro, trenza para padrillo
braid (to)	trenzar
braid the forelock (to)	trenzar el copete
braid the mane and forelock with tape (to)	trenzar la crin y el copete con cinta
braid the mane and forelock with yarn (to)	trenzar la crin y el copete con lana de tejer
braid the mane and tail (to)	trenzar la crin y la cola
clip the horse (to)	rasurar el caballo
blanket clip (to)	rasurar las piernas
body clip (to)	rasurar completo, trasquilar
full clip (to)	rasurar todo, rasurar completo
hunter clip (to)	rasurar para cacería
saddle-patch clip (to)	rasurar bajo la montura
trace clip (to)	rasurar pizca
clipper (person)	trasquilador
clipper blade	hoja de rastrillo, navaja de rasurar
change the clipper blade (to)	cambiar la navaja de rasurar

trace clip (to)
rasurar pizca

clippers	máquina de rasurar, maquinilla
body clippers	máquina para rasurar el cuerpo
electric clipper	rasurador eléctrico
face clippers	máquina para rasurar la cara
clipping and trimming equipment ...	equipo de recorte
comb (the)	peine, peineta
comb (to)	peinar
cut (to)	cortar
cut the mane (to)	cortar la crinera
dock (to)	descolar, recortar la cola
dock the tail (to)	descolar la cola
dressage cut the tail (to)	cortar la cola para adiestramiento
elastic/rubber band	banda elástica, banda de goma, liguillas
grow a coat (to)	dejarse pelo, crecer pelo
grow a heavy coat (to)	dejarse pelo espeso
grow a second coat (to)	dejarse pelo segundo
grow a winter coat (to)	dejarse pelo de invierno
hunter braid the tail (to)	trenzar la cola para cacería
plait (to)	trenzar
plait the mane (to)	trenzar la crin
plait the tail (to)	trenzar la cola
plaited tail	cola trenzada
pull the mane (to)	jalar crin, igualar crin, entresacar
roach the mane (to)	rozar la crin
scissors	tijeras
shed (to)	mudar
shed the coat (to)	mudar el pelo
shed to a summer coat (to)	mudar a pelo de verano
tape	cinta, huincha
thin the mane (to)	entresacar la crin
thinning shears	tijeras raleadoras
trim (to)	emparejar, recortar, atusar
trim the bridle path (to)	atusar la nuca
trim the ears (to)	atusar las orejas
trim the feathers (to)	atusar las cernejas

trim the muzzle (to)	atusar el hocico
trim the tail (to)	atusar la cola
yarn	lana de tejer

Tacking up the Horse
ensillando el caballo

adjust the bit (to)	ajustar el freno
adjust the bridle (to)	ajustar la brida
bit (the)	freno, filete
The bit hangs too low.	El freno está muy bajo.
The bit is too big.	El freno está demasiado grande.
The bit is too small.	El freno está demasiado pequeño.
bit (to use this)	usar este freno
bit up (to)	embocar, enfrenar
bit up the horse (to)	embocar el caballo
bridle (to)	embridar, poner la brida
bridle (to use this)	usar esta brida
buckle (to)	abrochar
buckle the girth (to)	abrochar la cincha
check (to)	chequear, inspeccionar
check the girth (to)	chequear la cincha, inspeccionar la cincha, revisar la cincha
cinch-bound horse	cinchonado, caballo sensitivo de barril
cinchy (to be)	estar sensitivo de barril
The horse is cinchy.	El caballo está sensitivo de barril.
cinchy horse	caballo sensitivo de barril
fit the saddle to the horse (to)	acomodar la montura al caballo
give a leg up (to)	dar una mano para montar, hacer estribo con las manos
halter the horse (to)	poner almartigón al caballo, encabaestrar
hand me	deme
Hand me my crop.	Deme mi fuete.
Hand me my gloves.	Deme mis guantes.
Hand me my hat.	Deme mi casco.
harness the horse (to)	aparejar el caballo
have the horse ready (to)	tener el caballo listo
Have the horse ready at . . . (to)	tener el caballo listo a . . .
hitch up the horses (to)	enganchar los caballos
hitch up the horses to the cart (to)	enganchar los caballos al carro
hobble (to)	manear, cojear
hold the horse when I mount (to)	sostener el caballo mientras monto
lead the horse (to)	conducir el caballo

loosen the girth (to)	soltar la cincha
pack a horse (to)	albardar
put a pack saddle on (to)	enalbardar
put a saddle on (to)	ensillar
put the back boots on (to)	poner las botas de atrás
put the boots on (to)	poner las botas
put the front boots on (to)	poner las botas de adelante
run the stirrups to the top of the leathers (to)	poner los estribos hasta arriba de los arciones, subir los estribos
run up the stirrups (to)	poner los estribos arriba, subir los estribos
saddle (to)	ensillar
saddle the horse (to)	ensillar
tack up (to)	ensillar
tack up my other horse (to)	ensillar mi otro caballo
tack up the horse (to)	ensillar el caballo
tie (to)	amarrar, atar
tie up the horse (to)	atar el caballo
tighten (to)	apretar
tighten the caveson (to)	apretar la cavesada, apretar el bosal
tighten the girth (to)	apretar la cincha, cinchar
unbridle (to)	desembridar
unharness the horse (to)	desaparejar el caballo
unhitch (to)	desenganchar
unhitch the horse (to)	desenganchar el caballo
unhitching	desenganche
unsaddle (to)	desensillar
unsaddle the horse (to)	desensillar el caballo
untie the horse (to)	desamarrar el caballo, soltar el caballo
unwrap the back legs (to)	desvendar las piernas de atrás
unwrap the front legs (to)	desvendar las piernas de adelante
unwrap the legs (to)	desvendar las piernas
use a foam pad (to)	usar el pelero de espuma de goma
use a lift-back pad (to)	usar el pelero acolchado atrás
wrap all legs with polo wraps (to)	vendar todas las piernas con vendas de polo
wrap the back legs (to)	vendar las piernas de atrás
wrap the front legs (to)	vendar las piernas de adelante
wrap the legs (to)	vendar las piernas

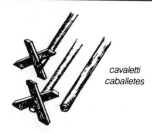

cavaletti
caballetes

Training the Horse
entrenando el caballo

blindfold (to)	vendar los ojos
break (to)	amansar, domar
broke to lead	manso de tiro, respecta la cabeza
bronco	bronco
busy colt	potrillo inquisitivo, potranca inquisitiva
cavaletti	caballetes
cavaletti work at a trot	trabajando caballetes al trote
cavaletti work at a walk	trabajando caballetes al paso
collection in hand	colección a mano
degree of training	grado de doma, grado de entrenamiento
easy to tie (to be)	ser fácil de amarrar
ground drive (to)	andar entre las líneas
ground work	trabajo a la mano
gymnastic work	trabajo gimnástico
halter broke	manso de tiro, respecta la cabeza
horse	caballo
exhausted horse	caballo exhausto, caballo agotado
fat horse	caballo gordo
fit horse	caballo en buena condición
green-broke horse	caballo recién amansado
green horse	caballo crudo, caballo redomón
halter horse	caballo de pose
lazy horse	caballo perezoso, caballo poltrón, caballo huevón arragán (Mex.)
made horse	caballo hecho, caballo bien domado, caballo de bien rienda
obedient horse	caballo obediente

overworked horse	caballo aplasto
push-button horse	caballo hecho
rideable horse	caballo que se puede montar
school horse	caballo de lección, caballo de instrucción
schooled horse	caballo bien riendado, caballo enseñado, caballo bien hecho
spoiled horse	caballo malogrado, caballo mañoso
stiff horse	caballo tieso
strong horse	caballo fuerte
submissive horse	caballo obediente
supple horse	caballo flexible
tired horse	caballo cansado
trained horse	caballo hecho, caballo entrenado
unfit horse	caballo fuera de condición
untrained horse	caballo sin entrenamiento, caballo sin trabajo, caballo crudo
well-made horse	caballo bien hecho
well-schooled horse	caballo de escuela, caballo bien trabajado, caballo de bien riendado
well-trained horse	caballo bien entrenado, caballo bien trabajado
wild horse	caballo salvaje, caballo ladino
horse at intense work	caballo con trabajo pesado
horse at light work	caballo con trabajo ligero
horse at moderate work	caballo con trabajo moderado
hung up (to be)	estar colgado/a
jumping without a rider	salto libre, salto sin jinete
leave in a bitting rig (to)	dejar en apero de embridar
line drive (to)	andar por las líneas, andar entre las líneas

line drive (to)
andar por las líneas

long rein (to)	trabajar con riendas largas, andar entre las líneas
longe (to)	trabajar a la cuerda, darle cuerda
longe over cavaletti (to)	trabajar a la cuerda por caballetes, darle cuerda por caballetes
longe the horse (to)	trabajar el caballo a la cuerda
loose jumping	salto de manera suelta
overwork (to)	aplastar
overwork the horse (to)	aplastar el caballo
sack out (to)	enmantar
school (to)	trabajar
school the horse (to)	trabajar el caballo, darle escuela
tie in single file (to)	reatar
tie to a patience post (to)	atar a poste de paciencia
train the horse (to)	entrenar el caballo, domar el caballo
training	entrenamiento, doma, adiestramiento
trotting poles	postes de trote, caballetes
work from the ground (to)	trabajar a la mano
work in a bitting rig (to)	trabajar con apero de embridar
work in long reins (to)	trabajar con riendas largas
work in the pillars (to)	trabajar en los pilares
work in the round pen (to)	trabajar en pista cerrada
work over cavaletti (to)	trabajar por caballetes

Gaits and Movements of the Horse
aires y movimientos del caballo

airs above the ground	aires sobre el piso, aires arriba de la tierra
amble (to)	amblar
back (to)	retroceder, andar atrás, recular
ballotade	balotada
beat (the)	tiempo
two beat	dos tiempos
three beat	tres tiempos
four beat	cuatro tiempos
canter (the)	galope
collected canter	galope reunido
counter canter	galope en falso, contra galope
cross canter	galope cruzado
disjointed canter	galope desunido
extended canter	galope largo

false canter	galope falso
medium canter	galope medio
true canter	galope, galope verdadero
working canter	galope ordinario
canter (to)	galopar
canter depart	salida al galope, partida al galope, rompe al galope, empieza a galope
canter simple change	cambio de galope simple
capriole	cabriola
change lead (to)	cambiar de la mano, cambiar del pie
circle (to)	dar la vuelta, dar vueltas, circular
counter change of hand	contracambio de mano
curvet	corveta
figure eight	figura ocho
flying change	cambio de pie en el aire
single flying change	cambio de pie simple
flying change of leg	cambio de pie en el aire volapié
gait (the)	aire, paso
good gait	buen aire, buen paso
gallop (the)	galope
full gallop	galope tendido, todo galope, galope de toda brida
full gallop (at a)	a toda brida, a todo galope, a galope tenido
gallop (at a)	a galope
hand gallop	galope sostenido, medio galope, galope a mano
hunting gallop	correr
racing gallop	correr
gallop (to)	galopar
gallop through	pasa la rienda
halt (the)	parada, alto
half halt	media parada
halt (to)	parar
half pass (to)	apoyar
half turn	media vuelta
half turn reverse	media vuelta reversa
haunches in	grupa adentro
haunches out	grupa afuera, grupa al muro
irregular gait	paso irregular
irregular steps	pasos irregulares
jig (to)	trotinar
jog (the)	paso lento
jog (to)	trotinar, andar a trote corto
lead change	cambio de la mano

leg yield	cesión a las piernas
levade	lanzada
movements	movimientos
High School movements	movimientos de alta escuela
lateral movements	movimientos laterales
school movements	movimientos escolares
pace	paso, aire
free and regular paces	aires regulares y libres
irregular paces	pasos irregulares
pace (to)	pasear
pacing	paseando
passage	pasage
pesade	grupa adentro
piaffe (the)	piaf
piaffe (to)	piafar
pirouette (the)	pirueta
canter pirouette	pirueta al galope
half pirouette	media pirueta
walk pirouette	pirueta al paso
pirouette (to)	hacer pirueta, hacer cabriola
prance (the)	cabriola
prance (to)	hacer cabriolas, encabritarse
renvers	grupa adentro
run (to)	correr
run at full speed (to)	correr a rienda suelta
school figures	figuras escolares
serpentine	serpentina
three-loop serpentine	serpentina de tres círculos
four-loop serpentine	serpentina de cuatro círculos
shoulder in	espaldas adentro
simple change of leg	cambio de pie simple, cambio sencillo de pierna
stop (the)	parada
stop (to)	parar
stop in time	parada a tiempo
stride	pisada
tempi changes	cambios a tiempos
transition	transición

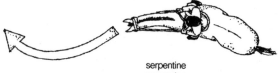

serpentine
serpentina

downward transition	transición por abajo
upward transition	transición por arriba
travers	cabeza afuera, cabeza al muro
turn (to)	dar vuelta
turn on the forehand (the)	vuelta sobre el anterior, vuelta en las manos
turn on the forehand (to)	dar vuelta sobre el anterior
turn on the haunches (the)	vuelta sobre el posterior, vuelta sobre la grupa
turn on the haunches (to)	dar vuelta sobre el posterior
trot (to)	trotar
trot (the)	trote
at an easy or slow trot	a trote corto
at the trot	al trote
break into trot (to)	empezar a trotar, comenzar el trote
collected trot	trote reunido
extended trot	trote largo, trote extenso
medium trot	trote medio
working trot	trote ordinario
volte	volte, vuelta (seis metros)
half volte	medio volte
increase the volte (to)	aumentar el volte
walk (the)	el paso
collected walk	paso reunido
extended walk	paso largo, paso extendido
free walk	paso libre
medium walk	paso medio
working walk	paso ordinario
walk (to)	caminar andar

Reactions of the Ridden Horse
reacciones del caballo montado

above the bit	sobre la brida
above the bit (to be)	estar sobre la brida, elevar la cabeza

above the bit
sobre la brida

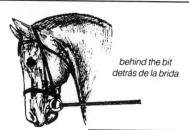

behind the bit
detrás de la brida

accept the bit (to)	aceptar el freno, aceptar la brida, aceptar el filete
action (to have)	tener movimiento, tener acción
active hocks (to have)	tener corvas activas, tener corvejos activos
active quarters (to have)	tener cuartos activos
airy movement (to have)	tener movimiento airoso, tener airosidad
balance	equilibrio, balance
balance (to have)	tener equilibrio, tener balance
balanced (to be)	equilibrar, balancear
behind the bit	detrás de la brida, detrás de la mano, detrás del freno
behind the bit (to be)	estar detrás de la brida, estar detrás de la mano, estar detrás del freno
bend (the)	curva, pliegue, doblez
bend (to)	curvar, plegar, doblar
bend at the poll (the)	flexión en la nuca
bend at the poll (to)	ceder la nuca
bob the head (to)	subir y bajar la cabeza
bolt (to)	desbocar
bolter	desbocado/a
bolting	desbocamiento
bolting horse	caballo desbocado
brush/knock (to)	rozar, tocar
buck (the)	corcovo
buck (to)	corcovear, desmontar, reparar, derribar
buck off (to)	desmontar de un corcovo
cadence	cadencia, ritmo medido
champ at the bit (to)	masticar el freno, masticar el filete
change leads	cambiar las manos
collected (to be)	estar reunido
overcollected (to be)	estar reunido excesivamente estar colectado excesivamente
collection (to have)	tener reunión

contact (to have)	tener contacto
contact	contacto
no contact	sin contacto
crack of the whip	chasquido de un látigo
crow hop (to)	reparar
disobedience	desobediencia
disobedient (to be)	ser desobediente
drag the feet (to)	arrastrar los pies
draw up the tongue (to)	levantar la lengua, hacer bola con la lengua
drop the back (to)	bajar la espalda, botar la espalda
drop the shoulder (to)	bajar el hombro, botar el hombro
elevated steps (to have)	tener pasos elevados, tener pasos erguidos
engage (to)	reunir, plegar, emplear
engage the haunches (to)	entrar el posterior, reunir el posterior
fear of water (to have)	tener miedo del agua
fight himself (to)	pelearse
flex the neck (to)	encorvar el pescuezo, encorvar la nuca
foam (to)	espumar
foaming	espumante
fresh mouth	boca fresca, boca nueva
good hock action (to have)	tener buena acción del garrón
grind the teeth (to)	rechinar los dientes
hang out the tongue (to)	poner afuera la lengua
hard mouth	boca dura
head in front of the verticle	cabeza adelante de la vertical, cabeza frente de la vertical
head set (the)	la cabeza en posición
head shy (to be)	tener miedo de la cabeza
hold the bit (to)	mantener el freno, mantener el filete
hollow back (to have a)	tener una espalda hueca, tener una espalda hundida
hollow the back (to)	hundir la espalda, hundir el lomo, botar la espalda
horse under saddle	caballo ensillado
impulsion (to have)	tener impulsión
in front of the bit	frente del freno, frente del filete, delante del freno, delante del filete
in front of the bit (to be)	estar frente del freno, estar frente del filete
inactive hind legs	pereza de las traseras
inactive hind legs (to have)	tener piernas traseras inactivas, tener traseras perezosas
jump (to)	saltar

kick (to)
dar una coz

kick (to)	dar una coz, patear, dar una patada
lean (to)	apoyar
lean on the bit (to)	apoyar en el freno
light in the forehand (to be)	estar liviano de anteriores
loss of gait	pierde el aire, pierde el paso
motionless (to be)	permanecer inmóvil, estar quieto/a
move forward (to)	mover adelante, avanzar, adelantar
move off the leg (to)	impulsar con las piernas
move with impulsion (to)	mover con impulsión
movement	movimiento
collected movement	movimiento reunido, movimiento colectivo
elastic movement	movimiento elástico
fluid movement	movimiento fluido
free movement	movimiento libre
obedient (to be)	ser obediente
obedient to the aids (to be)	ser obediente a las ayudas, ser obediente a las señales
on the bit (to be)	estar en la mano, estar enfrenado
on the forehand (to be)	estar sobre las manos
over the bit (to be)	estar sobre el freno, estar sobre el filete
overreach (to)	alcanzar, sobrepasar
play with the bit (to)	jugar con el freno
power (to have)	tener la fuerza, tener potencia
powerful (to be)	ser poderoso, ser fuerte, ser airoso
pull or bore (to)	jalar, timonear
pulling horse	caballo jalando a mano, caballo tirando de mano, caballo con tirón de mano
raise the head (to)	levantar la cabeza, engallarse
rear (to)	encabritar
refuse (to)	rehusar, parar
refuse the bit (to)	rehusar el freno
resist (to)	resistir

resist the action of the hand (to)	resistir la acción de la mano
resistance	resistencia
responsive (to be)	ser sensible, ser responsivo
responsive to the aids (to be)	ser sensible a las ayudas
rhythm (to have)	tener ritmo
round back (to have)	tener lomo redondo, tener espalda redonda
run away with (to)	desbocar
runaway horse	caballo desbocado
sensitive mouth	boca sensitiva
sensitive mouth (to have a)	tener una boca sensitiva
shake the head (to)	sacudir la cabeza
shy (to)	espantarse
soft mouth	boca suave, boca dulce
soft mouth (to have a)	tener una boca suave, tener una boca dulce
stampede (the)	estampida, desbocamiento
stampede (to)	estampidar, provocar una espantada
stand still (to)	parar
stiff back (to have a)	tener una espalda inflexible, tener una espalda tiesa
stubborn (to be)	ser terco/a
stumble (to)	tropezar
submissive horse	caballo obediente
submit to the aids (to)	someterse a las ayudas
supple (to be)	estar flexible
supple back (to have)	tener espalda flexible
supple horse	caballo flexible
suspension (to have)	tener suspensión
switch leads (to)	cambiar de pie, cambiar la mano
switch the tail (to)	menear la cola
switched the tail	meneó la cola
take the bit (to)	tomar el freno
tempo (to have)	tener ritmo
throw the rider (to)	tirar el jinete, derribar el caballista, derribar el jinete
tongue out (to put the)	sacar la lengua
tongue over the bit (to put the)	poner la lengua sobre el freno
track (to)	andar en las huellas
unbalanced (to be)	estar desequilibrado/a
untrack (to)	quitar del bilateral
wet mouth	boca húmeda, boca mojada
work on two tracks (to)	trabajar a dos pistas, pasar de costado
yield (to)	dar, ceder

Riding Technique
técnica de montar

aids	ayudas, señales
back aids	ayudas de espalda
body aids	ayudas de todo el cuerpo, ayudas de cuerpo, ayudas de peso del cuerpo
driving aids	ayudas de impulso
leg aids	ayudas de las piernas
rein aids	ayudas con la rienda, ayudas con la mano
simple aids	ayudas simples
voice aids	ayudas para la voz
aids (to apply the)	usar las ayudas, aplicar las ayudas
bend the horse (to)	plegar el caballo, doblar el caballo
bend the horse around the leg (to)	doblar el caballo sobre la pierna
bend the horse to the inside (to)	doblar el caballo hacia adentro
bend the horse to the outside (to)	doblar el caballo hacia afuera
bend the horse uniformly (to)	doblar el caballo con uniformidad
brace with your back (to)	afirmar la espalda
calm the horse (to)	calmar el caballo, sosegar el caballo
canter the horse (to)	galopar el caballo
change diagonal (to)	cambiar diagonal
change direction (to)	cambiar de dirección
change leads (to)	cambiar de pies
chin up	quijada arriba
click (to)	chasquear
cluck (to)	chascar
collect the horse (to)	reunir el caballo
cool out the horse (to)	enfriar el caballo, normalizar el caballo
cool the horse down (to)	enfriar el caballo, normalizar el caballo, refrescar el caballo
correct seat (to have)	tener un asiento correcto
cross the stirrups (to)	cruzar los estribos
decrease the circle (to)	disminuir el círculo
decrease the pace (to)	disminuir el paso, reducir el paso
deep seat (to have)	tener un asiento sólido, tener un asiento firme, tener un asiento, profundo
dismount (to)	desmontar
drive forward (to)	impulsar, empujar

dismount (to)
desmontar

elbows and arms close to the body	brazos y codos adentro, brazos y codos junto al cuerpo
engage the haunches (to)	emplear el posterior, emplear las ancas
exercise the horse (to)	trabajar el caballo
eyes down	ojos bajos
eyes forward	ojos delante
fall from the horse (to)	caer del caballo
He/she fell from the horse.	Se cayó del caballo.
feel the horse (to)	sentir el caballo, simpatizar con el caballo
flex to the left (to)	encorvar a la izquierda, requerir flexión a la izquierda
flex to the right (to)	encorvar a la derecha, requerir flexión a la derecha
gallop the horse (to)	galopar el caballo
give (to)	aflojar, soltar, dejarla
good hands (to have)	tener buenas manos
hack (to)	pasear, montar
hack out (to)	pasear a campo abierto
hack the horse (to)	pasear el caballo, montar el caballo
hands high	manos altas
hands low	manos bajas, manos abajo
hands together	manos juntas
head up	cabeza arriba
heels down	talones abajo
hold in the haunches (to)	sostener el posterior, mantener el posterior
hold the horse between the hands and legs	mantener el caballo entre las manos y las piernas
independent seat (to have)	tener un asiento independiente
in harmony with the horse (to be)	estar en armonía con el caballo
increase the circle (to)	aumentar el círculo

increase the pace (to)	aumentar el aire, acelerar el aire
jump (to)	saltar
lack of control (to have)	estar sin control, faltarle el control
lean over (to)	inclinarse
leg (to use)	usar la pierna
active leg	pierna activa
bending leg	pierna plegada
driving leg	pierna impulsada
inside leg	pierna interior, pierna interna, pierna de adentro
outside leg	pierna externa, pierna de afuera
passive leg	pierna pasiva
quiet leg	pierna tranquila, pierna relajada
leg contact (the)	contacto de la pierna
leg contact (to have)	tener contacto con las piernas
leg position	posición de la pierna
leg up (to give a)	dar una mano para montar, hacer estribo con las manos
lengthen the leg (to)	alargar la pierna
lengthen the stride (to)	alargar el paso
long rein (to give a)	dar
look down (to)	mirar abajo
maintain impulsion (to)	mantener la impulsión
mount the horse (to)	montar el caballo, montar
mounted	a caballo, montado a caballo montado
move the horse at an angle (to)	mover el caballo a ángulo, mover el caballo hacia un ángulo
on horseback	a caballo
overhorsed	no puede con el caballo
overwork the horse (to)	aplastar el caballo
pat the horse (to)	acariciar el caballo
perch (to)	encaramarse
pinched knee	rodilla adentro
post (to)	levantar al trote
prod with a spur	espolada
punish the horse (to)	castigar el caballo
quiet hands (to have)	tener manos suaves, tener manos quietas
react quickly (to)	responder rápido
reactions of the rider	responde del jinete, reacciones del jinete
rein (the)	rienda
active rein	rienda activa
bearing rein	rienda de una mano
direct rein	rienda directa
firm rein	manos firmes, rienda firme
inside rein	rienda interna, rienda de adentro

indirect rein	rienda indirecta
indirect rein behind the withers	rienda indirecta detrás de la cruz
indirect rein in front of the withers	rienda indirecta delante de la cruz
long rein	rienda larga
loose rein	rienda suelta
neck rein	rienda de una mano
open rein	rienda suelta, rienda abierta
outside rein	rienda exterior
passive rein	rienda pasiva
plow rein	rienda de conducción
rein back	rienda de paso atrás
rein (to)	enfrenar
adjust the reins (to)	ajustar las riendas
bridge the reins (to)	hacer puente con las riendas
change rein (to)	cambiar de mano, cambiar de rienda
give the reins (to)	aflojar las riendas, soltar las riendas, dejarla pasar
give with the reins (to)	aflojar con las riendas, soltar con las riendas, dejarla con pasar
hold the reins (to)	llevar las riendas, tomar las riendas
lengthen the reins (to)	soltar las riendas, aflojar las riendas
loosen the reins (to)	dar las manos, dar las riendas
play with the inside rein (to)	tentar con la rienda de adentro, jugar con la rienda de adentro
seesaw the reins (to)	aserruchar las riendas
shake the reins (to)	agitar las riendas, vibrar las riendas
shorten the reins (to)	cortar las riendas, tomar las riendas
support with the outside rein (to)	soportar con la rienda de afuera
rein in (to)	refrenar
rein in sharply (to)	sofrenar
remount the horse (to)	remontar, remontar el caballo
reward the horse (to)	premiar el caballo
ride (to)	montar, cabalgar
ride astride (to)	montar a horcajadas
ride back (to)	volver a caballo, regresar a caballo
ride bareback (to)	montar a pelo
ride by (to)	pasar a caballo
ride double (to)	montar en ancas
ride in (to)	llegar a caballo

ride off (to)	irse a caballo
ride on (to)	seguir adelante, montar adelante
ride on horseback (to)	montar a caballo
ride out (to)	salir a caballo
ride sidesaddle (to)	montar a la amazona, montar a mujeriegas
ride the transition (to)	montar la transición
ride to death (to)	montar hasta muerto
ride up (to)	llegar a caballo
ride without the stirrup (to)	montar sin estribos
riding position	posición de monta
riding style	estilo de montar
run the horse (to)	correr el caballo
run the horse at full speed (to)	correr el caballo a rienda suelta
seat	asiento profundo
correct seat	asiento correcto
deep seat	asiento sólido, asiento firme
dressage seat	asiento de adiestramiento
forward seat	asiento para saltar, posición de salto
independent seat	asiento independiente
jockey seat	asiento de carrera, asiento para correr
stiff seat	asiento rígido
supple seat	asiento flexible
set the head (to)	fijar la cabeza
shift the weight (to)	mudar el peso, influenciar con el peso, cambiar el peso
spur the horse (to)	espolear el caballo, picar el caballo con las espuelas, usar las espuelas
spurring the horse	espoleo del caballo
straighten the horse (to)	enderezar el caballo
steady legs and thighs (to have)	tener piernas y muslos tranquilos, tener piernas y muslos firmes
stiff seat (to have)	tener un asiento rígido, tener un asiento tieso, tener un asiento inflexible
stretch the legs (to)	estirar las piernas
stretch the neck (to)	estirar el cuello, alargar el cuello, estirar el pescuezo
supple hips (to have)	tener caderas flexibles
supple seat (to have)	tener un asiento flexible
supple the horse (to)	soltar al caballo, ablandar al caballo
suppling exercises	ejercicios de soltamiento
three point	pararse en el estribo, posición de salto

thrown from the horse (to be)	perder los estribos, ser tirado del caballo
toes out	talones adentro, pies afuera
tour on horseback	viajar a caballo
trick ride (to)	voltear
trick riding	volteo
trot (the)	trote
posting trot	trote levantado
rising trot	trote levantado
sitting trot	trote sentado
trot (to)	trotar
post the trot (to)	levantar al trote
sit the trot (to)	sentar el trote
trot the horse (to)	trotar el caballo
turn the horse (to)	voltear el caballo, dar vueltas al caballo
two point	monta de rodilla
underhorsed	no tiene suficiente caballo
use your leg (to)	usar su pierna
walk the horse (to)	caminar el caballo, andar el caballo
warm down the horse (to)	enfriar el caballo
warm up (the)	calentamiento, ejercicios de calentamiento, ejercicios de preparación
warm up (to)	calentar
warm up the horse (to)	calentar el caballo
well balanced	buen equilibrio, buen balance
whip (to)	azotar, fustigar, dar latigazos
whip on (to)	dar latigazos
whip the horse (to)	fustigar el caballo, azotar el caballo, dar latigazos al caballo
work	trabajo
fast work	trabajo rápido
flat work	trabajo de picadero, trabajo plano
work on two tracks (to)	trabajar en dos pistas
work the horse (to)	trabajar el caballo, usar el caballo

Dressage
adiestramiento

center line	línea central, centro del picadero
change of rein	cambio de rienda

change of rein down the center line	cambio de rienda por la línea central
change of rein from circle to circle	cambio de rienda de círculo a círculo
change of rein on the diagonal across half the arena	cambio de rienda por el diagonal atravesando por la mitad del cuadrángulo
change of rein on the diagonal across the whole arena	cambio de rienda por el diagonal atrevesando el cuadrángulo entero
change of rein through the circle	cambio de rienda dentro del círculo
circle	círculo
eight-meter circle	círculo de ocho metros
ten-meter circle	círculo de diez metros
fifteen-meter circle	círculo de quince metros
twenty-meter circle	círculo de veinte metros
collective marks	notas colectivas
diagonal (the)	diagonal
diagonal (to be on the)	estar en el diagonal
down the center line	por la línea central
dressage horse	caballo de adiestramiento, caballo de alta escuela
dressage test	lección de adiestramiento, prueba de adiestramiento
haute école	alta escuela
high school	alta escuela
manege	arena, ring de equitación
markers	señales, letras, marcas
middle line	línea central
pas a deux	pas de deux, paso doble
quadrille	cuadrilla
quarter line	línea cuarta
ride along the rail (to)	montar al riel
ride along the wall (to)	montar por la pared
ride down the center line (to)	montar por la línea central
test	examen, prueba
first-level test	examen de primer nivel
second-level test	examen de segundo nivel
third-level test	examen de tercer nivel
fourth-level test	examen de cuarto nivel
Grand Prix test	examen de Grand Prix
intermediere test	examen de intermedia
Prix St. Georges test	examen de premio San Jorge
training-level test	examen de nivel de entrenamiento

Eventing
prueba militar

advanced	avanzado
banks and steps uphill	talud y peldaños arriba
circle at the same obstacle	círculo antes del obstáculo, círculo al mismo obstáculo
combinations	combinaciones
competitions	pruebas, competencias
cross-country	campo abierto
enter or leave the penalty zone without addressing the obstacle (to)	tomar el área de penalidad sin tomar el obstáculo, tomar la zona sin intentar el obstáculo
event	prueba completa, prueba militar
one-day event	prueba de un día
three-day event	prueba de tres días
event horse	caballo de prueba completa, caballo de prueba militar
event rider	jinete de prueba completa, jinete de prueba militar
eventing	prueba completa, prueba militar
exceed the time limit (to)	exceder el tiempo, exceder el límite de tiempo
fall of horse	caída del caballo
fall of rider	caída del jinete
faults	faltas, errores, fallos
fences	vallas, saltos
jump-through fences	saltos de pasada
spread fences	saltos anchos
steps down and drop fences	peldaños abajo y saltos botados
water fences	saltos de agua
foot in the water	pie en el agua
halfway	media cancha, medio camino
jump an obstacle in the wrong order (to)	saltar un obstáculo fuera de orden, saltar un obstáculo fuera de secuencia
jumping derby	derby de salto
knockdown	botada, tirada
levels of competition	niveles de competición
novice	novicios
obstacles	obstáculos
phase	fase
cross-country phase	fase de cross, fase de campo abierto

dressage phase	fase de adiestramiento
show-jumping phase	fase de salto, fase de concurso de salto
speed and endurance phase	fase de velocidad y resistencia
steeplechase phase	fase de steeplechase
refusal	rehusada
retake an obstacle (to)	retomar un obstáculo, repetir un obstáculo
roads and tracks	caminos y pistas
run out	evasión, salida de cancha
uprights	verticales, postes
veterinary check	examen veterinario
veterinary inspection	inspección veterinario

Hunting
cazando

at bay	acosado, a la tierra
bitch/gyp	perra
brush	matorral
capping fee	tarifa de caza
couple	pareja, un par
cross-country (to ride)	montar a campo traviesa, montar a campo abierto
cub hunt (to)	cazar por cachorro
cubbing	zorrilando
cunning	astuto
ditch	zanja
dogs	perros
drag hunt (to)	cazar por arrastre
field (country)	campo
field (persons)	grupo de los cazadores
fox	zorro
fox hole	zorrera
fox hound	perro raposero
fox hunt (the)	caza por zorros
fox tail	cola de zorro
hedge	seto
hounds	perros de caza, mastines
hunt (to)	cazar
fox hunt (to)	cazar por zorros
stag hunt (to)	cazar de cierro
hunt an area for foxes (to)	recorrer una región en busca de zorros, cazar una región de zorro

hunt cap	trago
hunt trials	pruebas de caza
hunter (horse)	caballo de caza
hunter (person)	cazador/a, montera
hunting	caza, cacería, montería
cub hunting	caza de cachorro
drag hunting	caza de arrastre
fox hunting	caza de zorros
stag hunting	caza de ciervo
hunting dogs	perros de caza
hunting dress	traje de caza
hunting field	terreno de caza, terreno de cacería, campo de caza
hunting horn	cuerno de caza
hunting manners	modales de caza, etiqueta de caza
huntsman	cazador
kennel huntsman	cazador de perrera
kennel	perrera
kill (the)	muerte
kill (to)	matar
kill the fox (to)	matar el zorro
master of the hounds	maestro de los perros
master of the hunt	maestro de la caza
pack (the)	perrada, jauría, perrería
pick up the scent (to)	encontrar el rastro, ollar el rastro
quarry	presa
ride cross-country (to)	montar a campo traviesa, montar a campo libre, montar a campo abierto
ride to the hounds (to)	cazar con jauría
scent	rastro, olfato
second horse	segundo caballo
stag hunt (the)	cazar de cierro
trophy	trofeo
whelp	cachorro
whipper-in	montero

Jumping
saltando

angle of the approach	ángulo del aproche, enfoque
approach the fence (to)	aproximarse al obstáculo, acercarse al obstáculo
banks, slopes, and ramps	banquetas, cuestas y rampas

bar	vara, barreta, caña
bent line ...*.....................	línea chueca
bounce in the cups (to)	saltar en los soportes
bring down a fence (to)	botar un obstáculo, bajar el salto
brush (to)	rozar, tocar
brush box	muro de ramas
bury the horse (to)	hundir el caballo
calcutta	calcuta
center of the jump	centro del salto
chef d'Équipe	jefe de equipo
chip (to)	astillar
circling	rodeando, circulando
clear the fence (to)	saltar limpio
competitions	concursos
count the strides of the horse (to) ...	contar las pisadas del caballo
course	recorrido, curso
off course	fuera del recorrido
on course	en el recorrido
course plan	plano del recorrido, plano por el curso
cups (the)	soportes
deep cups	soportes profundos
flat cups	soportes planos
shallow cups	soportes llanos, soportes poco profundos
cut the corner (to)	cortar la esquina, abreviar la esquina
distance between the fences	distancia entre los saltos
estimate (to)	estimar, calcular
estimate the distance (to)	estimar la distancia
exceed the time allowed (to)	exceder el tiempo permitido
fall (the)	caída
fall of horse	caída del caballo
fall of rider	caída del jinete
fall (to)	caer
faults	errores, faltas
fence	salto, obstáculo, valla
artificial fence	obstáculo artificial
combination fence	combinación, salto compuesto
double fence	salto doble
fixed fence	salto fijo
spread fence	salto ancho
straight fence	salto recto, salto derecha
triple bar fence	salto de barra triple
foot in the water	pie en el agua, pisar agua
gates	puertas
ground line	cuerda
hog's back	salto de lomo de chancho

hog's back
salto de lomo de chancho

in-and-out	salto de dentro y fuera
jump (the)	salto
water jump	salto de agua
jump (to)	saltar
jump (to have a lot of)	tener mucho salto
jump off (the)	desempate
first jump off	primer desempate
jump off (to)	desempatar
jump standards	postes que soportan la barra de salto, postes verticales
jump stands	postes, verticales
jump the horse over the fence (to)	hacer saltar el caballo sobre el salto
jumper	caballo de salto
Grand Prix jumper	caballo de salto de gran premio, caballo de salto de Grand Prix
intermediate jumper	caballo de salto intermedio
open jumper	caballo de salto abierto
preliminary jumper	caballo de salto preliminario
speed/modified jumper	caballo de salto modificado
jumping	saltando
Grand Prix jumping	salto de gran premio, salto de Grand Prix
open jumping	salto abierto
show jumping	concurso hípico, concurso de saltos
speed jumping	salto de velocidad
team jumping	salto por equipos
jumping ability	habilidad de salto, talento de salto
knock down (to)	derribar, botar
knock down a fence (to)	derribar un salto, botar un obstáculo
knock over (to)	botar, tirar
know the course (to)	conocer el curso
land (to)	llegar, caer
land on the tape (to)	pisar la cinta, tocar la cinta

landing	llegada, caída
line	línea
liverpool	liverpool
miss the spot (to)	errar la distancia, faltar la distancia
multiple obstacles	saltos múltiples
obstacle	salto, obstáculo, valla
closed obstacle	salto cerrado
natural obstacle	salto natural
open ditch	zanja abierta
oxer	oxer
ramped oxer	oxer de rampa, oxer oblicuo
Swedish oxer	oxer sueco
pole	vara, barreta, caña
rap pole	caña
tack pole	caña con clavos
Prix de Nations	Premio de Naciones, Prix de Nations
puissance	salto de potencia
rail (the)	riel, reja, barra
back rail	riel de atrás
front rail	riel de adelante, riel de frente
ground rail	riel de tierra
side rail	riel del lado, riel cerca
top rail	riel de arriba
rap (to)	rozar
refusal	rehusada
refuse a fence (to)	rehusar un salto
release (the)	aflojamiento
neck release	rienda a la crin
secondary release	afloja secundaria
release (to)	dar las riendas, aflojar las riendas
review the course (to)	revisar el curso
ride a turn (to)	hacer un recorrido, montar la vuelta
roll a bar (to)	voltear la vara, rollar un riel
roll top	rodón
rub (to)	tocar
run out	salida de cancha, evasión del obstáculo
school on the flat (to)	trabajar sin saltos, trabajar en picadero, ensayar movimientos planos
see a spot (to)	ver un lugar, conocer el punto
standards	postes verticales
straight line	línea recta
strides	pisadas
How many strides?	¿Cuántas pisadas?

triple combination
combinación triple

take off	punto de picar, punto de saltar
trebles	triples
triple combination	combinación triple
turn (the)	vuelta
short turn	vuelta corta
wide turn	vuelta abierta, vuelta ancha
turn (to)	volver
turn quickly (to)	volver rápidamente
turn wide (to)	volver ancho
unauthorized assistance	ayuda externa, ayuda sin autorización
uprights	verticales
walk the course (to)	caminar la cancha, caminar el curso
walk off the stride (to)	caminar las batidas, pisar distancia
wall	pared, muro, muralla
weight requirement	peso reglamentario, peso requerido
work over fences (to)	calentar sobre saltos, trabajar sobre saltos

Polo
polo

arena polo	polo de arena
back the ball	tiro para atrás
chukka, chucker	chukka, entrada
forward	delantero
free hit from center	tiro libre del centro
free hit from a spot	tiro libre del lugar
goal	gol, tanto, meta
high goal	juego de polo alta categoría
low goal	juego de polo baja categoría

medium goal	juego de polo mediana categoría
handicap	valor en goles de cada jugador, handicap, desventaja
collective handicap	handicap colectivo, suma de valores individuales
team handicap	handicap de equipo, la suma de los cuatro goles
hit out from behind	saque
hook (to)	enganchar
hooking	enganche con el mazo
How much time is left to play?	¿Cuánto tiempo queda de juega?
infringement	infracción, violación
match	juego
offside, forehand stroke	golpe por la derecha
ones	uno delantero
penalty	castigo
penalty three (3)	castigo tres (3)
penalty four (4)	castigo cuatro (4)
penalty five-a (5a) (thirty (30)-yard hit)	castigo cinco a (5a) (tiro de treinta (30) yardas)
penalty five-b (5b) (forty (40)-yard hit)	castigo cinco be (5b) (tiro de cuarenta (40) yardas)
penalty six (6) (sixty (60)-yard hit)	castigo seis (6) (tiro de sesentall (60) yardas — con defensores, tiro de sesentall (60) yardas con poder intercepción)
penalty seven-a (7a) (another hit)	castigo siete a (7a) (otro tiro)
penalty seven-b (7b) (hit in by defenders)	castigo siete be (7b) (tiro de un defensor)
penalty seven-c (7c) (hit in from the thirty (30)-yard line)	castigo siete ce (7c) (tiro de treinta (30) yardas, gol abierto)
penalty seven-d (7d) (unnecessary delay)	castigo siete de (7d) (retraso innecesario de juego, espera innecesaria)
penalty eight (8) (player to retire)	castigo ocho (8) (jugador expulsado)
penalty nine-a (9a) (pony disqualified)	castigo nueve a (9a) (caballo descalificado, poney descalificado)

penalty nine-b (9b) (pony ordered off)	castigo nueve be (9b) (caballo que se autoriza a cambiar)
penalty nine-c (9c) (player ordered off)	castigo nueve ce (9c) (jugador que se autoriza a cambiar)
penalty ten (10) (player excluded)	castigo diez (10) (jugador excluído)
penalty goal	gol de castigo, gol abierto
penalty hit	tiro de castigo
period	tiempo
play (the)	juego
play (to)	jugar
play polo (to)	jugar polo
player	jugado
eight (8)-goal player	jugado de ocho (8) goles
ten (10)-goal player	jugador de diez (10) goles
nineteen (19)-goal player	jugado de diecinueve (19) goles
playing field	campo de jugar polo
polo club	club de polo
polo field	campo para polo
polo lessons	lecciones de polo
polo pitch	campo de polo
polo player	jugador de polo, polista
polo pony	poney de polo, caballo de polo
polo pony market	mercado del poney de polo
polo strokes	golpes
polo team	equipo de polo
position	posición
professional polo	polo de profesión, polo profesional
ride off (the)	caballazo, carga
safety zone	contra cancha, zona de seguridad
score a goal (to)	marcar un gol
sixty (60)-yard hit	tiro de sesenta (60) yardas
sixty (60)-yard hit with defenders	tiro de sesenta (60) yardas, con poder de intercepción
team captain	capitán del equipo
threes	tres delantero
throw in	bola puesta in juego por árbitro o juez
twos	dos delantero
umpire	árbitro, árbitro de polo

Racing
carreras

added	extra para ganador
all-ages sale	venta de todas las edades
also eligible	elegibles
backstretch	estero de atrás
bad ride (to have a)	tener mala montura
bear out	se tira para afuera
bet (the)	apuesta
bet (to)	apostar
place a bet (to)	apostar
Where can I place a bet?	¿Dónde está la ventanilla de apuestas?
betting	apostando
off-track betting	apuestas afuera del hipódromo
betting shop	agencia de apuestas hípicas
betting window	ventana de apuestas
bettor	apostante
break post (to)	empezar la carrera
break the maiden (to)	correr la primera vez
breakage	quebrada
Breeder's Cup	Copa de Criadores
breeding-stock sale	venta de criadores
breeze (to)	galopar ligero
carry weight (to)	cargar peso
chute	cajón
claimer	caballo de reclamo
claiming price	precio de reclamo
classic	clásico/a
come in first (to)	llegar primero
coupled	acoplado/a
course	pista
racecourse	pista
turf course	pista de grama, pista de sacate, pista de pasto
crowd (to)	empujar
dead heat	empate
disqualification	descalificación
dope (to)	endrogar, drogar
draw the race (to)	seleccionar los caballos en la carrera
drug (to)	endrogar, drogar
entry	entrada, apunte
exacta	exactamente
excluded	fuera de la carrera

favorite	favorito
field	grupo del los caballos en la carrera
tough field	grupo difícil de los caballos en la carrera
field horse	caballo en la carrera
film patrol	patrulla cinematográfica, patrulla de filmación
finish (the)	el final
finish (to)	finalizar
finish line	línea de final
finish strong (to)	finalizar fuerte
first running	primera vez, corriendo primero
foul	falta
front stretch	el derecho de atrás, recta inicial
furlong	estadio, medida de doscientos y un metros
futurity	carrera del futuro
gamble (to)	apostar, jugar
gate (the)	gatera
to the gates/post	a la gatera
go to the inside (to)	correr hacia adentro
go to the outside (to)	correr hacia afuera
go to the races (to)	ir a las carreras
good ride (to have a)	tener buena montura
graded stakes	carreras de grados
grass horse	caballo carrera en la pista de pasto
guaranteed	garantizado
handicap	desventaja, handicap
hold the position (to)	mantener la posición
infield	medio de la pista
in the body	dentro de la carrera
inquiry	averiguación
jockey	jinete, jockey, vaquerillo (Mex.)
apprentice jockey	aprendiz de jockey
jockey fees	sueldo del jinete
jockey valet	mozo, mozo de jockey
leading money earner (the horse)	caballo ganador de más dinero
leading money earner (the rider)	jinete ganador de más dinero
length (a)	un cuerpo, echada
one length	un cuerpo
long shot (to be a)	tener poco oportunidad de ganar, tener poco chance de ganar
maiden horse	caballo sin ganancia
minimum weight	peso mínimo
mixed meeting	pura sangre y cuarto de milla

move along the inside (to)	mover por adentro, mover hacia adentro
move along the outside (to)	mover por afuera, mover hacia afuera
nomination	nominación
nomination fee	paga de nominación, paga para nominación
nomination form	forma de nominación
outrider	jinete para ayudar
owner	dueño
pace (the)	el paso
partnership	un conjunto de dueños
pay (to)	pagar
perfecta	apuesta perfectamente
photo finish	final de carrera muy reñido
place (to)	llegar en segundo lugar
play the horses (to)	apostar en las carreras de caballos
post position	posición para arancar
purse (the)	premio
race (the)	carrera
added money race	carrera de extra dinero
allowance race	carrera de allowance
claiming race	carrera de reclamación
combination race	carrera combinada, carrera de combinación
flat race	carrera plana
grade-one race	carrera a grado uno
grade-two race	carrera a grado dos
grade-three race	carrera a grado tres
horse race	carrera de caballos
horse race (as sport)	hipismo
hurdle race	carrera de salto
jump race	carrera de salto
listed race	carrera listada, carrera anunciada
maiden allowance race	carrera de allowance para no ganadores
maiden race	carrera de no ganadores
match race	carrera al pelo
non-qualified, added-money race	no cualificado, carrera de dinero extra
Q race	carrera de más de treinta mil dolares
restricted race	carrera restringida
selling race	carrera de reclamación
stakes race	carrera de premio mayor

race (to)	correr
race a horse (to)	correr un caballo
race card	programa de carreras, tarjeta de carreras
race course	pista
race goer	aficionado a las carreras de caballos
race horse	caballo de carrera
race program	programa de carreras
race steward	juez de carreras
racer	corredor
races (the)	carreras
racetrack (facility)	hipódromo
racetrack (the track)	pista de carreras
racing	carreras
harness racing	carreras de los trotones, carreras de trote, carreras de trotadores
horse racing	carreras
pacer racing	carreras de caballos de paso
quarter horse racing	carreras de cuarto de milla
standardbred racing	carreras de sangre estándard
thoroughbred racing	carreras de pura sangre
trotter racing	carreras de trote
racing age	edades de carreras
racing commission	comisión hípica, comisión de carreras
racing committee	comité de carreras
racing office	oficina de carreras
racing official	oficial de carreras, funcionario hípico
racing schedule	programa de carreras
racing silks	colores
save ground (to)	ganar terreno
scratch (to)	retirarse
second running	segunda vez, segunda corrida
set down	suspensión
set down (to be)	estar suspendido
show (to)	tercer lugar, llegar en tercer lugar
shut off (to be)	estar cerrado
silks	colores
sprint (to)	sprinter, correr
sprinter	corredor, sprinter
stakes book	libro de premio mayor
stakes winner	ganador de premio mayor
start (to)	empezar
starter's orders	orden para empezar
starting gate	gatera, barrera, en línea de salida

starting time	tiempo de carrera
stayer	caballo de larga distancia
steeple chase	carrera de obstáculos
take down the number (to)	descalificar el numero, descalificar
take position (to)	tomar posición
test (the)	examen, prueba
drug test	examen para droga, examen de drogas
saliva test	examen de saliva
urine test	examen de orina
test the horse (to)	examinar el caballo, hacer un análisis de caballo
throw the jockey (to)	derribar al jinete
The horse threw the jockey.	El caballo derribó al jinete.
ticket	boleto
ticket window	taquilla
Where is the ticket window?	¿Dónde está la taquilla?
track (the)	pista
dirt track	pista de tierra
fast track	pista rápida, pista veloz
grass track	pista de pasto
main track	pista de carreras
major track	pista mayor
muddy track	pista fangosa, pista lodoso
off track	pista mala
sloppy track	pista resvalosa
slow track	pista despacio
training track	pista de entrenamiento
wet track	pista mojada
track steward	juez de la pista
turf	hipódromo
turn (the)	curva
turn (to)	volver
weigh in (to)	pesar
weight allowance	autorización de peso
weight cloth	faldón de pesas
win (to)	ganar

ground tie (to)
amarrar al piso

win by a length (to)	ganar por un cuerpo
win by a neck (to)	ganar por un cuello
win by a nose (to)	ganar por una nariz
win by half a length (to)	ganar por un medio cuerpo
winner's circle	círculo de ganadores
winner's picture	fotografía de ganadores
yearling sale	venta de potrillos de un año

Western
vaquero

barrel racing	carrera de baril
bowline knot	nudo de rosa
calf roping	piales
cutting	cortando
cutting horse	caballo de aparta, caballo para cortar
dally (to)	afirmar la reata
dally roping	dar la vuelta, enlazar a reata suelta
dodge (to)	esquivar
duck (to)	agachar, esquivar agachando la cabeza
gaucho life	vida gauchesca, vida de gaucho
give enough rope (to)	darle suficiente cuerda
ground tie (to)	amarrar al piso, amarrar en tierra
gymkhana	gymkhana
hackamore horse	caballo de falsa rienda, caballo de jáquima
have enough cow (to)	saber vaquera
header (to be a)	enlazador de cabeza
heel loop	pial
heeler (to be a)	enlazador de patas, pillador
hitch a horse to a tree (to)	atar un caballo a un árbol
lasso (to)	coger con el lazo, lazar

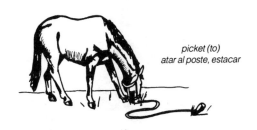

picket (to)
atar al poste, estacar

neck rein (to)	riendar una mano, riendar sobre el cuello
picket (to)	atar al poste, estacar
picket the horse (to)	atar un caballo a la estaca
pleasure horse	caballo de paseo, caballo de placer
rein hand	mano de rienda
reiner	calador
reiner (to be)	estar arrendado, ser calador
reining horse	caballo arrendado, caballo bien riendado
ride barrels (to)	correr barriles
rodeo	rodeo
roll back (the)	volapié
rope (the)	cuerda, lariat, lazo
rope (to)	enlazar
roper	enlazador, de lazo, lazador
roping	enlazando, lazando
roping horse	caballo de lazo
round up (to)	rodear
set and turn	sentado y volapié
sliding stop	sentada enalgada
wild sliding stop	sentada enalgada descontrolada, enalgada fuera de control
stock horse	caballo vaquero
team pen (to)	acorralar por equipos
trail horse	caballo hullero

Transporting the Horse
transportando el caballo

air transport	transporte aéreo
clean the trailer (to)	limpiar el acoplado, limpiar el

sliding stop
sentada enalgada

trailer (the)
acoplado

	trailer, limpiar el remolque
haul (to)	transportar
hitch the trailer to the truck (to)	enganchar el remolque al camión
horse passport	pasaporte de caballo
horse van	furgón para el transporte de los caballos
horse wagon (train)	vagón para transportar caballos
load (to)	cargar
load the horses (to)	cargar los caballos
quarantine	cuarentena
quarantine regulations	reglamentos de cuarentena
ramp	rampa
trailer (the)	acoplado, remolque, trailer
goose-neck trailer	acoplado de quinta rueda, remolque de quinta rueda
horse trailer	acoplado, trailer (Mex.), remolque para caballos
two-horse trailer	acoplado para dos caballos
trailer (to)	transportar
truck (the)	camión
truck (to)	transportar los caballos por camión
unload (to)	descargar
unload the horses (to)	descargar los caballos
van (the)	camioneta
van (to)	transportar por camioneta

Showing the Horse
concursando el caballo

announcer	anunciador, locutor
bell (the)	timbre, campana
clear round	recorrido sin faltas
compete	competir
competition	concurso, competición

competitor	concursante
course	curso, recorrido
off course	fuera de recorrido, fuera de curso
on course	en recorrido, en curso
course (to set the)	afilar el curso
course designer	diseñador
disqualification	descalificación
disqualified (to be)	ser descalificado/a
eliminate (to)	eliminar
elimination (the)	eliminación
enter the ring (to)	entrar a la cancha, entrar a la arena
entry (the)	inscripción, entrada
entry fee	costo de la inscripción
error	error
error of the course	error de recorrido
error of the test	error en la lección
event (the)	concurso, evento
Federation (FEI) rules	reglamento de la Federación Internacional Ecuestre, reglas de la Federación
finish (the)	llegada
finish (to)	llegar, terminar
flag	bandera
red flag	bandera roja
white flag	bandera blanca
horse show	concurso, hípico
in gate	puerta de entrada
judge (the)	juez
judge (to)	juzgar
judge's sheets	planillas
judge's stand	caseta del jurado
judging	juzgando
leave the ring (to)	abandonar la cancha, salir de la cancha
nomination fees	costos de nominación
opening ceremony	comienzo de la ceremonia
out gate	puerta de salida
penalty	falta, penalidad, pena
penalty points	puntos penales, penalidades
penalty seconds	penalidades, segundos de penalidad
percentage	porcentaje
performance	actuación
place (the)	lugar
first place	primer lugar
second place	segundo lugar
third place	tercer lugar

fourth place	cuarto lugar
fifth place	quinto lugar
place (to)	premiar
present the horse (to)	presentar el caballo
prize	premio
regulations	reglamento
ribbon	tirón
riding accident	accidente de montar
riding time	tiempo del recorrido, tiempo de la lección, tiempo acordado
ring steward	juez de cancha
rules	reglas
salute (the)	saludo
salute (to)	saludar
salute the judge (to)	saludar al juez
scratch (to)	retirarse
scoring	resultados
show (the)	concurso
away show	concurso afuera, concurso distante
indoor show	concurso adentro
show (to)	concursar
show circuit	circuito
showing	concursando
showmanship	talento
sound the bell (to)	tocar el timbre, tocar la campana, sonar la campana
speed	velocidad
time	tiempo
interrupted time	tiempo interrumpido
time allowed	tiempo permitido, tiempo reglamentario, límite de tiempo
time limit	tiempo limitado, límite de tiempo
time of resistance	tiempo de resistencia
time on the clock	tiempo en el reloj de reglamento
time penalty	falta por tiempo, falta de tiempo, pena de tiempo
time clock	cronómetro, reloj registrador
turned out (to be)	estar bien presentado
turned out horse	caballo bien presentado, caballo bien aseado
turned out rider	jinete bien presentado
vaccination certificate	certificado de vacuna, historia de vacunación
vaccination records	registro de vacuna
win (to)	ganar
win a ribbon (to)	ganar una cinta, ganar un tirón
withdraw (to)	retirar

field boots
botas camperas

Riding Habit
traje de montar

back protector	protector de la espalda
bandaid	vendita, curita (Mex.)
bat	fusta, fuete, plano
belt	cinto, cinturón
blouse	blusa
body protector	protector del cuerpo
bombachas	bombachas
boots	botas
ankle boots	botas al tobillo, botas cortas
cowboy boots	botas vaqueras
cuff-lined boots	botas medio forradas
custom boots	botas hechas a la medida
dressage boots	botas para adiestramiento botas para dressage
field boots	botas camperas, botas de campo
hunt boots	botas para caza
jodhpur boots	botín
lined boots	botas forradas
paddock boots	botín
polo boots	botas para polo
racing boots	botas para jockey
rubber riding boots	botas de goma para montar
stiff boots	botas duras, botas rígidas
top boots	botas altas
unlined boots	botas sin forro
boot bag	bolsa para bota
boot brush	cepillo para bota
boot hook	tirabotas, gancho para botas, gancho
boot jack	sacabotas
boot lace	cordón
boot legs	piernas de botas

boot polish	betún, grasa
boot rubbers	galochas
boot straps	orejas, orejas de mulo
boot tree	horma de bota
boots (to dust off my)	limpiar el polvo de mis botas, quitar el polvo a mis botas, sacudir mis botas
bowler	bombín, sombrero hongo
bow tie	corbata de lazo
breeches	pantalones de montar
cotton breeches	pantalones de algodón para montar
full-seat breeches	pantalones de montar con asiento completo
half-seat breeches	pantalones de montar con medio asiento
riding breeches	pantalones de montar
synthetic breeches	pantalones sintéticos de montar
tailor-made breeches	pantalones hechos a la medida
breeches leather	remonta
change clothes (to)	cambiar las ropas
chaps	chaparreras, zajones (Sp.)
custom chaps	chaparreras a la medida
English chaps	chaparreras inglesas
half chaps	chaparreras a la mitad
western chaps	chaparreras de vaquero
choker tie	corbata ahogadera
clean the boots (to)	limpiar las botas
clothes bag	bolsa de ropa
coat	saco, chaqueta
black coat	saco negro
dressage coat	saco de adiestramiento, saco de dressage, saco de vestir
hunt coat	saco de caza, saco para cazar
melton hunt coat	saco de paño
overcoat	abrigo
pink coat	saco rojo
raincoat	saco impermeable
riding coat	saco de montar
tailcoat	frac
tailor-made coat	saco hecho a la medida
tuxedo coat	saco de smoking
waist coat	chaleco
crop	fuete, fusta

crop
fuete, fusta

dress (to)	vestir
face guard	máscara protectora
garter	liga
gloves	guantes
hairnet	redecilla
hairpin	horquilla
hat	sombrero
cowboy hat	sombrero vaquero, sombrero de cowboy
silk top hat	sombrero de copa, sombrero de seda
top hat	sombrero de copa, chistera
hat guard	guardia para sombrero protectora para sombrero
hatbox	sombrerera
helmet	casco, casco de caza
helmet cover	cubierto para casco
helmet harness	harness de casco
hunt cap	casco
hunt-cap cover	cubierto para casco
hunt crop	fuete de caza, látigo de caza
hunt derby	tongo, hongo
hunt flask	frasco, licorera
hunt thongs	traíllas
hunt vest	chaleco de caza
jeans	pantalones de mezclilla, jeans
western-cut jeans	pantalones corte de vaquero
jewelry	joyería, joyas
jockey cap	casco
jodhpurs	jodhpurs
jodhpur knee straps	ligas
kerchief	pañuelo
leather knee pad	rodillera
leggings	polainas
long underwear	ropa interior larga
mule ears	orejas de mulo, orejas

shadbelly
frac

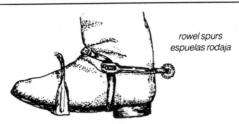

rowel spurs
espuelas rodaja

neck wear	corbata
pant clips	clips de pantalón
polish the boots (to)	brillar las botas, dar grasa a las botas, lustrar las botas
poncho	poncho
pull on boots (to)	ponerse las botas
quirt	cuarta
racing colors	colores
racing silks	colores
rain pants	pantalones de lluvia
rain suit	traje de lluvia
rat catcher (blouse)	blusa a la inglesa
rat catcher (tie)	corbata a la inglesa
riding habit	traje de montar
riding skirt	pollera de montar, falda para montar
rope	cuerda
safety pin	alfiler, gancho, afiler de broche, imperdible
shadbelly	frac
shine the boots (to)	sacar brillo a las botas
shirt	camisa
shirt studs	gemelos, colleras
silk scarf	pañuelo de seda
spur straps	correas para espuela, cintos para espuela
spurs	espuelas
children's spurs	espuelas de niños
dummy spurs	espuelas falsas
men's spurs	espuelas de hombres
rowel spurs	espuelas rodaja
sharp spurs	espuelas puntadas, espuelas con punta
western spurs	espuelas de vaquero
women's spurs	espuelas de mujer
stock pin	alfiler

stock tie	corbata
take off the boots (to)	quitarse las botas, sacarse las botas
tie bar	barra
undress (to)	desnudar
wear a size . . . (to)	usar una talla . . .
whip	fusta, látigo
dressage hip	fuete de adiestramiento, fuete de dressage, fusta de adiestramiento, fusta de dressage
driving whip	fuete de tiro
longe whip	látigo largo, huasca larga
racing whip	fuete de carreras

Tack
equipo

back jockey	sobrefalda
bandage	venda
anti-inflammatory bandage	venda anti-inflamatoria
cast bandage	venda de enyesar, venda de yeso
exercise bandage	venda de ejercicio
fetlock bandage	venda de cuartilla
hock bandage	venda de garrón
knee bandage	venda de rodilla
poultice bandage	venda de cataplasma
pressure bandage	venda de presión
running bandage	venda de carrera
shipping bandage	venda de transporte, venda de embarque
spider-web bandage	venda de telaraña
standing bandage	venda de descanso
support bandage	venda de descanso, venda de soporte
sweat bandage	venda de sudar
tail-wrap bandage	venda de la cola
wound bandage	venda de herida
bib	babero
billet straps	correas de barriguera, látigos
bit	freno, filete
curb bit	freno de palanca, freno de curva
jointed curb bit	freno de palanca con bocado accionado

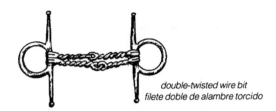

double-twisted wire bit
filete doble de alambre torcido

straight curb bit	freno de palanca con bocado recto
double-twisted wire bit	filete doble de alambre torcido
Dr. Bristol bit	freno Bristol
elevator bit	freno de elevador, levantador
English bit	filete
full-cheek bit	freno con patas
gag bit	ahogador, filete para ahogador
generic bit	freno
German-made bit	freno hecho en Alemania
kimberwicke bit	freno Kimberwick, freno de palanca corta
leverage bit	freno
pelham bit	freno para dos riendas, pollero, pelham
pony bit	freno de poney, filete de poney
rubber bit	freno de goma
silver bit	freno de plata
snaffle bit	filete
spade bit	freno de cuchara
sweet-steel bit	freno de fierro dulce
training bit	freno de trabajo, freno de entrenamiento
western bit	freno de vaquero
Weymouth bit	bocado doble, bocado completo, freno y filete
bit burr	guarda cepillada
bit guard	guarda de freno
bit mouthpiece	bocado
bit parts	partes de freno
bit port	portalón
bit rings	anillos, argollas
bitting harness	arnés de embridar, arreos de embridar, jaez
bitting rig	apero de embridar
blanket	manta, manta para caballos (Sp.), camisa (Mex.), cobija, frazada

bell boots
campanas de hule

light blanket	manta ligera
waterproof blanket	manta impermeable
blanket hood	capucha de la manta
blindfold	venda
blinkers	mascarillas, anteojeras
boots	botas, protectores, zapatillas
back boots	botas traseras, botas de atrás
bell/coronet boots	campanas de hule, botas de goma cubrecascos
brushing boots	rozadoras
easy boots	zapatillas para cascos
front boots	botas delanteras
galloping boots	galopadoras, botas para galope
hind boots	botas traseras
hock boots	garroneras
kicking boots	pateadoras
knee boots	rodilleras
leather boots	botas de cuero
open-front boots	botas con frente abierto
overreach boots	alcanzadoras
polo boots	botas de polo
poultice boots	botas de medicación
service boots	botas de servicio
sheepskin boots	botas de piel de oveja
shin boots	botas de huesos
shipping boots	botas de embarque, botas de transporte, cañeras de viaje
shoe-boil boots	botas para bursitis del codo, botas de descanso
splint boots	cañeras, botas contra sobrehueso
treatment boots	botas para tratamiento
breastplate	pechera, pretal
bridle	brida
double bridle	brida doble
full bridle	brida completa
racing bridle	brida de carreras
snaffle bridle	brida de filete
split-ear bridle	brida de oreja partida

bridle
brida

bridle cover	cubierta de brida
bridle parts	partes de la brida
bridle rack	gancho para la brida, gancho para la cavesada
bridoon	bridón
egg-butt bridoon	bridón ovalado, filete ovalado
ordinary bridoon	bridón ordinario, filete ordinario
two-joint bridoon	bridón con doble articulación
bridoon with cheeks	bridón con patas
browband	frontalera
buckle	hebilla
bucket heater	calentador
cantle	cantileja, borrén, teja (Mex.), copa (Ch., Arg.)
carriage	coche
hackney carriage	coche de alquiler
cart	carretilla, carreta
two-wheeled cart	calesa, carreta de dos ruedas
cavesson	cavesada, cabezón (Sp.)
longeing cavesson	cavesada de torneo, cavesada de trabajo a cuerda
training cavesson	cavesada de entrenamiento, cavesada de trabajo
chain	cadena
curb chain	cadena
kicking chains	cadenas de patear, cadenas de cocear
stud chain	cadena de caballo semental
chambon	chambón
cheek piece	mejillera, pieza para mejilla
collar	collar
cooler	manta para enfriar
cribbing strap	collar para el chupador
crown piece	nuquera, corona
crupper	grupera
driving crupper	grupera para tiro

three-folded girth
cincha de tres partes

riding crupper	grupera para montar
feed bag	morral
fender	falda, arción
fetlock ring	anillo de nudo
flank cinch	barriguera
front jockey	sobrefalda
girth	cincha
breastgirth	pechera
elastic girth	cincha elástica
foregirth	cincha delantera
leather girth	cincha de cuero
nylon girth	cincha de nilón
overgirth	sobrecincha
regular girth	cincha regular
three-folded girth	cincha de tres partes
girth cover	cubierta para la cincha
girth extender	alargador de la cincha
girth tube	cubierta de la cincha
hackamore	jáquima
halter	cabestro, ronzal, almartigón, cavesada
adjustable halter	almartigón ajustable
grooming halter	almartigón de aseo
horse halter	almartigón del caballo, almartigón
leather halter	almartigón de cuero
nylon halter	almartigón de nilón
pony halter	almartigón del poney
show halter	almartigón de concurso, cabezón de lujo
halter tube	tubo de almartigón
harness	arreo, arnés, jaez
racing harness	arnés de carrera
head bumper	protectora para la cabeza
headstall	cabezada
hobble strap	tira de la manea

hobbles
maneas

hobble strap (saddle)	porta manea, porta cuarta, tiro de la manea
hobbles	maneas
hooks	ganchos
irons	estribos
keeper	pasadores
knee roll	rollo
lariat	reata
lasso	lazo
lead rope	cuerda
lead shank	cadena
leather oil	aceite para cuero
leather punch	punzón para hacer agujeros
leathers	arciones, aciones
lip strap	correa labial
longe line	cuerda larga
longe whip	látigo largo, huasca larga
martingale	martingala
DeGogue martingale	martingala DeGogue
German martingale	martingala alemana
running martingale	martingala de anillos
standing martingale	martingala de bajador
mouthpiece	bocado
muzzle	bozal
neck cradle	collar de cuna
neck guard	manta de cuello, protector
neck sweat	sudador de pescuezo
nose bag	morral
noseband	bozal, bozalillo, cavesada, muserola
drop noseband	muserola
figure-eight noseband	cavesada de ocho
flash noseband	cavesada doble, cavesada alemana
lever noseband	cavesada de plancha
padded noseband	cavesada acolchada
numnah	sudadero

overcheck	rienda engalladura
pad	sudadero, mantilla, manta, frazada, pelero
all-purpose pad	sudadero
bareback pad	sudadero con cincha
close-contact pad	sudadero de silla de salto
contour pad	sudadero conformado
cotton pad	sudadero de algodón
dressage pad	sudadero para silla de adiestramiento
fleece pad	sudadero de vellón
foam pad	sudadero de espuma de goma
half pad	medio sudadero
harness pad	almohadilla
lift-back pad	sudadero acolchado de atrás, pelero levantador
partial pad	sudadero parcial
pommel pad	sudadero de arzón, sudadero de cabecilla
quilted pad	sudadero acolchonado
square pad	sudadero cuadrado
thick pad	sudadero grueso, sudadero espeso
thin pad	sudadero delgado
western pad	sudadero, sudadero vaquero
withers pad	sudadero para cruz
polo mallet	martillo para polo
pommel	cabecilla
port	portalón
rein stops	topes
reins	riendas
braided reins	riendas trenzadas
bridoon reins	riendas de bridón
double reins	riendas dobles
draw reins	riendas de plancha
driving reins	riendas de tiro
hackamore reins	riendas falsas, mecate
hair reins	riendas de pelo, riendas de crin
laced reins	riendas pasadas
leather reins	riendas de cuero
long reins	riendas largas, riendas de cuerda
longeing rein	riendas a la cuerda
plain reins	riendas comunes
plaited reins	riendas trenzadas
roping reins	riendas de lazo
rubber reins	riendas de goma
side reins	riendas de atar
split reins	riendas divididas

Western saddle
silla, montura vaquera

web reins	riendas de tela, riendas de lona
riata	reata
rings	anillos, argollas
roller	rodillos
anti-cast roller	aparato contra atorado
body roller	rodillo de cuerpo
longeing roller	rodillo de trabajo a cuerda
padded roller	rodillo acolchado
training roller	rodillo de entrenamiento
rope	lazo, cuerda
rubber rings	anillos de goma
rubber stops	topes de hule (Mex.), topes de goma
saddle	silla de montar, montura, albardón
dressage saddle	silla de dressage
endurance saddle	silla de resistencia, silla de adiestramiento
English saddle	silla inglesa
flat saddle	silla plana, silla inglesa
hunt saddle	silla de cacería, albardón de cazamiento
jumping saddle	silla de salto
pack saddle	albarda, basto, enjalma de carga
polo saddle	silla de polo
race saddle	silla de carrera
sidesaddle	silla de lado, silla de amazona
small riding saddle	sillín
stock saddle	silla, montura vaquera, montura australiana
synthetic saddle	montura sintética
Western saddle	silla, montura vaquera
saddle cover	cubierta de montura
saddle flap	falda
saddle horn	cacho cabeza, cuerno
saddle horn neck	cuello de cacho, garacanta

saddle stand
caballete

saddle pad	sudadero, mantilla, manta, frazada, pelero
saddle-pad cover	cubierta del sudadero
saddle-pad liner	forro del sudadero
saddle rack	portasilla
saddle seat (the)	asiento
saddle seat size	talles del asiento de la silla
saddle soap	glicerina, jabón de calabasa (Mex.)
saddle stand	caballete
saddle strings	correas
saddle tree	fuste
saddle with a deep seat	silla con asiento profundo
saddle with a flat seat	silla con asiento plano
saddle with a hard seat	silla con asiento duro
saddle with a long flap	silla con falda larga
saddle with a narrow tree	silla con fuste angosto
saddle with a padded seat	silla con asiento acolchado
saddle with a regular tree	silla con fuste normal, silla con fuste regular
saddle with a wide tree	silla con fuste ancho
saddlebag	alforja, cantinas
saddlecloth	pelero, sudadero, corona (Mex.)
saddlery	herraje de sillero
seat	asiento
fifteen and a half (15.5)-inch seat	asiento de quince punto cinco (15.5) pulgadas o treinta y nueve punto siete (39.7) centímetros
sixteen (16)-inch seat	asiento de dieciséis (16) pulgadas o cuarenta y uno punto tres (41.03) centímetros
sixteen and a half (16.5)-inch seat	asiento de dieciséis punto cinco (16.5) pulgadas o cuarenta y dos punto (42.31) treinta y uno centímetros

seventeen (17)-inch seat	asiento de diecisiete (17) pulgadas o cuarenta y tres punto cincuenta y nueve (43.59) centímetros
seventeen and a half (17.5)-inch seat	asiento de diecisiete punto cinco (17.5) pulgadas o cuarenta y cuatro punto ochenta y siete (44.87) centímetros
eighteen (18)-inch seat	asiento de dieciocho (18) pulgadas o cuarenta y seis punto quince (46.15) centímetros
shadow roll	rollo de sombra
sheet	manta, manta para caballos (Sp.), camisa (Mex.), cobija
day sheet	manta para día, manta ligera
fly sheet	manta para proteger de moscas
quarter sheet	manta grupera
side jockey	sobre falda
skirt	falda
snaffle	filete
full-cheek snaffle	filete con patas
loose-ring snaffle	filete de anillos sueltos
snap	cierre
stall guard	guardia de la puerta, guardia del establo, pechera
stirrup	estribo
aluminum stirrup	estribo de aluminio
stirrup bar	barra de estribo
stirrup leathers	arciones, aciones
lined stirrup leathers	arciones forrados
synthetic stirrup leathers	arciones sintéticos
stirrup pads	colchoneta de los estribos
stirrup tread	piso del estribo
surcingle	sobrecincha
training surcingle	sobrecincha de escuela
vaulting surcingle	sobrecincha de acrobacia
swell	borrén, delantero, hombro
tack trunk	caja para equipo
tail wrap	venda para la cola
throatlatch	fiador
tie-down	bajador
trace	tirante
tug	tirante
turnout rug	manta de potrero
twist/waist	angostura, cintura

waist of the saddle	cintura
wash the wraps (to)	lavar las vendas
whipcracker	tronador
wraps	vendas
jumping wraps	vendas de salto
polo wraps	vendas de polo
race wraps	vendas de carrera
standing wraps	vendas de medicación, vendas de descanso, vendas de reposo

Equine Personnel
personal ecuestre

apprentice	aprendiz
boot maker	zapatero, botero
braider	trenzador/a
breeches maker	pantaloner/a
buckaroo	vaquero
cart driver	calesero/a
clipper	trasquilador/a
coach driver	conductor/a de carruaje
competitor	concursante
course builder	constructor/a del curso, armador/a de cancha, armador/a de pista
course designer	diseñador/a
cowboy	vaquero
equestrian	ecuestre, caballista, jinete
equestrienne	amazona, caballista
farrier	herrero/a
feeder	alimentador/a de caballos
foreman	supervisor, mayordomo
gaucho	gaucho
good judge of horseflesh (a)	un entendido en caballos
good judge of horses (a)	un buen entendido de caballos
groom	mozo de caballos, caballerango/a, cuidador de caballos, caballerizo
harness maker	talabartero, guarnicionero
horse agent	agente de caballos
horse breaker	domador/a de caballos, caballerango/a, petisero (Arg.)
horse breeder	criador/a de caballos
horse chiropractor	quiropráctico de caballos

horse dealer	comerciante de caballos, vendedor/a de caballos, negociante de caballos, chalán, tratante de caballos
horse dentist	dentista de caballos
horse doctor	veterinario/a
horse guards	guardia montada
horse handler	caballerango, caballerizo
horse hauler	transportador/a de caballos
horse manager	manejador/a de caballos, administrador/a de caballos
horse owner	dueño de caballo
horse person	persona a caballo, aficionado/a al caballerismo
horse thief	cuatrero/a, ladrón de caballos
horse trader	comerciante de caballos, vendedor/a de caballos, negociante de caballos
horseman	equitador, caballisto, jinete
horsewoman	caballista, equitadora
horsey person	persona a caballo
hot walker	paseador/a, caminador/a
international competitor	concursante internacional
jockey	vaquerillo (Mex.), jinete, jockey
apprentice jockey	jockey de aprendiz
landowner	terrateniente
absentee landowner	ausente
leather worker	talabartero
liveryman	propietario de caballo de alquiler
mule driver	mulero, muletero, arriero
muleskinner	mulero, muletero, arriero
muleteer	mulero, muletero, arriero
owner of horses	dueño de caballo
rancher	ranchero/a
rider	jinete, equitador/a
amateur rider	caballista aficionado/a
beginning rider	jinete novicio/a, jinete en entrenamiento
circus rider	jinete de circo
novice rider	jinete novicio/a, jinete en entrenamiento
professional rider	profesional, jinete profesional
skilled rider	jinete, caballero, amazona, equitador/a de experiencia
trick rider	jinete de circo
riding instructor	instructor/a de equitación
riding master	maestro/a de equitación
riding student	estudiante de equitación, discípulo/a de equitación

saddle maker	guarnicionero, monturero, talabartero
pack saddle maker	enjalmero
saddler	monturero, sillero, talabartero
student	estudiante
working student	discípulo/a de maestro
tailor	sastre
teacher	profesor/a, maestro/a
trainer	domador/a de caballos, entrenador
assistant trainer	asistente de entrenador, asistente de entrenamiento, ayudante de entrenador, asistente
dressage trainer	entrenador/a de adiestramiento, entrenador/a de dressage
English trainer	entrenador/a de inglesa
horse trainer	entrenador/a de caballos, domador/a de caballos
hunter trainer	entrenador/a de caza
jumper trainer	entrenador/a de salto
Peruvian trainer	chalán
western trainer	entrenador/a de vaquero
veterinarian	veterinario/a
wrangler	caballerango/a

Equine Words and Expressions
palabras y expresiones equinas

bray (the)	rebuzno
bray (to)	relinchar
cart rut	carril, rodada
equine insurance	seguro equino
harness shop	guarnicionería, talabartería
hee-haw (the)	rebunzo
hee-haw (to)	rebunzar
hoofbeat	ruido de cascos
horse drawn	tirado por caballos
horse flesh	carne de caballo
horse management	administración de los caballos
horse sense	sentido común
horse trade	comercio en caballos, cambio de caballos, negocio de caballos, chalaneo
horse trading	comercio en caballos, cambio de caballos, negocio de caballos

horseless	sin caballo
horseless carriage	automóvil
horsemanship	equitación
horsepower	caballo de vapor
horse's ass	necio
horsey	caballuno
horsey smell	olor a caballo
horsiness	afición
lead horse	caballo que va en cabeza
lead mule	mulo que va en cabeza
leather shop	talabartería
mounting block	arrimadero
mule track	camino carretero
neigh (the)	relincho
neigh (to)	relinchar
pack saddle (to make)	enjalmar
packtrain	reata de caballos, reata de mulos
pull a carriage (to)	arrastrar un carruaje
riding is easy	es fácil montar a caballo
saddle repair	reparación de montura
saddle shop	monturía, talabartería, tienda de monturas
tack shop	talabartería
Where is the tack shop?	¿Dónde está la talabartería?
tailor shop	sastrería
whinny (the)	relincho
whinny (to)	relinchar
whoa!	¡so!

3
Equestrian Facility Management
administración de
instalaciones ecuestres

The Equine Facility
la instalación equina

aisle	pasillo
aqua tred	máquina con banda para ejercicio en el agua
arena	arena
covered arena	arena cubierta
enclosed arena	arena cerrada
practice arena	arena para ensayar, arena para practicar, ring de ensayo
automatic waterer	agua automática, abrevadero automático
barn	galpón
grain barn	granero
hay barn	galpón de forraje
horse barn	cuadril
training barn	cuadril de entrenamiento, centro hípico
bathroom	baño, cobertizo
Where is the bathroom?	¿Dónde está el baño?
bedding storage	galpón
boarding facility	cuadril, instalación, edificio para mantener caballos
bridle path	senda, sendero, huella, caminito
buildings	edificios
bull pen	corral redondo, corral toril
cattle guard	guardavaca
corral	corral
cross-ties	amarraderos, amarras cruzadas
dirt	tierra
equestrian center	centro equestre
farm	finca, granja, fundo
breeding farm	yeguada, criadero, rancho de criadero

cooperative farm	finca cooperativa
lay-up farm	campo de descanso, rancho de descanso
stud farm	yeguada
farmhouse	casa
feed room	granero, cuarto de alimento
feed trough	artesa, comedero
feed tub	tina de comida
feeding manger	pesebre
feeding rack	pesebre
fence	cerca, alambrado
barbed wire fence	cerca de púas
board fence	cerca de tabla
chain link fence	cerca de malla
concrete fence	cerca de concreto, cerca de material
electric fence	cerca eléctrica
nylon fence	cerca de nilón
pipe fence	cerca de pipa, cerca de tubo
plastic fence	cerca de plastico, cerca de PVC
rubber fence	cerca de hule, cerca de goma
wire fence	cerca de alambre
field	campo
open field	campo abierto
gate	puerta, paso
grain silo	silo para granos
grassland	pastizal
ground	tierra
hard ground	terreno duro
grounds	las tierras
hacienda	hacienda
hay loft	henil, galpón de forraje
hitching post	poste de amarre
hitching rack	amarradero, palenque

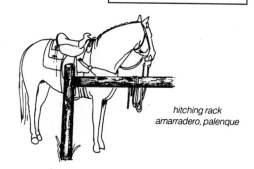

hitching rack
amarradero, palenque

holding	propiedad
hot walker (device)	mecánica para pasear, caminante
horse swimming pool	alberca para caballos, piscina para caballos
meadow	prado
large meadow	pradera, pradería
small meadow	prado pequeño
manège	manage, picadero de equitación
manger	pesebre, comedero
office	oficina
barn office	oficina, oficina de establo
Where is the office?	¿Dónde está la oficina?
office (to lock the)	cerrar la oficina con llave
office (to unlock the)	abrir la oficina
paddock	potrero
pasture	pasto, pastizal, pastura
summer pasture	agostadero, veraneo
plot	parcela
pond	charca
practice area	área para ensayar, área para practicar, área de ensayo
prairie	pradera
race track	pista de carrera
ranch	rancho
horse ranch	rancho de caballos
riding path	camino de herradura
riding school	escuela de equitación, picadero
ring	arena, pista de montar, picadero, cancha
covered ring	arena cubierta
dressage ring	pista de adiestramiento
jumper ring	picadero, cancha de salto, arena de salto
round ring	arena redonda
schooling ring	arena de entrenamiento, picadero de trabajo
warm-up ring	arena de practicar, arena de calentamiento
saddle room	cuarto de equipo, cuarto de monturas
saddling area	área para ensillar
sand	arena
snubbing post	poste para amarrar, poste de atar
stable	cuadra, establo, caballeriza
livery stable	establo de caballo de alquiler
rental stable	caballeriza para alquilar
training stable	establo de entrenamiento, centro hípico

stall	caballeriza, chiquero
box stall	caballeriza cerrada, caballeriza
covered stall	caballeriza cubierta
in-and-out stall	caballeriza con corral
pipe stall	corral de tubo
temporary stall	caballeriza temporánea, caballeriza temporal
stall mats	pisos de hule, pisos de goma
station (large operation)	estancia
sun pen	corral
swinging rail	tranca, tranquera
tack room	cuarto de equipo, cuarto de aperos, cuarto de arreos
telephone	teléfono
Where is the telephone?	¿Dónde está el teléfono?
trail	sendero, vereda, huella
training facility	instalación de entrenamiento
turn-out pen	corral de ejercicio
wash rack	lavadero
water bucket	balde de agua
water tank	aljibe, tanque de agua
water trough	abrevadero

Facility Maintenance and Equipment
mantenimiento de la instalación y equipo

barbed wire	alambre de púas
bedding	cama
replace the bedding (to)	reemplazar el aserrín, cambiar la cama
bolt (the)	cerrojo
broom	escoba
car	carro, auto, máquina, coche
clean (to)	limpiar
clean the stall (to)	limpiar la caballeriza
clean the stall later (to)	limpiar la caballeriza más tarde
clean the tack room (to)	limpiar el cuarto del equipo
closed	cerrado
Always keep the door closed.	Mantenga siempre la puerta cerrada.
close the door (to)	cerrar la puerta
crowbar	palanca
dirt	tierra
dirt floor	piso de tierra
dirty	sucio

disc harrow	rastra de discos
droppings	cagajones, estiércol
dung	cagajón, bosta, mierda
electricity	electricidad
extension cord	extension eléctrica, cordón eléctrico
fence	barda, cerca, valla, pared
check the fences (to)	chequear las bardas, revisar las bardas
paint the fence (to)	pintar la cerca, pintar la pared
repair the fence (to)	reparar la cerca, reparar la pared
set the jumps/fences (to)	poner los saltos
fix (to)	arreglar, componer
fix this (to)	arreglar éste/ésta/esto, componer éste/ésta/esto
garbage bag	bolsa de basura
garbage can	lata para basura, cubo de la basura, basurero
empty the garbage can (to)	vaciar el basurero
gasoline	gasolina, petroleo, bencina
get hot water (to)	traer agua caliente
hammer	martillo
hose (the)	manguera, manga
hose (to)	regarpa
hose down the barn aisles (to)	regar los pasillos de cuadril para limpiar
irrigation system	sistema de riego
light bulb	bombillo, eléctrica, ampolleta
maintain the track (to)	mantener la pista
manure	abono, cagajón, estiércol, mierda
manure heap	estercolero
nail	clavo
peat moss	viruta
pitchfork	horqueta, horca, yeldo (Mex.)
May I use your pitchfork?	¿Podría yo usar su horca? ¿Puedo usar su horca?

pitchfork
horqueta, horca, yeldo (Mex.)

plow	arado
power mower	motosegadora, segadora motorizada
rake	rastrillo, rastra
repair (to)	reparar
repair this (to)	reparar éste/ésta/esto
rice hulls	cáscara de arroz
ring	arena, picadero
drag the ring (to)	emparejar la arena
groom the ring (to)	relimpiar el picadero
maintain the ring (to)	mantener la arena, mantener el picadero
rake the ring (to)	rastrillar el picadero
seal the ring (to)	sellar el picadero
water the ring (to)	regar la arena
saw	sereta, serrucho
screwdriver	desatornillador
shavings	aserrín
The shavings are dirty.	El aserrín está muy sucio. La cama está sucia.
The shavings are wet.	El aserrín está muy mojado.
shavings (to give more)	dar más aserrín, poner más viruta
shavings (to replace the)	reemplazar el aserrín
shovel	pala
sledgehammer	combo
sprinkling system	sistema de aspersión
stall	caballeriza
The stall door is broken.	La puerta de la caballeriza está quebrada.
The stall smells.	La caballeriza huele.
stall (to muck out the)	vaciar el aserrín, limpiar el guano, limpiar la caballeriza
stall (to remove the horse from the)	sacar el caballo de la caballeriza, sacar el caballo del box
stall door (to close during the night)	cerrar la puerta de la caballeriza durante la noche
stall door (to open during the day)	abrir la puerta durante el día
stall mats (to lay the)	extender los pisos
stalls (to check at night)	chequear los establos por la noche
straw	paja
sweep (to)	barrer
sweep later (to)	barrer más tarde
tools	herramientas
tractor	tractor
trash can	balde de la basura
truck	camión, troque
water truck	camión aguador

wheelbarrow
carretilla

turn off (to)	apagar
turn on (to)	encender
turn on the ring lights (to)	encender las luces del picadero
urine	orina, meado, orín
vacuum (to)	limpiar con aspiradora, aspirar
vacuum the office (to)	limpiar con aspiradora la oficina
wash (to)	bañar
water (the)	agua
water (to)	regar
water the pasture/lawn (to)	regar el pasto, regar el césped
wet	mojado
wheelbarrow	carretilla
Where is the wheelbarrow?	¿Dónde está la carretilla?
wirecutter	corta alambre
wrench	llave para las tuercas

Staff Management
administración de personal

alien	extranjero/a, ajeno/a
citizen	ciudadano/a
Are you a U.S. citizen?	¿Es Ud. ciudadano? ¿Es Ud. ciudadano de los Estados Unidos?
citizenship	ciudadanía
deport (to)	deportar
deportation	deportación
deported	deportado/a
deported (to be)	ser deportado/a
discharge (to)	perforar su carta (Mex.), despedir
Do you know how to ride?	¿Sabe Ud. montar a caballo?
drink (to)	beber
driver's license	licencia para manejar, licencia de conductor, licencia de cunducir

Do you have a driver's license?	¿Tiene Ud. una licencia para manejar? ¿Tiene Ud. una licencia de conducir, una licencia de manejar?
drunk	borracho/a
drunkard	borracho/a
experience (to have)	tener experiencia
Do you have experience with horses?	¿Tiene Ud. experiencia con caballos?
family	familia
Do you have family here?	¿Vive aquí su familia? ¿Tiene Ud. familia aquí?
fire (to)	darle aire (Mex.), despedir
fired (to be)	ser despedido/a
You are fired.	Está despedido/a.
hired (to be)	ser contratado/a
You are hired.	Está contratado/a.
How old are you?	¿Cuántos años tiene?
immigrant	inmigrante
immigrate (to)	inmigrar
Immigration and Naturalization Service (INS)	la "migra"
immigration office	oficina de inmigración
immigration officer	oficial de inmigración
In emergency call . . .	En caso de emergencia llame . . .; En emergencia llame . . .
last name	apellido
My telephone number is . . .	Mi numero de teléfono es . . .; Mi teléfono es . . .
No sir.	No señor.
papers (the)	papeles, papeles de inmigración
Do you have papers?	¿Tiene Ud. papeles? ¿Tiene Ud. papeles de inmigración?
papers (to have)	tener papeles, tener mica
The stable is closed on . . . (day) and/or (time)	El establo está cerrado el . . .; El establo se cierra a las . . .
What is your address?	¿Dónde vive Ud.? Deme, por favor, su dirección.
What is your name?	¿Cómo se llama Ud.?
What is your telephone number?	¿Cuál es su número de teléfono? ¿Cuál es su teléfono?
Where are you from?	¿De dónde es Ud.?
Where have you worked before?	¿Dónde trabajó anteriormente?
Where were you yesterday?	¿Dónde estaba Ud. ayer?
work (the)	trabajo
Call me if you cannot work.	Llámeme si no puede trabajar.
You do good work.	Ud. trabaja bien, trabajas bien.

work (to)	trabajar
do good work (to)	hacer buen trabajo
When can you start work?	¿Cuándo podría comenzar su trabajo?
work with horses	trabajo con caballos
Have you worked with horses before?	¿Ha trabajado con caballos antes?
Yes sir.	Sí señor.
You finish work at . . .	Termina de trabajar a las . . .
You start work at . . .	Empieza a trabajar a las . . .
Your day off is . . .	Su día de descanso es . . .; Su día libre es . . .
Your hours are . . .	Sus horas de trabajo son . . .

Payroll Management
administración de pagos

cash	dinero
cents	centavos
charge (to)	cobrar
How much do you charge to blanket?	¿Cuánto cobra por poner la manta?
How much do you charge to feed a horse?	¿Cuánto cobra por alimentar un caballo? ¿Cuánto cobra por darle de comer al caballo?
How much do you charge to turn out a horse?	¿Cuánto cobra por soltar el caballo?
check	cheque
deductions	deducciones
dependents	dependientes
dollars	dólares
money	dinero
owe (to)	deber
How much do I owe you?	¿Cuánto le debo?
pay (the)	pago, dinero, sueldo, lana
How much do you pay?	¿Cuánto paga Ud.?
How much do you pay per day?	¿Cuánto paga Ud. por día?
How much do you pay per hour?	¿Cuánto paga Ud. por hora?
I will pay you . . .	Yo le voy a pagar . . .; Le pagaré . . .
take-home pay	sueldo neto

pay (to)	pagar
pay every . . . (to)	pagar cada . . .
pay in cash (to)	pagar en efectivo
pay monthly (to)	pagar mensualmente
pay plus room and board	sueldo más borde
pay weekly (to)	pagar cada semana, pagar semanalmente
pay with a check (to)	pagar con cheque
payday	el día de pago
Payday is . . .	El día de pago es . . .
rate per day	sueldo por día
rate per hour	sueldo por hora
rate per month	sueldo por mes
rate per week	sueldo por semana
rate per year	sueldo por año
salary	sueldo, salario
taxes	impuestos
tip (the)	propina
This tip is for you.	Esta propina es para Ud.
tip (to)	propinar, dar propina
split this tip with (to)	dividir la propina con . . .; compartir la propina con . . .
wage	salario
minimum wage	salario mínimo
Minimum wage is . . .	El salario mínimo es . . .

4
Conversation Basics
conversación básica

Colors
colores

black	negro
blue	azul
brown	colorado, café, marrón
dark	obscuro
green	verde
light	claro
orange	naranja
pink	rosa, rosado
purple	morado
red	rojo
white	blanco
yellow	amarillo

Communication
comunicación

all	todo/a, todos/as
backwards	hacia atrás
Be careful.	¡Tenga cuidado/a!
because	porque
because of	a causa de, a causa por, debido a
before (in front of)	adelante de, por delante de
belong to	pertenecera
enough	bastante, suficiente
everybody	todo el mundo, todos
everything	todo, todo lo que
everywhere	por todas partes
forward	hacia adelante
front	frente
in front of	en frente de

have	tener
Do you have?	¿Tiene Ud.?
help	ayudar
Help me, please.	Ayúdeme por favor.
here	aquí
How awful!	¡Qué horrible!
Hurry!	¡Apúrese!
I don't believe it.	No lo creo.
left	izquierda
many	muchos/as
My goodness!	¡Dios mío!
name	nombre
My name is . . .	Me llamo . . .; Mi nombre es . . .
no	no
please	por favor
would you please	si es Ud. tan amable
right	derecho
say (to)	decir
How do you say?	¿Cómo se dice?
someone	alguien
sorry	perdone, perdón
speak	hablar
Do you speak English?	¿Habla inglés? ¿Habla Ud. inglés?
Do you speak Spanish?	¿Habla español? ¿Ud. habla español?
I do not speak English.	No hablo inglés.
I do not speak Spanish.	No hablo español.
Speak slowly, please.	Hable despacio, por favor.
thank you	gracias
no thank you	no gracias
Thank you very much.	Muchas gracias.
that	ése/ésa/eso
What's that?	¿Qué es eso?
there	allá
Let's go over there.	Vamos hacia allá.
over there	por allá
this	este/esta/esto
this way	hacia acá
What's this?	¿Qué es esto?
understand (to)	comprender
Do you understand?	¿Comprende Ud.?
I do not understand.	No comprendo.
I understand.	Comprendo.
what	cómo, qué
What is the matter?	¿Qué pasa?
What are you doing?	¿Qué está haciendo?
where	dónde

Where is . . . ?	¿Dónde está . . . ?
who	quién
why	por qué
why not	por qué no
yes	sí
Yes, I am speaking to you.	Sí le estoy hablando.
you're welcome	de nada, por nada

Expressions of Time
expresiones de tiempo

after	después de, después que
afternoon	tarde
in the afternoon	por la tarde, en la tarde
again	otra vez
April	abril
at last	finalmente, al fin, por fin
at once	al instante, enseguida
August	agosto
before (time)	antes de
clock	reloj
It is one o'clock.	Es la una.
It is three o'clock.	Son las tres.
day	día
daybreak	amanecer, alba
days of the week	días de la semana
December	diciembre
evening	tarde, anochecer
this evening	esta tarde
fall	otoño
February	febrero
Friday	viernes
hour	hora
How long ago?	¿Hace cuánto tiempo? ¿Cuándo ha? ¿Hace cuándo?
January	enero
July	julio
June	junio
last minute	de última hora
later	después
a little later	un poco después
March	marzo
May	mayo
midnight	medianoche
midday	medio día

minute	minuto
wait a minute	horita, un momento
Monday	lunes
month	mes
morning	mañana
in the morning	por la mañana, en la mañana
this morning	esta mañana
next	próximo
night	noche
at night	por la noche, en la noche
last night	anoche
nightfall	anochecer, crepúsculo
noon	media día
November	noviembre
now	ahora
October	octubre
once	una vez
Saturday	sábado
seasons	estaciones
September	septiembre, setiembre
spring	primavera
summer	verano
Indian summer	veranillo de San Martín
Sunday	domingo
sunrise	salida del sol
sunset	puesta del sol, ocaso
Thursday	jueves
time	tiempo
At what time?	¿A qué hora?
each time	cada vez
from time to time	de vez en cuándo
How many times?	¿Cuántas veces?
What time is it?	¿Qué hora es? ¿Qué hora son?
today	hoy
tomorrow	mañana
day after tomorrow	pasado mañana
tomorrow morning	mañana por la mañana
tonight	esta noche
Tuesday	martes
Wednesday,	miércoles
week	semana
last week	semana pasada
next week	semana entrante, semana que viene
this week	esta semana
weekend	fin de semana
next weekend	próximo fin de semana
this weekend	este fin de semana

when	cuándo
while (time)	tiempo
a little while ago	hace un poco, un momento
in a little while	dentro de un momento, dentro de poco
winter	invierno
year	año
last year	año pasado
next year	año entrante, año que viene
this year	este año
years	años
yesterday	ayer
day before yesterday	anteayer
yesterday afternoon	ayer por la tarde, ayer en la tarde
yesterday morning	ayer por la mañana, ayer en la mañana

Expressions of the Weather
expresiones del clima

breeze	brisa
changeable weather	tiempo variable
cloud	nube
rain cloud	nubarrón
cloudburst	chaparrón
cloudy	nublado/a
It is cloudy today.	Hoy está nublado.
cold (to be)	hacer frío
It is very cold.	Hace mucho frío.
cyclone	ciclón
dew	rocío
downpour	aguacero
drought	sequía
fine weather	buen tiempo
freeze (a)	helada
frost	escarcha
hail	granizo
hot (to be)	hacer calor
It is very hot.	Hace mucho calor.
humid	húmedo/a
It is humid today.	Hoy hay humedad. Hoy está húmedo.
humidity	humedad
hurricane	huracán
lightning	relámpago
rain	lluvia

drizzling rain	llovizna
in the rain	bajo la lluvia
It is about to rain.	Está para llover.
rain belt	zona de lluvias
rain drop	gota de lluvia
rainfall	precipitación
raining	lloviendo
Is it raining?	¿Está lloviendo?
sower (rain)	chaparrón
snow	nieve
snowfall	nevada
snowflake	copo de nieve
sun	sol
temperature	temperatura
thunder	trueno
warm (to be)	hacer calor
It is very warm.	Hace mucho calor.
weather	tiempo, clima
changeable weather	tiempo variable
fine weather	buen tiempo
in sucn weather	con semejante tiempo
The weather kept us in.	El mal tiempo nos retuvo en casa.
What is the weather like?	¿Cómo está el tiempo? ¿Cómo está el clima? ¿Qué tiempo hace?
weather conditions	condiciones atmosféricas
weather permitting	si el tiempo no lo impide, si el tiempo lo permite
wind	viento
gust of wind	ráfaga de viento
whirlwind	torbellino, manga de viento

Measures
medidas

acre	acre
one acre = 40.468 areas	un acre = 40.468 áreas
bale	bala, fardo
cup	taza
foot	pie
one foot = 0.3 meters	un pie = 0.3 metros
gallon	galón
one gallon = 3.785 liters	un galón = 3.785 litros
gram	gramo

inch	pulgada
one inch = 0.025 meter	una pulgada = 0.025 metro
kilogram	kilogramo
one kilogram = 2.204 pounds	un kilogramo = 2.204 libras
liter	litro
one liter = 1.057 quarts	un litro = 1.057 cuartos de galón
ten liters = 2.2 gallons	diez litros = 2.2 galones
meter	metro
one meter = three feet, three (3) inches	un metro = tres pies, tres pulgadas
mile	milla
one mile = 1,760 yards = 1,609 meters	una milla = 1,760 yardas = 1,609 metros
one-eighth	un octavo
one-quarter	un cuarto
one-third	un tercio
one-half	un medio
three-quarters	tres cuartos
seven-eighths	siete octavos
ounce	onza
one ounce = 28.35 grams	una onza = 28.35 gramos
pint	pinta
pound	libra
one pound = 0.4536 kilogram	una libra = 0.4536 kilógramo
quart	cuarto de galón, un cuarto
scoop	pala
tablespoon	cuchara de mesa, cucharón
ton	tonelada
volume	capacidad, volumen
weight	peso
yard	yarda
one yard = 0.91 meter	una yarda = 0.91 metro

Numbers
números

one (1)	uno, una (1)
two (2)	dos (2)
three (3)	tres (3)
four (4)	cuatro (4)
five (5)	cinco (5)
six	(6) seis (6)

seven (7)	siete (7)
eight (8)	ocho (8)
nine (9)	nueve (9)
ten (10)	diez (10)
eleven (11)	once (11)
twelve (12)	doce (12)
thirteen (13)	trece (13)
fourteen (14)	catorce (14)
fifteen (15)	quince (15)
sixteen (16)	dieciséis (16)
seventeen (17)	diecisiete (17)
eighteen (18)	dieciocho (18)
nineteen (19)	diecinueve (19)
twenty (20)	veinte (20)
twenty-five (25)	veinticinco (25)
thirty (30)	treinta (30)
forty (40)	cuarenta (40)
fifty (50)	cincuenta (50)
sixty (60)	sesenta (60)
seventy (70)	setenta (70)
eighty (80)	ochenta (80)
ninety (90)	noventa (90)
one hundred (100)	cien, ciento (100)
one thousand (1,000)	mil (1,000)
first	primero/a
second	segundo/a
third	tercero/a
fourth	cuarto/a
fifth	quinto/a
sixth	sexto/a
seventh	séptimo/a
eighth	octavo/a
ninth	noveno/a
tenth	décimo/a

Salutations
saludos

Congratulations!	¡Enhorabuena! ¡Felicitaciones!
good afternoon	buenas tardes
good evening	buenas noches
good morning	buenos días
good bye	adiós
I'm sorry	lo siento
Happy Birthday.	Feliz cumpleaños.

Happy New Year.	Feliz año nuevo.
Happy Thanksgiving.	Feliz día de dar las gracias. Feliz día de gracias.
hello	hola, qué hubo
How are you?	¿Cómo está Ud.?
How do you do?	¿Cómo ha estado?
Merry Christmas	Feliz Navidad
see you later	hasta luego
thank you	gracias
No thank you.	No gracias.
Yes thank you.	Sí, gracias.
Thank you very much.	Muchas gracias.

5
Illustrations
Ilustraciónes

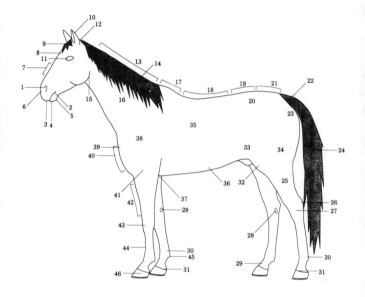

Points of the Horse
puntos del caballo

1. Nostril • *Ollar, Nariz*
2. Mouth • *Boca*
3. Upper Lip • *Labio Superior*
4. Lower Lip • *Labio Inferior*
5. Under Lip • *Labio Bajo*
6. Muzzle • *Hocico, Boca*
7. Bridge of the Nose • *Puente de la Nariz*
8. Forehead • *Frente*
9. Forelock • *Copete, Chasca, Mechón, Tupe*
10. Ear • *Oreja*
11. Eye • *Ojo*
12. Poll • *Nuca*
13. Crest • *Cresta, Cresta del Cuello*
14. Mane • *Crin, Crinera, Tuse/a*
15. Throatlatch • *Friador, Ahogador, Gargantilla*
16. Neck • *Cuello, Pescuezo*
17. Withers • *Cruz*
18. Back (Upper) • *Espalda*
19. Loin • *Lomo, Ijada*
20. Point of the Hip • *Punta de la Cadera*
21. Croup • *Grupa, Rabadilla*
22. Dock • *Maslo, Maslo de Cola*
23. Buttock • *Nalga, Grupa*
24. Tail • *Cola, Rabo*

25. Gaskin • *Muslo de la Pierna, Muslo*
26. Point of the Hock • *Punto del Corvejón, Punto del Garrón*
27. Hock • *Corvejón, Garrón*
28. Chestnut • *Ergot, Castaña, Espejuelo*
29. Pastern • *Cuarta, Cuartilla*
30. Fetlock • *Nudo, Nudillo*
31. Coronet • *Corona del Casco, Corona, Margen Superior del Casco*
32. Stifle • *Babilla*
33. Flank • *Flanco*
34. Thigh • *Muslo*
35. Barrel/Ribs • *Costilla*
36. Belly • *Barriga*
37. Elbow • *Codo, Codillo*
38. Shoulder • *Hombro*
39. Point of the Shoulder • *Punto del Hombro, Punta del Pecho*
40. Chest/Breast • *Pecho*
41. Arm • *Brazo, Paleta*
42. Forearm • *Antebrazo, Brazuelo, Brazo*
43. Knee • *Rodilla*
44. Cannon • *Caña*
45. Ergot • *Ergot*
46. Hoof • *Casco, Pezuña*

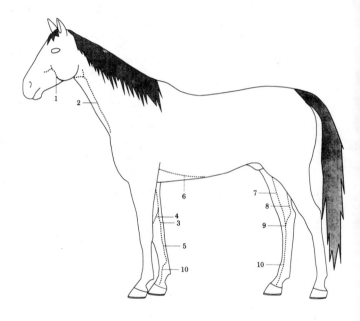

Primary Veins of the Horse
venas primarias del caballo

1. Facial Vein • *Vena Facial*
2. Jugular Vein • *Vena Jugular*
3. Cephalic Vein • *Vena Cefálica*
4. Accessory Cephalic Vein • *Vena Cefálica Accesoria*
5. Metacarpal Vein • *Vena Metacarpiana*
6. External Thoracic Vein • *Vena Torácica Externa*
7. Saphenous Vein • *Vena Safena*
8. Posterior Tibial Vein • *Vena Tibial Posterior*
9. Metatarsal Vein • *Vena Metatarsiana*
10. Digital Vein • *Vena Digital*

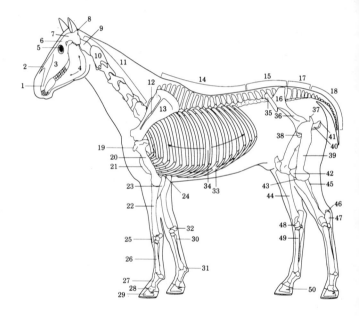

Bone Structure of the Horse
esqueleto del caballo

1. Premaxillary • *Premaxilar*
2. Nasal • *Nasal*
3. Maxillary • *Maxilar Superior*
4. Mandible • *Mandíbula*
5. Orbit • *Porción Orbitaria del Frontal*
6. Frontal • *Frontal*
7. Temporal Fossa • *Escama del Temporal*
8. Occipital • *Cresta Occipital*
9. Atlas • *Atlas*
10. Axis • *Axis*
11. Cervical Vertebrae (7) • *Vértebras Cervicales (7)*
12. Scapular Spine • *Espina de la Escápula*
13. Scapula • *Escápula*
14. Thoracic Vertebrae (18) • *Vértebras Torácicas (18)*
15. Lumbar Vertebrae (6) • *Vértebras Lumbares (6)*
16. Tuber Sacrale • *Tuberosidad Sacra*
17. Sacral Vertebrae (5) • *Vértebras Sacras (5)*
18. Coccygeal Vertebrae (17-20) • *Vértebras Coccígeas (17-20)*
19. Tuberosity of Humerus (Point of the Shoulder) • *Tuberosidad Húmero*
20. Humerous • *Húmero*
21. Sternum • *Esternón*
22. Radius • *Radio*
23. Ulna • *Cúbito*
24. Olecranon • *Olécranon*
25. Carpus • *Carpo*
26. Large Metacarpal • *Gran Metacarpiano*
27. First Phalanx (Pastern) • *Primera Falange (Cuarta)*
28. Second Phalanx, Middle Phalanx (Short Pastern) • *Segunda Falange*

29. Third Phalanx, Distal Phalanx (Pedal Bone) • *Tercera Falange*
30. Proximal Sesamoid • *Sesamoideo Proximal*
31. Small Metacarpal • *Pequeño Metacarpiano, Metacarpiano Externo, Segundo Metacarpiano*
32. Accessory Carpal • *Accesorio*
33. Costal Cartilages • *Cartílagos de la Costilla*
34. Ribs (18) • *Costillas (18)*
35. Tuber Coxae • *Tuberosidad Coxal*
36. Ilium • *Ilión*
37. Greater Trochanter of the Femer • *Trocanter Mayor*
38. Pubis • *Pubis*
39. Femer • *Femer*
40. Ischium • *Isquión*
41. Tuber Ischii • *Tuberosidad Isquiática*
42. Patella • *Rótula*
43. Femoral Trochlea • *Tróclea Femoral*
44. Tibia • *Tibia*
45. Fibula • *Peroné*
46. Tuber Calcanei (Point of the Hock) • *Tuberosidad Calcánea (Punto del Corvejón)*
47. Calcaneus • *Tarsoperoneo*
48. Talus (Tibial Tarsal) • *Tarsotibial*
49. Large Metatarsal • *Gran Metatarsiano (Tercer Metatarsiano)*
50. Distal Sesamoid Bone (Navicular Bone) • *Hueso Navicular, Sesamoideo Distal*

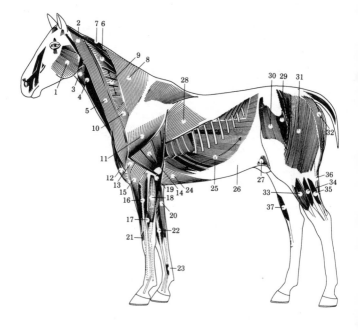

Muscles of the Horse
músculos del caballo

1. Masseter M. • *M. Masetero*
2. Wing of the Atlas • *M. Ala del Atlas*
3. Sternothyrohyoid/Omohyoid M. • *M. Omohioideo*
4. Sternocephalic M. • *M. Esternofálico*
5. Brachiocephalic M. • *M. Braquiocefálico*
6. Splenius M. • *M. Esplenio*
7. Rhomboid M. • *M. Romboides*
8. Trapezius M. • *M. Trapecio*
9. Ventral Serate M. • *M. Serrato Cervical*
10. Cranial Deep Pectoralis M. • *M. Pectoral Profundo Anterior*
11. Deltoid M. • *M. Deltoides*
12. Cranial Superficial Pectoral M. • *M. Pectoral Superficial Anterior*
13. Brachialis M. • *M. Braquial*
14. Triceps M. • *M. Triceps*
15. Radial Carpal Extensor M. • *M. Extensor Carporradial*
16. Common Digital Extensor M. • *M. Extensor Digital Común*
17. Lateral Digital Extensor M. • *M. Extensor Digital Lateral*
18. Lateral Carpal Flexor M. • *M. Flexor Carporlateral*
19. Deep Digital Flexor M. • *M. Flexor Digital Profundo*
20. Middle Carpal Flexor M. • *M. Cubital Lateral*
21. Oblique Carpal Extensor M. • *M. Extensor Oblícuo del Carpo*
22. Medial Carpal Flexor M. • *M. Flexor Carpormedial*
23. Digital Flexor Tendon • *Tendón Flexor Digital*
24. Pectoral M. • *M. Pectoral Profundo*
25. External Abdominal Oblique M. • *M. Oblícuo Abdominal Externo*
26. Aponeurosis of External Abdominal Oblique M. • *Aponeurosis de M. Oblícuo Abdominal Externo*
27. Cutaneous M. • *M. Cutáneo Abdominal*
28. Latissimus Dorsi M. • *M. Gran Dorsal*
29. Superficial Gluteal M. • *M. Glúteo Superficial*
30. M. Tensor Fasciae Latae • *M. Tensor de la Fascia Lata*
31. Biceps Femoris M. • *M. Biceps Femoral*
32. Semitendinous M. • *M. Semitendinoso*
33. Long Digital Extensor M. • *M. Extensor Digital Largo*
34. Lateral Digital Extensor M. • *M. Extensor Digital Lateral*
35. Long Digital Flexor M. • *M. Flexor Digital Profundo*
36. Achilles Tendon • *M. Tendón de Aquiles*
37. Anterior Tibial M. • *M. Tibial Anterior*

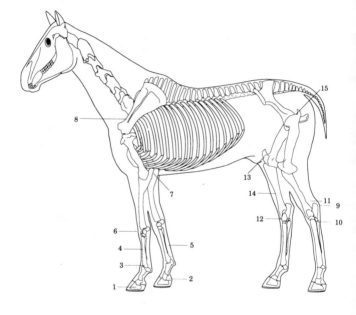

Sites of Lameness of the Horse
puntos cojos del caballo

1. Bruised Sole • *Contusión de la Suela, Planta Contusa*
   Corns • *Callos*
   Contracted Heel • *Talón Encogido, Talón Contraído*
   Cracked Heels • *Talones Rajados*
   Cracked Hoof • *Casco Rajado, Vaso Partido, Fisura del Casco*
   Dropped Sole • *Suela Caída*
   Founder/Laminitis • *Aguado, Laminitis, Infosurado*
   Gravel • *Arenilla*
   Keratoma • *Queratoma*
   Navicular Disease • *Enfermedad Navicular, Navicular*
   Pedal Osteitis • *Osteítis Podal*
   Pumiced Hoof • *Casco Pómez*
   Pyramidal Disease • *Enfermedad Piramidal*
   Quarter Crack • *Cuarto Rajado, Fisura del Cuarto*
   Sand Crack • *Rajadura de Arena, Fisura del Casco*
   Scratches • *Rasguños, Raspaduras*
   Seedy Toe • *Separación de la Uña, Hormiguillo*
   Sesamoid Fracture • *Fractura Sesamoideo*
   Side Bones • *Endurecimiento de los Cartílagos Laterales de las Patas*
   Stone Bruise • *Contusión de Piedra*

   Thrush • *Afta, Enfermedad del Pie del Caballo con Discarga Fétida*
2. Ring Bone • *Sobrehueso, Sobrehueso de la Cuartilla, Sobrehueso de la Corona*
3. Osselets • *Osteítis, Huesecillos*
   Sesamoiditis • *Sesamoiditis*
   Stocking Up • *Hinchando*
   Wind Puffs • *Bolsas de Aire*
4. Bucked Shins • *Periostitis de los Huesos Metacarpianos*
   Splints • *Sobrehuesos*
5. Bowed Tendon • *Tendinitis, Tendón Botado (Arg., Ch., Ven.), Tendón Arqueado*
6. Carpitis • *Carpitis, Rodilla Dislocada*
   Epiphysitis • *Epifisitis*
7. Capped Elbow • *Capelet (Sp., Arg.), Higroma del Codo, Bursitis del Codo*
8. Sweeny • *Atrofia de los Músculos del Hombro*
9. Capped Hock • *Higroma del Corvejón, Bursistis del Corvejón*
10. Curb • *Corva, Corvaza*
11. Thoroughpin • *Hinchazón Tarsal*
12. Bog Spavin • *Esparaván Falso*
    Bone Spavin • *Esparaván Óseo*
    Occult Spavin • *Esparaván Oculto*
13. Gonitis • *Gonitis*
14. Stringhalt • *Mioclonía de las Patas Traseras*
15. Coxitis • *Coxitis*

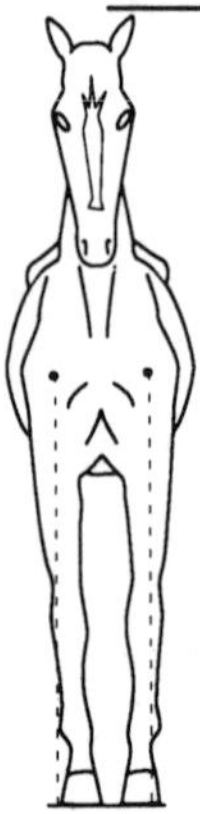

1

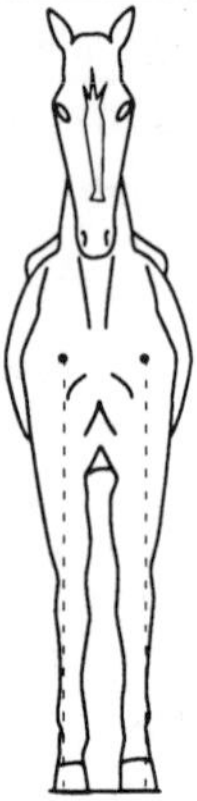

2

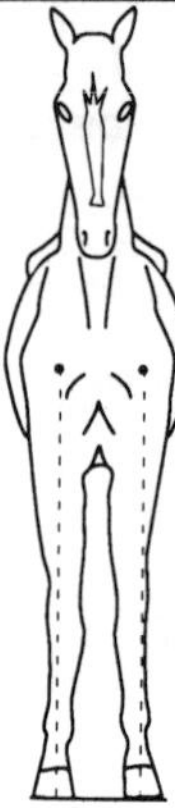

3

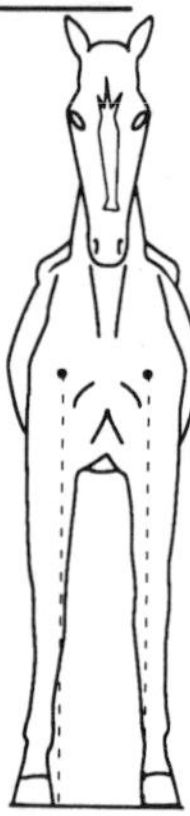

4

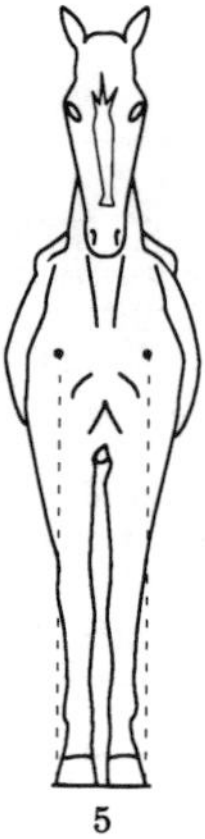

5

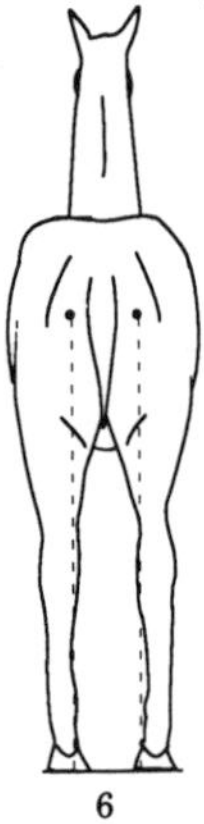

6

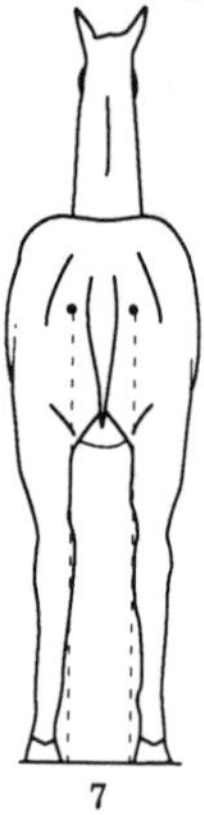

7

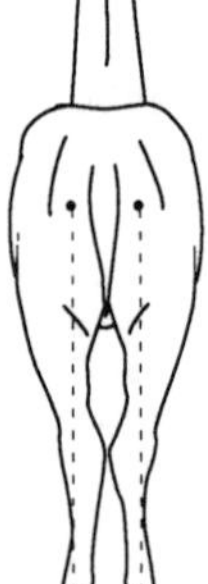

8

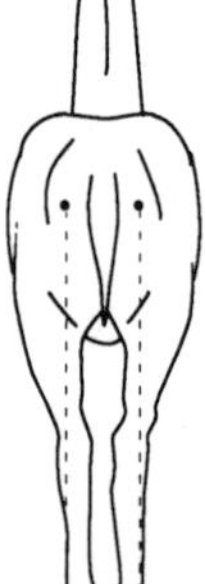

9

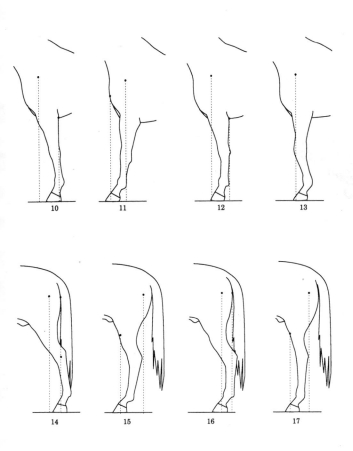

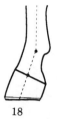

18

19

20

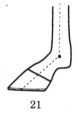

21

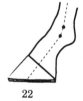

22

Set of the Legs
aplomas

1. Pigeon Toed • *Pie de Paloma*
2. Crooked Legged • *Piernas Chuecas*
3. Knock Kneed • *Patizambo*
4. Open in Front • *Abierto de Adelante*
5. Closed in Front • *Cerrado de Adelante*
6. Bow Legged • *Curvada, Rodilla Arqueada*
7. Open Behind • *Piernas Abiertas de Atrás*
8. Cow Hocked • *Patizambo, Corva de Vaca*
9. Closed Behind • *Cerrado de Atrás, Piernas Cerradas de Atrás*
10. Camped under in Front • *Remitido de Adelante*
11. Camped out in Front • *Plantado de Adelante*
12. Hollow Kneed • *Rodilla Transcorta, Rodilla Hueca*
13. Sprung Kneed • *Transcorto*
14. Camped out Behind • *Plantado de Atrás*
15. Camped under Behind • *Remitido de Atrás*
16. Sickle Hock • *Pata de Sable*
17. Straight Hock • *Corvejón Derecho, Corvejón Erguido*
18. Stumpy Pastern • *Corto de Cuartilla*
19. Broken-Forward Foot • *Inclinación Excesiva Hacia Adelante*
20. Broken-Back Foot • *Inclinación Excesiva Hacia Atrás*
21. Sloping Pastern • *Corto Angulada*
22. No Heel • *Destalonado*

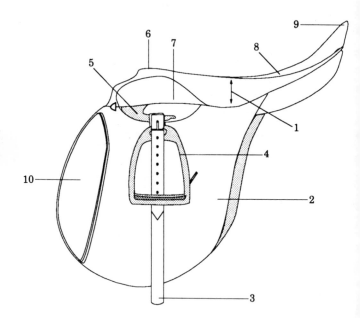

Parts of the English Saddle
partes de la silla inglesa

1. Waist • *Cintura*
2. Saddle Flap • *Falda*
3. Leathers • *Arciones*
4. Irons • *Estribos*
5. Stirrup Bar • *Barra de Estribo*

6. Pommel • *Cabecilla*
7. Skirt • *Falda*
8. Seat • *Asiento*
9. Cantle • *Cantileja, Borrén*
10. Knee Roll • *Rollo*

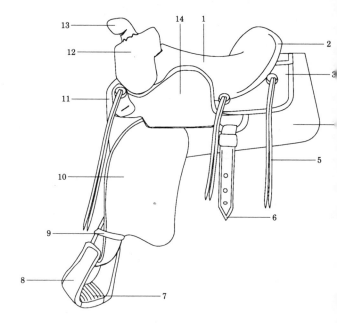

Parts of the Stock Saddle
partes de la silla vaquera

1. Seat • *Asiento*
2. Cantle • *Cantileja, Borrén, Copa, Teja*
3. Back Jockey • *Sobrefalda*
4. Skirt • *Falda*
5. Saddle Strings • *Correas*
6. Flank Cinch • *Barriguera*
7. Stirrup Tred • *Piso del Estribo*

8. Stirrup • *Estribo*
9. Hobble Strap • *Porta Manea, Porta Cuarta*
10. Fender • *Falda, Arción*
11. Front Jockey • *Sobrefalda*
12. Swell • *Borrén, Delantero, Hombro*
13. Horn • *Cacho, Cuerno, Cabeza*
14. Side Jockey • *Sobrefalda*

6
5,000 Everyday Words
5,000 palabras de cada día

A

a, un
abandon, abandono
abandoned, vicioso
abbey, abadía
abbreviation, abreviación
abdominal, abdominal
ability, habilidad
able, capaz
abnormal, anormal
aboard, a bordo
abolition, abolición
about, acerca de
above, sobre
abroad, fuera de casa
abscess, absceso
absence, ausencia
absent, ausente
absolute, absoluto
absolutely, absolutamente
absorb, absorber
absorbed, absorbido
absorbent, absorbente
absorption, absorción
abstract, abstracto
abstraction, abstracción
absurd, absurdo
abundant, abundante
abuse, abuso
academic, académico
academy, academia
accent, acento
acceptable, aceptable
acceptance, aceptación
access, acceso
accessories, accesorios
accident, accidente
accommodate, acomodar

accommodation, acomodación
accompany, acompañar
accomplished, cumplido
accordance, acuerdo
according, acorde
accordingly, de conformidad
account, cuenta
accumulation, acumulación
accuracy, exactitud
accurate, exacto
accused, acusado
accustomed, acostumbrado
acetylene, acetileno
ache, dolor
achieve, lograr
achievement, logro
acid, ácido
aclamation, aclamación
acquaintance, conocido
acquire, adquirir
acquisition, adquisición
acre, acre
acreage, extensión en acres
across, a través
act, acto
acting, interino
action, acción
active, activo
actively, activamente
activity, actividad
actor, actor
actress, actriz
actual, efectivo
actually, realmente
acute, agudo
adaptation, adaptación
adapter, adaptador
add, agregar

addiction, afición
addition, añadidura
additional, adicional
address, dirección
adequate, adecuado
adhesive, adhesivo
adjacent, adyacente
adjective, adjetivo
adjoining, contiguo
adjustment, ajustamiento
administration,
    administración
administrative,
    administrativo
administrator, administrador
admirable, admirable
admiral, almirante
admiralty, almirantazgo
admiration, admiración
admire, admirar
admission, admisión
admit, admitir
adolescent, adolescente
adopt, adoptar
adult, adulto
adultery, adulterio
advance, avance
advanced, avanzado
advantage, ventaja
advent, advenimiento
adventure, aventura
advertisement, anuncio
advertising, publicidad
advice, consejo
advisable, aconsejable
advise, aconsejar
advised, avisado
adviser, aconsejador
advisory, asesor
advocate, abogado
aerial, aéreo
aesthetic, estético
affair, asunto
affect, influir
affected, afectado
affecting, conmovedor
affection, afecto
affix, añadidura

affluent, abundante
afford, proporcionar,
    permetirse
afraid, asustado
Africa, Africa
African, africano
after, después de
aftershave, loción
afternoon, la tarde
afterward, después
again, de nuevo
against, contra
age, edad
aged, viejo
agency, acción
agent, agente
aging, envejeciendo
ago, atrás, hace
agony, agonía
agree, asentir, acordar
agreeable, agradable
agreement, pacto
agricultural, agrícola
agriculture, agricultura
ahead, delante
aid, ayuda
aim, puntería
air, aire
aircraft, aeronave o avión
airline, línea aérea
airmail, correo, aéreo
airplane, aeroplano, avion
airport, aeropuerto
airship, aeronave
alarm clock, despertador
alarm, alarma
alas, ¡ay!
alcoholic, alcohólico
alert, alerta
alien, ajeno
alight, encendido
alike, igual
alive, vivo
all, todo
alleged, alegado
allergic, alérgico
alley, calleja
alliance, alianza

allied, aliado
allies, aliados
allocation, distribución
allotment, reparto
allow, conceder
allowance, concesión
alloy, impureza
almond, almendra
almost, casi
alone, solo
along, a lo largo
alongside, al costado
aloud, alto
alphabet, alfabeto
already, ya
also, también
alter, modificar
alteration, modificación
alternative, alternativo
although, aunque
altogether, en conjunto
aluminium, aluminio
always, siempre
amateur, amateur
amazed, asombrado
amazing, asombroso
ambassador, embajador
amber, ámbar
ambition, ambición
ambitious, ambicioso
ambulance, ambulancia
amendment, enmienda
America, América
American, americano
among, entre
amongst, entre
amount, cantidad
ample, amplio
amplifier, amplificador
amusement park, parque de
   atracciones
amusement, solaz
amusing, divertido
an, un
analogous, análogo
analogy, analogía
analysis, análisis
ancestor, progenitor

anchovy, anchoa
ancient, antiguo
and, y
angel, ángel
anger, cólera
angle, ángulo
angry, colérico
angular, angular
animal, animal
ankle, tobillo
anniversary, aniversario
announcement, anuncio
annual, anual
anonymous, anónimo
anorak, anorak
another, otro
answer, respuesta
antibiotic, antibiótico
anticipation, intuición o
   impresión de lo que va a
   suceder
antidepressant, antidepresivo
antiseptic, antiséptico
anxiety, ansiedad
anxious, ansioso
any, cualquier
anybody, alguien
anyone, alguien
anything, algo
anyway, de todos modos
anywhere, doquiera
apart, aparte
apartheid, aparteid
apartment, departamento
apology, apología
appalling, espantoso
apparatus, aparato
apparent, claro
apparently, claramente
appeal, apelación
appealing, atrayente
appear, aparecer
appearance, aparición
appendicitis, apendicitis
appendix, apéndice
appetite, apetito
appetizer, aperitivo
apple, manzana

appliance, instrumento
applicable, aplicable
application, aplicación
apply, aplicarse
appointment, señalamiento, cita
appreciate, estimar, apreciar
appreciation, aprecio
apprentice, aprendiz
approach, proximidad
appropriate, apropiado
approval, aprobación
approve, aprobar
approximately, aproximadamente
approximation, aproximación
apricot, albaricoque
April, abril
apron, delantal
apt, apto
Arabic, arábigo
archaeology, arqueología
archbishop, arzobispo
archer, arquero
architect, arquitecto
architecture, arquitectura
arctic, ártico
area, área
area code, código de zona
area, área
argue, argumentar
argument, debate
arise, subir
arm, brazo
armistice, armisticio
army, ejército
around, en derredor
arrange, arreglar
arrangement, ordenamiento
arrival, llegarda
arrive, llegar
art gallery, museo de pintura
art, arte
artery, arteria
article, artículo
artificial, artificial
artist, artista
artistic, artístico

as, como
ash, ceniza
ashamed, avergonzado
ashore, en tierra
ashtray, cenicero
Asia, Asia
Asian, asiático
aside, al lado
ask, preguntar
asleep, dormido
asparagus, espárrago
aspect, aspecto
aspirin, aspirina
assembly, asamblea
assertion, aserto
assess, amillarar
assessment, avalúo
asset, ventaju, posesión
assist, asistir
assistance, asistencia
assistant, ayudante
associate, asociado
association, asociación
assume, asumir
assumed, supuesto
assuming, arrogante
assumption, asunción
assurance, seguridad
assure, asegurar
assured, seguro
asthma, asma
at least, al menos
at once, a la vez
at, en
Atlantic, Atlántico
atmosphere, atmósfera
atomic, atómico
attack, ataque
attain, lograr
attempt, intento
attend, asistir
attendance, asistencia
attention, atención
attic, ático
attitude, actitud
attract, atraer
attraction, atractivo
audience, auditorio

aunt, tía
Australia, Australia
Australian, australiano
author, autor
authoritative, autorizado
authority, autorización
automatic, automático
autumn, otoño
available, aprovechable
avalanche, avalancha
avenue, avenida
average, promedio
avoid, evitar
awake, vigilante
award, premio
aware, enterado
awareness, conocimiento
away, lejos
awful, atroz
awkward, torpe
axis, eje

B

baby, criatura
babysitter, niñera
bachelor, soltero
back, trasero
backache, dolor de espalda
background, fondo
backward, havia atrás
bacon, tocino
bad, malo
badge, divisa
bag, saco
baggage check, talón de
    equipaje
baggage, equipaje
baker, panadero
bakery, panadería
balance, equilibrio
balcony, galería
ball, bola
ball point pen, bolígrafo
ballet, baile de espectáculo
ban, prohibición
banana, plátano
band, faja

band-aid, tirita
bandage, venda
bank, banco
baptism, bautismo
bar, barra
barber, barbero
bare, desnudo
barely, apena
bargain, trato
barge, barcaza
bark, corteza
barn, granero
barrier, barrera
base, base
basic, básico
basically, fundamentalmente,
    basicamente
basil, albahaca
basin, pilón
basket, cesta
batch, hornada
bath, baño
bath towel, toalla de baño
bathing suit, traje de baño
bathrobe, bata
bathroom, cuarto de baño
battery, batería
battle, batalla
bay leaf, hoja de laurel
bay, bayo
be, ser
beach, playa
beam, viga
bean, haba
bear, oso
beard, barba
bearing, porte, conducta
beast, bestia
beat, latido
beaten, batido, golpeado
beating, paliza
beautiful, bello
beautifully, maravillosamente
beauty salon, salón de belleza
beauty, belleza
because, porque
become, convenir
becoming, que sienta

bed, cama
bedroom, dormitorio
beef, carne de vaca
beer, cerveza
before, delante
beforehand, de antemano,
begin, comenzar
beginner, principiante
behalf, de parte de
behave, portarse
behavior, conducta
behind, detrás
beige, beige
belief, creencia
believe, creer
bell, campana
bellboy, botones
belong, pertenecer
beloved, querido
below, abajo
belt, cinturón
bench, banco
bend, inclinación, torcer
bending, acción de torcer
beneath, abajo
benefit, beneficio
Berlin, Berlín
beside, cerca de
best, mejor
bet, apuesta
better, mejor
between, en medio
beverage, bebida
beyond, salvo
bias, sesgo
Bible, Biblia
bicycle, bicicleta
bid, licitación
big, grande
bill, pico
billion, billón
binding, atadura
biography, biografía
biological, biológico
bird, ave
birth, nacimiento
birthday, natalicio, dio de
  nacimiento, cumpliaño

biscuit, galleta
bishop, obispo
bit, trozo
bitter, amargo
bitterness, amargor
black, negro
blackberry, zarzamora
bladder, vejiga
blade, hoja
blame, culpa
blank, en blanco
blanket, manta
blast, explosión
bleach, lejía
bleed, sangrar
blend, mezcla
bless, bendecir
blessing, bendición
blind, ciego
block, bloque
blonde, rubio
blood pressure, presión
  arterial
blood transfusion, transfusión
blood, sangre
bloody, sangriento
blouse, blusa
blow dry, secar con secador
blow, golpe, soplar
blown, rendido
blue, azul
blueberry, arándano
boar, verraco
board, tabla
boarding house, casa de
  huéspedes
boarding, tablazón
boat, barco
body, cuerpo
boil, divieso, hervir
bold, valiente
bomb, bomba
bone, hueso
bonus, plus, bono
book, libro
booklet, folleto
bookshop, librería
boom, en prosperidad rápida y
  creciente

boot, bota
border, borde
bore, taladro
born, nacido
borough, villa
borrow, tomar o pedir prestado
borrowed, prestado
botany, botánica
both, ambos
bother, preocupación
bottle opener, abrebotellas
bottle, botella
bottom, fondo
bound, obligado
boundary, linde
bout, rato
bow, inclinación
bow tie, corbata de lazo
bowel, intestinos
bowl, cuenco
box, caja
boxing, boxeo
boy, niño
boyfriend, amigo
bra, sostén
bracelet, pulsera
brain, cerebro
brake, freno
brake fluid, líquido para frenos
branch, rama
brand, marca
brandy, coñac
brass, latón
brave, valiente
breach, abertura
bread, pan
breadth, anchura
break, descanso
breakdown, caída
breakfast, desayuno
breast, pecho
breath, hálito, respiro
breathe, alentar
breathing, respiración
breed, casta
breeding, cría
breeze, brisa
brewery, cervecería

brick, ladrillo
bride, novia
bridge, puente
brief, breve
briefcase, cartera
briefly, brevemente
brigade, brigada
bright, brillante
brilliant, brillante
bring, traer
briskly, enérgicamente
broad, ancho
broadcast, sembrado a voleo
bronze, bronce
brook, arroyo
brother, hermano
brother-in-law, hermano político
brown, moreno
bruise, contusión
brush, cepillo
brussels sprouts, coles de Bruselas
bubble, burbuja
bubble bath, baño de espuma
bucket, cubo
buckle, hebilla
budget, presupuesto
build, estructura
builder, constructor
building, construcción
bulb, bombilla
bulk, bulto
bullet, bala
bunch, manojo
bunny, conejito
burden, carga
bureau, escritorio
burial, entierro
burn, quemadura
burner, mechero
burning, ardiente
burst, reventón
bus, autobús
bush, arbusto
business, comercio
business trip, viaje de negocios

busy, ocupado
but, sólo
butane gas, butano
butcher's, carnicería
butler, mayordomo
butter, mantequilla
button, botón
buy, compra
by, cerca de

C

cabbage, col
cabin, cabaña
cabinet, gabinete
cable, cable
cable-car, coche de teleférico
cage, jaula
cake shop, pastelería
cake, pastel
calculation, cálculo
calculator, calculadora
calendar, calendario
calf, ternero
call, llamada
calm, tranquilo
calmly, con calma
calves, ternero
camera, despacho particular
   del juez
camp, campamento
camp site, camping
campaign, campaña
campbed, cama de campaña
camping, campamento
can opener, abrelatas
can, vaso
Canada, Canada
Canadian, canadiense
canal, acequia
candidate, candidato
candle, vela
candy, azúcar cande
canned, en conserva
canvas, lona
cap, gorra
capable, capaz
capacity, capacidad

cape, capa
capital, capital
captain, capitán
captive, cautivo
capture, apresamiento
car, coche, carro
car hire, alquiler de automóviles
car park, aparcamiento,
   estacionamiento
caravan, carromato
card, tarjeta
cardigan, chaqueta de punto
care, preocupación
career, carrera
careful, cuidadoso
carefully, cuidadosamente
careless, descuidado
carpet, alfombra
carriage, carruaje
carrier, porteador
carrot, zanahoria
carry, transporte en hombros
carving, entalladura
case, caso
cash, numerario
cassette, casete
castle, castillo
casual, informal
cat, gato
catalogue, catálogo
catch, cogedura
catching, contagioso
category, categoría
cathedral, catedral
catholic, católico
cattle, ganado
cauliflower, coliflor
cause, causa
caution, caución
cave, cueva
cease, cesación
celebrated, célebre
celebration, celebración
celery, apio
cell, celda
cemetery, cementerio
cent, centavo
centimeter, centímetro

central, central
center, centro
century, siglo
cereal, cereal
ceremonial, ceremonial
ceremony, ceremonia
certain, fijo
certainly, ciertamente
certainty, certeza
certificate, certificado
Ceylon, Ceilán
chain, cadena
chair, silla
chairman, presidente
challenge, desafío
chamber, cámara
chamberlain, chambelán
champagne, champán
champion, campeón
championship, campeonato
chance, ventura
chancellor, canciller
change, cambio
channel, lecho
chaos, caos
chapel, capilla
chapter, capítulo
character, carácter
characteristic, característica
charcoal, carbón de leña
charge, carga
charm, encanto
chase, persecución
chat, charla
chauffeur, chofer
cheap, barato
check, cheque
checkbook, talonario
check, contratiempro
check in, facturar
check out, pagar y
    marcharse
check up, comprobar
cheek, mejilla
cheer, grito de entusiasmo
cheerful, alegre
cheese, queso
chef, jefe de cocina

chemical, químico
chemistry, químca
cherry, cereza
chess, ajedrez
chest, pecho
chewing gum, goma de
    mascar
chicken, pollo
chicory, achicoria
chief, principal
chiefly, principalmente
child, niño
childhood, infancia
childish, infantil
childless, sin hijos
children, niño
chimney, chimenea
chin, barba
China, China
Chinese, chino
chips, patatas fritas
chisel, cincel
chloride, cloruro
chocolate, chocolate
choice, escogimiento
choose, escoger
chop, corte
chorus, coro
Christ, Cristo
Christian, cristiano
Christianity, cristianidad
Christmas, Navidad
church, iglesia
cider, sidra
cigar, puro
cigarette, cigarrillo
cigarette lighter, mechero
cine camera, cámara
cinema, cine
cinnamon, canela
circle, círculo
circuit, circuito
circular, circular
circulation, circulación
circumstance, circumstancia
citizen, ciudadano
city, ciudad
civic, cívico

civil, civil
civilian, paisano
civilization, civilización
claim, reclamación
clam, almeja
clarity, claridad
clash, ruido
clasp, broche
class, clase
classic, clásico
classical, clásico
classification, clasificación
clause, oración breve
clay, arcilla
clean, limpio
cleaning, limpieza
clear, claro
clear-cut, bien perfilado
clearance, despejo
clearly, claramente
clergy, clero
clerical, clerical
clerk, empleado
clever, diestro
cliff, risco
climate, clima
climax, climax
climb, trepar, escalar
clinging, adhesivo
clinic, clínico
clip, grapa
cloak, capa
cloakroom, guardarropa
clock, reloj
clock radio, radio-despertador
close, cerca
closely, fielmente
cloth, paño
clothes, ropa
clothes peg, pinza
cloud, nube
club, club
clue, indicio
coach, coche
coal, carbón
coast, costa
coat, cubierta
cock, gallo

coconut, coco
cod, bacalao
code, código
coefficient, coeficiente
coffee, café
cognac, coñac
coin, moneda
coincidence, coincidencia
cold, frío
collapse, derrumbamiento
collar, cuello
colleague, colega
collect, reunir
collection, acumulación
college, colegio
color, color
color film, película
color television, TV en colores
colorful, lleno de color
column, columna
comb, peine
combination, combinación
combine, asociación
come, venir
comedy, comedia
comfort, consuelo
comfortable, confortable
comfortably, cómodamente
comic, cómico
coming, próximo
command, orden
commander, jefe
commanding, que manda
commend, recomendar
comment, comento
commentary, comentario
commerce, comercio
commercial, comercial
commission, comisión
commit, cometer
committee, comité
commodity, producto
common, común
commonly, comúnmente
commonwealth, nación
communication, comunicación
communion, comunión
communism, comunismo

communist, comunista
community, común
compact disc, disco compacto
compact, pacto
companion, compañero
company, compañía
comparable, comparable
comparative, comparativo
comparatively,
    comparativamente
compare, comparación
comparison, comparación
compartment, departamento
compass, compás
compensation, compensación
compete, competir
competence, competencia
competition, competición
competitive, de competición
complain, quejarse
complaint, queja
complement, complemento
complete, entero
completely, completamente
completion, terminación
complex, complejo
compulsory, obligatorio
computer, ordenador
concentrate, concentrar
concept, concepto
concern, asunto
concert, acuerdo
conclude, concluir
conclusion, decisión final
concrete, concreto
condemn, condenar
condition, condición
conduct, conducta
conductor, conductor
conference, conferencia
confess, confesar
confession, confesión
confidence, confianza
confident, seguro
confidential, confidencial
confirm, confirmar
confirmation, confirmación
confirmed, confirmado

conflict, conflicto
conformity, conformidad
confused, confuso
confusion, confusión
congestion, congestión
congratulation, congratulación
congregation, congregación
congregational, de
    congregación
congress, congreso
consider, considerar
consist, consistir
constable, condestable
constant, constante
constipation, estreñimiento
constituency, distrito electoral
constitute, constituir
constitution, constitución
constitutional, constitucional
construct, construir
construction, construcción
constructive, constructivo
consult, consultar
consultation, consultación
consumer, consumidor
consumption, consunción
contact, contacto
contain, contener
container, recipiente
contamination, contaminación
contemporary, coetáneo
contempt, desprecio
content, contenido
contention, contención
contest, contienda
context, contexto
continent, continente
continental, continente
continual, continuo
continue, continuar
continued, continuado
continuity, continuidad
continuous, continuo
contraceptive,
    anticoncepcional
contract, contrato
contraction, contracción
contrary, contrario

contrast, contraste
contribute, contribuir con
contribution, aportación
control, mando
convenient, cómodo
cook, cocinero
cookie, galleta
cool, fresco
cooperate, cooperar
cooperation, cooperación
cope, capa
copper, cobre
copy, copia
cork, tiznar con corcho
      quemado
corkscrew, sacacorchos
corn, grano, maíz
corner, ángulo
corporation, corporación
correct, correcto
correction, enmienda
correlation, correlación
correspond, corresponder
correspondence,
      correspondencia
correspondent,
      correspondiente
corresponding,
      correspondiente
corridor, corredor
corrosion, corrosión
corruption, corrupción
cost, coste
costly, costoso
costume, traje
cottage, casita
cotton wool, algodón
cotton, algodón
cough, toser
count, cuenta
country, país
couple, par
courage, valor
court, tribunal
covenant, contrato
cover, tapa
covering, cubierta
cow, vaca

crack, crujido
craft, arte
cramp, calambre
cranberry, arándano agrio
crane, grulla
crash, estallido
crayon, crayola, pastel
crazy, agrietado
cream, crema
create, crear
creation, el universo
creative, creador
creature, criatura
credit card, tarjeta de crédito
credit, crédito
crime, crimen
criminal, criminal
crowd, multitud
cruel, cruel
cruelty, crueldad
cruise, crucero
cry, grito
crystal, cristal
Cuban, cubano
cucumber, pepino
cuisine, cocina
cultivated, cultivado
culture, cultivo
cup, taza
cupboard, aparador
currency, moneda
cut off, cortar
cut, lámina
cutlery, cuchillería
cutting, cortante
cycle, ciclo
cycling, ciclismo
cynical, cínico
Cyprus, Chipre

D

daily, diario
dairy, lechería
damage, daño
damn, maldito
damned, condenado
damp, húmedo

dance, danza
dancing, baile
danger, peligro
dangerous, peligroso
Danish, danés
dare, reto
daring, atrevido
dark, oscuro
darkness, oscuridad
darling, amado
data, datos
date, fecha
daughter, hija
dawn, alba
day off, día de descanso
day, día
daylight, luz del día
dazzling, deslumbrador
dead, muerto
deadly, mortal
deal, porción
dealing, proceder
dear, querido
death, muerte
debate, debate
debt, deuda
debut, estreno
decade, década
decay, decaimiento
December, diciembre
decent, decente
decide, decidir
decision, decisión
decisive, decisivo
deck, cubierta
declaration, declaración
declare, declarar
decline, declinación
decoration, ornamentación
defeat, derrota
defense, defensa
defend, defender
defendant, que defiende
deficiency, deficiencia
define, definir
definite, preciso
definition, precisión
deflection, desvío

degree, grado
delay, dilación
delegate, delegado
delegation, delegación
deliberate, deliberado
deliberately, deliberadamente
delicate, delicado
delicatessen, fiambre
delight, deleite
delightful, deleitoso
deliver, libertar
delivery, liberación
demand, demanda
demonstration, manifestación
    pública
dental, dental
dentist, dentista
denture, dentadura
deny, negar
deodorant, desodorante
department, ministerio
departure, marcha
depend, pender
dependence, confianza
dependent, dependiente
deposit, depósito
deposition, destitución
depreciation, depreciación
depression, abatimiento
depth, profundidad
deputy, diputado
derelict, derrelicto
derive, derivar
derived, derivado
descendant, descendiente
describe, describir
description, género
desert, mérito
deserve, merecer
desperate, desesperado
despite, apesarde
dessert, postres
destination, destinación
destiny, sino
destroy, destruir
destruction, destrucción
destructive, destructivo
detail, detalle

detect, descubrir
detective, detective
detention, detención
deterioration, deterioración
determination, determinación
determine, determinar
determined, determinado
detour, desvío
develop, desenvolver
development,
    desenvolvimiento
device, artificio
devil, demonio
devote, consagrar
devoted, consagrado
devotion, devoción
diabetic, diabético
diagram, diagrama
dial, cuadrante
dialect, dialecto
diameter, diámetro
diamond, diamante
diaper, pañal
diarrhea, diarrea
diary, diario
dictionary, diccionario
die, dado
diet, dieta
differ, diferir
difference, diferencia
different, diferente
differential, diferencial
difficult, trabajoso
difficulty, obstáculo
digital, digital
dignity, dignidad
dill, eneldo
dinner, banquete
diploma, diploma
direct, directo
direction, consejo de
    administración
directly, directamente
director, director
directory, directorio
disc, disco
discharge, descarga
disciple, seguidor, discípulo

discipline, disciplina
discover, descubrir
discretion, discreción
discrimination,
    discernimiento
discuss, discutir
disease, enfermedad
disguise, disfraz
disgust, aversión
dish, plato
disorder, desorden
displacement, traslado
display, despliegue
disposal, disposición
disposition, arreglo
dispute, disputa
distance, distancia
distant, distante
distinct, distinto
distinction, distinción
distinguish, distinguir
distinguished, distinguido
distress, dolor
district, partido
disturb, turbar
disturbance, perturbación
diversion, diversión
divide, divisoria de aguas
divine, divino
division, división
divorce, divorcio
dizzy, mareo
do, do
doctor, doctor
doctrine, doctrina
document, documento
dog, perro
doing, acción
doll, muñeca
dollar, dólar
domestic, doméstico
dominant, dominante
done, hecho
door, puerta
doorway, puerta
dose, dosis
double, doble
doubt, duda

doubtful, dudoso
doubtless, indudable
down, abajo
downstairs, de abajo
downtown, el centro de la ciudad
downward, descendente
downwards, hacia abajo
dozen, docena
draft, acción de sacar
drag, rastra, arrastrar
drain, drenar
drama, drama
drastic, drástico
draught, acción de sacar
draw, arrastre
drawing, dibujo
drawn, arrastrado
dreadful, espantoso
dream, sueño
dreary, triste
dress, vestido
dressing gown, bata
dried, seco
drift, lo arrastrado
drill, taladro
drink, bebida, beber
drip, chorreadura
drive, conducir, manejar
driver, carretero, conductor
drop, gota
drove, manada
drug, droga
drugstore, farmacia
drunk, borracho
dry, seco
dual, dual
dubious, dudoso
duchess, duquesa
duck, duck
due, debido
duke, duque
dull, embotado
dummy, mudo
duration, duración
during, durante
dusk, oscuro
dust, polvo

dusty, polvoriento
duty, deber
dwelling, morada
dye, tintura
dying, moribundo

E

each, cada
eager, ávido
ear, oreja
earache, otalgia
earl, conde
early, antiguo
earn, ganar
earnest, formal
earring, arete
earth, tierra
ease, alivio
east, este
Easter, Pascua de Resurrección o florida, semanasanta
eastern, oriental
easy, fácil
eat, comer
eccentric, excéntrica
echo, eco
economic, económico
economy, economía
eczema, eczema
edge, filo
editor, redactor, editor
editorial, editorial
educated, educado
education, educación
educational, educativo
eel, anguila
effect, efecto
effective, real
efficiency, eficiencia
efficient, eficiente
effort, esfuerzo
egg, huevo
eggplant, berenjena
eight, ocho
eighteen, diez y ocho
eighteenth, decimoctavo
eighty, ochenta

either, uno y otro
elaborate, trabajado
elastic, elástico
elbow, codo
elder, mayor
elderly, mayor
eldest, primogénito
elect, elegido
electrician, electricista
electricity, electricidad
electron, electrón
electronic, electrónico
elegance, elegancia
elegant, elegante
element, elemento
elementary, elemental
elevator, elevador
eleven, once
eliminate, eliminar
else, más
elsewhere, en o a otra parte
embark, embarcar
embarrassment, compromiso
embassy, embajada
embroidery, bordado
emerald, esmeralda
emerge, emerger
emergency, emergencia
emergency exit, salida de emergencia
emotion, emoción
emotional, emocional
emphasis, énfasis
empire, imperio
employ, empleo
employee, dependiente
employer, dueño
employment, ocupación
empty, vacío
enable, habilitar
enamel, esmalte
encounter, encuentro
encourage, alentar
encouragement, ánimo
encouraging, alentador
end, fin
endeavor, esfuerzo

ending, fin
endless, inacabable
endure, soportar
energy, energía
enforce, dar fuerza a
engage, comprometer
engagement, compromiso
engine, ingenio
engineer, ingeniero
engineering, ingeniería
English, inglés
Englishman, inglés
enjoy, gozar o disfrutar de
enjoyable, agradable
enjoyment, uso
enlarge, agrandar
enormous, enorme
enough, bastante
ensure, asegurar
enter, entrar en o por
enterprise, empresa
entertain, entretener
entertainment, acogida
enthusiasm, entusiasmo
entire, entero
entirely, enteramente
entrance, entrada
entry, entrada
envelope, envoltura
environment, ambiente
envy, envidiar
episode, episodio
epoch, época
equal, igual
equality, igualdad
equation, ecuación
equilibrium, equilibrio
equipment, equipo
equity, equidad
equivalent, equivalente
era, era
eraser, borrador
erect, derecho
error, error
escalator, escalera mecánica
escape, escape
escort, escolta
especially, especialmente

essay, tentativa
essence, esencia
essential, esencial
establish, establecer
establishment, casa
estate, estado
estimate, estimación
Europe, Europa
European, europeo
evaporation, vaporización
Eve, Eva
even, igual
evening dress, traje de noche
evening, tarde
event, caso, evento
eventually, eventualmente
ever, siempre
every, cada
everybody, todos
everyday, diario
everyone, todos
everything, todo
everywhere, por o en todas
    partes
evidence, evidencia
evident, evidente
evil, aciago
evolution, evolución
exact, exacto
examination, examen
examine, examinar
example, dechado
exceed, exceder
excellency, excelencia
excellent, excelente
except, excepto
exception, excepción
exceptional, excepcional
excess, exceso
excessive, excesivo
exchange rate, tipo del cambio
exchange, cambio
exchequer, tesorería
excitement, agitación
exciting, excitante
exclusive, exclusivo
excursion, excursión
excuse, excusa

execution, embargo
executive, ejecutivo
exercise, ejercicio
exhaust, escape
exhausted, agotado, consado
exhaustion, agotamiento
exhibit, expuesto, objeto
exhibition, exhibición
exist, existir
exit, salida
expand, extender
expanding, que se extiende o
    ensancha
expansion, expansión
expect, esperar
expectant, expectante
expectation, espera
expedition, expedición
expenditure, gasto
expense, gasto
expensive, caro
experience, experiencia
experienced, experimentado
experiment, experimento
experimental, experimental
expert, experimentado, experto
expiration, expiración
explain, explicar
exploit, hazaña
explosion, explosión
explosive, explosivo
export, exportación
exposed, expuesto
exposure, exposición a la
    intemperie
express, expreso
expressly, expresamente
expulsion, expulsión
exquisite, exquisitez
extend, extender
extended, extendido
extension, extensión
extensive, extensivo
extent, extensión
external, externo
extra, extra
extract, extracto
extraordinary, extraordinario

extravagant, extravagante, pródigo
extreme, extremo
extremely, extremadamente
eye, ojo
eyed, de ojos

F

fabric, tejido, tela
face, cara
faced, de cara
facing, paramento
fact, hecho
factor, factor
factory, fábrica
fall, caer
falling, cayendo
false, falso
fame, fama
familiar, familiar
familiarity, familiaridad
family, alcurnia
famous, famoso
fan, abanico
fancy, fantasía
fantasy, ensueño, fantasía
far, lejos
fare, precio
farm, granja
farmer, granjero
farmhouse, granja
farming, cultivo
farther, más lejos
fashion, moda
fashionable, a la moda
fast, rapido
faster, ayunador
fat, gordo
fatal, fatal
fate, hado
father, padre
father-in-law, suegro
fatigue, fatigar
faucet, grito
fault, falta
favor, favor
favorable, favorable

favored, favorecido
favorite, favorito
fear, miedo
fearful, espantoso
feast, fiesta
feather, pluma
feature, rasgo
February, febrero
federal, federal
federation, federación
fee, honorarios
feed, alimentar
feeding, alimento
feel, palpamiento
feeling, sentimiento, tacto
feet, pies
fellow, compañero
fellowship, compañerismo
feminine, femenino
fence, empalizada
fennel, hinojo
ferry, transbordador
festival, festival
fetch, buscar
fever, fiebre
few, pocos
fewer, menos
fibre, fibra
fiction, ficción
field, campo
fierce, fiero
figure, cuerpo
figured, figurado
file, lima
fill, llenar
fill in, insertar
filling, relleno
film, película
filter, filtro
fin, aleta
final, final
finally, finalmente
finance, ciencia y práctica financiera
financial, financiero
find, hallazgo
finding, hallazgo
fine, multa

finger, aguja indicadora
finish, fin
finishing, acabando
finite, finito
fire, fuego
fireplace, hogar
firing, encendiendo
firm, firme
firmly, firmemente
first name, nombre de pila
first, primero
first-class, de primera clase
firstly, primero
fish, pez
fishing tackle, avíos de pescar
fishing, pesca
fist, puño
fit, ataque
fitting, propio
fix, apuro
fixed, fijo
flame, llama
flannel, franela
flash, llamarada
flashlight, linterna eléctrica
flat, plano
flavor, sabor
flea, pulga
flesh, carne
flexibility, flexibilidad
flight, volada
flock, bandada
flood, inundación
floor, suelo
flounder, forcejeo
flour, harina
flow, flujo
flower, flor
flu, gripa
fluctuation, fluctuación
fluid, fluido
fly, mosca
flying, vuelo
foam, espuma
focus, foco
fog, niebla
fold, doblez
folding chair, silla plegable o de tijera

folk music, música popular
folk, gente
follow, seguir
following, siguiente
folly, tontería
fond, aficionado
food, alimento
foodstuff, comestible
fool, necio
foolish, tonto
foot, pie
football, fútbol
footpath, senda
footstep, paso
for, por
forbid, prohibir
forbidden, prohibido
force, fuerza
forced, forzado
forecast, pronóstico
foregoing, anterior
forehead, frente
foreign, extranjero
foreigner, extranjero
forest, bosque
forester, guardabosque
forever, siempre
forget, olvidar
forgive, perdonar
fork, horcón
form, forma
formal, formal
format, formato
formation, formación
former, pasado
formerly, anteriormente
formidable, formidable
forth, delante
forthcoming, venidero
fortnight, quincena
fortress, fortaleza
fortunate, afortunado
fortune, suerte
forty, cuarenta
forward, delantero
foster, fomentar
found, fundar
foundation, fundación

founder, fundidor
fountain, fuente
fountain pen, pluma fuente
four, cuatro
fourteen, catorce
fourteenth, catorceno
fourth, cuarto
fowl, gallo
fraction, fragmento
fragment, fragmento
frame, armazón
framework, esqueleto
France, Francia
Frank, franco
free, libre
freedom, libertad
freely, libremente
frequency, frecuencia
frequent, frecuente
fresh, fresco
Friday, viernes
fried egg, huevo frito o
    estrellado
fried, freído
friend, amigo
friendly, amistoso
friendship, amistad
fringe, franja
frog, rana
from, de
front, frente
frontier, frontera
frost, escarcha
fruit, fruto
frustrate, frustrar
frustration, frustración
fry, freir
fuel, combustible
fulfilment, cumplimiento
full, lleno
fully, plenamente
fun, diversión
function, función
fund, fondo
fundamental, fundamental
funeral, entierro
funny, cómico
fur, piel

furious, furioso
furnished, amueblado
furniture, ajuar
further, adicional
furthermore, además
fuss, alboroto
future, futuro

G

gag, mordaza
gain, ganancia
gallery, galería
game, juego
gang, pelotón
gap, boquete
gap, portillo
garage, garaje
garden, jardín
garlic, ajo
garment, vestido
gas, gas
gasoline, gasolina
gasp, boqueada
gastritis, gastritis
gate, puerta
gather, frunce
gathering, acumulación
gauge, medida
gauze, gasa
gay, alegre
gaze, mirada fija
gear, engranaje
geese, ganso
gem, gema
general, general
generally, generalmente
generation, generación
generous, generoso
genetic, genético
genius, genio
gentle, suave
gentleman, caballero
gently, mansamente
gentry, señorío
genuine, genuino
geology, geología
geometry, geometría

gesture, gesto
get, conseguir
get up, levantarse
ghastly, horrible
gherkin, pepinillo
ghost, espíritu
giant, gigante
gift, donación
gigantic, gigantesco
gin, ginebra
ginger, jengibre
girdle, cinto
girl, niña
give, dar
give way, ceder
given, dado
glad, alegre
gladly, alegremente
glance, mirada
gland, glándula
glass, vidrio
glassware, cristalería
glimpse, resplandor fugaz
gloomy, oscuro
glorious, glorioso
glory, gloria
glove, guante
glow, resplandor
glue, cola
go away, irse
go, ir
go out, salir
goal, meta
God, Dios
gold, oro
golden, de oro
golf course, campo de golf
golf, golf
gone, ido
good, bueno
good-bye, adiós
goodness, bondad
goods, mercancias
gooseberry, grosellero
  silvestre
gospel, evangelio
gossip, chismografía
govern, gobernar

government, gobernación
governor, gobernador
grace, gracia
gracious, gracioso
grade, grado
gradual, graduado
grain, grano
grammar, gramática
grand, grandioso
grandparents, abuelos
grant, concesión
grape, uva
grapefruit, pomelo
grasp, agarro
grass, hierba
grateful, agradecido
gratitude, gratitud
grave, grave
gravity, gravedad
gravy, salsa
gray, gris
graze, rozamiento
greasy, grasiento
great, grande
greater, mayor
greatly, muy
Greece, Grecia
Greek, griego
green, verde
greeting, saludo
grid, rejilla
grief, dolor
grill, parrillas
grim, torvo
grip, agarro
grocery, comestibles
gross, grueso
ground, tierra
group, grupo
grow, crecer
growing, creciente
grown, crecido
growth, crecimiento
gruff, brusco
guarantee, garantía
guard, guardia
guarded, defendido
guardian, guardián

guess, conjetura
guest, huésped
guidance, guía
guide, guía
guidebook, guía de turismo
guild, gremio
guilt, culpa
guilty, culpable
gum, encía
gun, pistola
gynecologist, ginecólogo

H

habit, hábito
hair, cabello
hairbrush, cepillo para el pelo
haircut, corte de pelo
hairdresser, peluquero
half, mitad
halibut, especie de lenguado
hall, vestíbulo
halt, alto
ham, pernil
hammer, martillo
handsome, hermoso
hang, colgar
hanger, soporte colgante
happen, acontecer
happiness, ventura
happy, feliz
harbor, puerto
hard, duro
hard-boiled, duro
hardly, difícilmente
hare, liebre
harm, mal
harmless, inofensivo
harmony, armonía
harsh, áspero
haste, prisa
hat, sombrero
hate, odio
hatred, odio
have, haber, tener
hay fever, fiebre del heno
hay, heno
hazard, azar
he, él

head, cabeza
headache, jaqueca
header, cabecilla
heading, título
headline, título
headquarters, cuartel general
heal, curar
health, salud
healthy, sano
heap, montón
hear, oír
hearing, oído
heart, corazón
hearth, hogar
heartily, sinceramente
heat, calor
heath, brezo
heating, calefacción
heaven, gloria
heavenly, celestial
heavily, pesadamente
heavy, pesado
hedge, seto vivo
heel, talón
height, altura
helicopter, helicóptero
hell, infierno
hello, ¡hola!
help, ayuda
helpful, útil
helping, racion
her, ella
herb, hierba
herd, rebaño
here, aquí
heritage, herencia
hero, héroe
herring, arenque
hesitate, vacilar
hesitation, duda
hidden, escondido
hide, cuero
hiding, ocultamiento
high tide, pleamar
high, alto
higher, más alto
highly, altamente
hike, marcha

hill, colina
him, él
himself, solo
hinge, gozne
hint, indicación
hire, alquilar
historian, historiador
history, historia
hit, golpe
hobby, alcotán
hold, agarrar
holding, tenencia
hole, agujero
holiday, fiesta
hollow, hueco
holy, santo
home, hogar
honest, honrado
honesty, honradez
honey, miel
honeymoon, luna de miel
honorary, honorario
honor, honor
hook, gancho
hope, esperanza
hopeless, desesperado, sin esperanza
hopper, saltador
horizon, horizonte
horizontal, horizontal
horror, horror
horse, caballo
horseback, lomo de caballo
horseradish, rábano picante
hospital, hospital
hospitality, hospitalidad
host, hospedero
hostess, posadera
hostile, hostil
hostility, hostilidad
hot, caliente
hotel, hotel
hour, hora
house, lugar donde se aloja
household, casa
housing, alojamiento
how far, cuán lejos
how many, cuántos

how, cómo
however, de cualquier modo que
huge, grande
hull, cáscara
human, humano
humanity, humanidad
humble, humilde
humor, humor
hundred, cien
hunger, gana
hungry, hambriento
hunt, caza
hunting, caza
hurried, precipitado
hurry, premura
hurt, herida
husband, marido
hut, choza
hydraulic, hidráulico
hypothesis, hipótesis

I

I, yo
ice cream, helado de crema
ice, hielo
icing, carpa de azucar
idea, idea
ideal, ideal
ideology, teorización
if, si
ignition, ignición
ignorance, ignorancia
ignorant, ignorante
ignore, desconocer
ill, enfermo
illegal, ilegal
illness, enfermedad
illusion, ilusión
illustrate, ilustrar
illustration, ilustración
image, imagen
imagination, imaginación
imaginative, imaginativo
imagine, imaginar
immediate, inmediato
immediately, inmediatamente

immense, inmenso
immigrant, inmigrante
immigration, inmigración
immortal, inmortal
impact, golpe
impatience, impaciencia
impatient, impaciente
imperial, imperial
impersonal, impersonal
implication, implicación
implied, implícito
imply, implicar
import, importancia
importance, importancia
important, importante
impose, imponer
imposing, impresionante
impossible, imposible
impress, impresión
impression, impresión
impressive, impresionante
imprisonment,
    encarcelamiento
improbable, improbable
improve, mejorar
improvement,
    perfeccionamiento
impulse, impulso
in, en
inadequate, inadecuado
incentive, incitativo
inch, pulgada
incidence, acto o manera de
    afectar o modificar
incident, incidente
inclination, inclinación
inclined, inclinado
include, incluir
inclusion, carta que acompaña
    a otra
income, entrada
incomplete, incompleto
increase, aumento
incredible, increíble
indeed, realmente
independence, independencia
independent, independiente
index, índice

India, India
Indian, indio
indicate, indicar
indication, indicio
indicator, indicador
indifferent, indiferente
indigestion, indigestión
indignation, indignación
individual, individual
indoor, interior
industrial, industrial
industry, industria
inevitable, inevitable
inexpensive, barato
inexperienced, inexperto
infant, infante
infect, infectar
infection, contaminación
inferior, inferior
infinite, infinito
inflammation, inflamación
inflation, inflación
influence, influencia
influenza, influenza
inform, informe
informal, que no se ajusta a
    formalidades o ceremonias
informant, informador
information, información
informed, informado
ingenious, ingenioso
ingenuity, ingenio
ingredient, ingrediente
inhabitant, habitante
inherent, inherente
inheritance, herencia
initial, inicial
initiative, iniciativo
injection, inyección
injure, dañar
injury, daño
injustice, injusticia
ink, tinta
inland, interior
inn, posada
inner, interior
innocence, inocencia
innocent, inocente

innumerable, innumerable
inquest, información o
   pesquisa judicial con ayuda
   de un jurado
inquiry, indagación
inscription, título
insect, insecto
inside, interior
insight, discernimiento
insignificant, insignificante
insist, insistir
inspection, inspección
inspector, inspector
inspiration, inspiración
installation, instalación
instance, ejemplo
instant, instante
instantly, al instante
instead, en cambio
instinct, instinto
institute, instituto
institution, institución
instruction, enseñanza
instrument, instrumento
instrumental, instrumental
insufficient, insuficiente
insurance, seguro
insured, asegurado
intact, intacto
integral, integrante
intellectual, intelectual
intelligence, inteligencia
intelligent, inteligente
intend, tener la intención de
intended, propuesto
intense, intenso
intensity, intensidad
intensive, intenso
intention, intención
interest, interés
interfere, interponerse
interference, interposición
interim, interino
interior, interior
intermediate, intermedio
intermittent, intermitente
internal, interior
international, internacional

interpret, interpretar
interpretation, interpretación
interruption, interrupción
intersection, intersección
interval, intervalo
intervention, intervención
interview, entrevista
intimate, íntimo
into, en
intricate, intrincado
introduce, introducir
invasion, usurpación
invention, invento
invest, investir
investigate, investigar
investigation, averiguación
investment, inversión
invisible, invisible
invitation, invitación
invite, invitar
invoice, factura
involve, envolver
involved, envuelto
iron, fierro
irregular, irregular
irrelevant, impertinente,
   irrelevante
irrigation, irrigación
island, isla
isle, isla
isolation, soledad
issue, asunto
it, el/lo
Italian, italiano
Italy, Italia
item, item
its, su
itself, él mismo
ivory, marfil

J

jacket, chaqueta
jade, jade
jam, compota
January, enero
jar, jarra
jaw, quijada
jazz, jazz

jealous, celoso
jealousy, celos
jelly, jalea
Jesus, Jesús
jet, avion jet
Jew, judío
jewellery, pedrería
Jewish, judaico
job, obra
jockey, jockey
join, punto de unión o de encuentro
joint, articulación
joke, chiste
journal, diario
journey, camino
joy, gozo
Judaism, judaísmo
judge, juez, juzgar
judgment, juicio
judicial, judicial
jug, jarro
juice, jugo, zumo
July, julio
jump, salto
June, junio
jungle, selva virgen
junior, menor
juniper, junípero
just, justo
justice, justicia
justification, justificación
justify, defender, justificar

K

keen, agudo
keep, guardar
kerosene, petróleo para lámparas
key, llave
kick, puntapié
kid, cabrito
kidney, riñón
kill, muerte
killing, muerte
kilo, kilo
kilogram, kilogramo
kilometer, kilómetro

kin, parientes
kind, bueno
kindly, bondadoso
kindness, bondad
king, rey
kingdom, reino
kinship, parentesco
kiss, beso
kit, avíos
kitchen, cocina
knee, rodilla
knife, cuchillo
knight, caballero
knob, perilla
knock, golpe
know, conocer
knowing, inteligente
knowledge, conocimiento
label, marbete

L

labor, trabajo
lace, cordón
lack, falta
lacking, carente
lad, muchacho
lady, señora
lake, lago
lamb, cordero
lamp, lámpara
land, tierra
landed, hacendado
landing, desembarco
landlord, propietario
landmark, mojón
landscape, paisaje
lane, senda
language, lenguaje
lantern, linterna
lap, falda, regazo
large, grande
last, último
lasting, durable
late, tarde
lately, últimamente
latent, latente
latter, más reciente
laugh, risa

laughing, risueño
laughter, risa
launch, lanzamiento
laundry, ropa sucia
law, ley
lawn, césped
lawyer, abogado
laxative, laxativo
lay, laico
layer, colocador
laying, colocación
layout, arreglo
lazy, perezoso
lead, plomo
leader, conductor
leadership, dirección
leading, objetos de plomo
leaf, hoja
league, liga
lean, delgado
leaning, ladeo
leap year, año bisiesto
leap, salto
learn, aprender
learned, ilustrado
learning, instrucción
lease, arrendamiento
least, mínimo
leather, cuero
leave, salir
lecture, conferencia
lecturer, disertante
leek, puerro
left, izquierdo
leg, pierna
legal, legal
legend, leyenda
legislation, legislación
legislative, legislativo
legitimate, legítimo
leisure, ocio
leisurely, lento
lemon, limón
lemonade, limonada
lend, prestar
length, longitud
lens, lente
lentil, lenteja

less, menos
lesser, menor
lesson, lección
let, permitir
letter box, buzón
letter of credit, carta de crédito
letter, letra
level, llano
liability, riesgo
liable, expuesto
liberal, liberal
liberty, libertad
librarian, bibliotecario
library, biblioteca
license, licencia
lie down, acostarse
lie, mentira
life belt, cinturón salvavidas
life, vida
lifetime, vida
lift, alzamiento
light, luz
lighter, encendedor
lighting, iluminación
lightly, ligeramente
lightning, relámpago
like, igual
likely, probable
likewise, lo mismo
liking, inclinación
lime, cal
limestone, caliza
limit, límite
limitation, limitación
limited, constitucional
line, cuerda
linear, lineal
linen, hilo de lino
link, eslabón
lion, león
lip, labio
lipstick, lápiz para los labios
liqueur, licor
liquid, líquido
list, lista
listen, escuchar
lit, amaneramiento
literary, literario

literature, literatura
liter, litro
little, pequeño
live, vivo
lively, vivo
liver, viviente
lives, vida
load, carga
loading, carga
loan, préstamo
lobster, langosta
local train, tren suburbano
local, local
locality, situación
lock, candado
lodging, alojamiento
logic, lógica
logical, lógico
loneliness, soledad
lonely, solo
long, largo
long-sighted, présbita
long-term, a largo plazo
longer, más largo
longing, ansia
look for, buscar
look, mirar
loop, curva
loose, suelto
lord, señor
lose, perder
losing, pérdida
loss, pérdida
lost, arruinado
lot, lote
loud, fuerte
lounge, salón
love, amor
lovely, amable
lover, enamorado
loving, amante
low tide, bajamar
low, bajo
lower, más bajo
loyal, leal
loyalty, lealtad
luck, suerte
luckily, afortunadamente

lucky, afortunado
luggage, equipaje
lump, trozo
lunch, almuerzo
lung, pulmón
luxury, lujo
lying, mentiroso

M

machine, máquina
machinery, maquinaria
mad, loco, enojado
madam, señora
made, hecho
madness, locura
magazine, almacén
magic, magia
magistrate, magistrado
magnetic, magnético
magnificent, magnífico
mahogany, caoba
maid, doncella
maiden, doncella
mail, malla
mailbox, buzón
main, primero
mainly, principalmente
maintain, mantener
maintenance, sostenimiento
majesty, majestad
major, mayor
majority, mayoría
make up, hacer
make, hechura
maker, hacedor
making, hechura
male, macho
man, hombre
manage, manejar
management, dirección
manager, director
manicure, manicura
mankind, género humano
manner, manera
manual, manual
manufacture, manufactura
manufacturing, fabril
manure, abono

manuscript, manuscrito
many, muchos
map, mapa
March, marzo
margin, margen
marine, marinero, marítimo
marked, marcado
market, mercado
marmalade, mermelada
marriage, matrimonio
married, casado
marry, casar
marsh, marjal
marshal, mariscal
Marxist, marxista
mass, masa
massive, macizo
master, amo
match, fósforo
material, material
mathematics, matemáticas
matrix, matriz
matter, materia
mattress, colchón
mature, maduro
maturity, madurez
May, mayo
maybe, acaso
mayor, alcalde
me, me
meadow, prado
meal, comida, harina
mean, bajo
meaning, mezquino, significado
meaningful, significante
meanwhile, entretanto
measure, medida
measured, medido
measurement, medición
meat, carne
mechanic, mecánico
mechanical, mecánico
mechanism, mecanismo
medal, medalla
medieval, medieval
medical, médico
medicine, medicina

Mediterranean, Mediterránea
medium, medio
meet, apropiado
meeting, reunión
melancholy, melancolía
melody, melodía
melon, melón
melt, fusión
member, miembro
membership, miembredad
memoir, memoria
memorial, conmemorativo
memory, memoria
men, hombre
menace, amenaza
mend, arreglar
mental, mental
mention, mención
menu, lista de platos
merchant, mercader
mercy, misericordia
mere, mero
merely, meramente
merger, unión
merit, mérito
merry, alegre
mess, desorden
message, mensaje
metal, metal
meter, medidor
method, método
meter, metro
metropolitan, metropolitano
middle, medio
middle-aged, de mediana edad
middle-class, de la clase media
midnight, medianoche
midst, centro
might, poderío
mighty, poderoso
migration, migración
mild, apacible
mildly, suavemente
mile, milla
mileage, longitud o recorrido en millas

military, militar
milk, leche
milking, ordeñar
mill, molino
million, millón
mind, mente
minded, dispuesto
mine, mío
miner, minero
mineral water, agua mineral
mineral, mineral
miniature, miniatura
minimum, minimum
mining, minería
minister, ministro
ministry, ministerio
minor, menor
minority, minoridad
mint, casa de moneda
minute, minuto
miracle, milagro
mirror, espejo
miscellaneous, misceláneo
miserable, miserable
misery, miseria
Miss, señorita
missile, proyectil
missing, extraviado
mission, misión
mist, niebla
mistake, equivocación
mistaken, equivocado
Mister, Señor
mistress, ama
mix, mezcla
mixed, mezclado
mixture, mezcla
mobility, movilidad
mode, modo
model, modelo
moderate, templado
moderation, moderación
modern, moderno
modest, recatado
modification, modificación
moisture, humedad
mole, mola
moment, momento

momentum, ímpetu
monarch, monarca
monarchy, monarquía
monastery, monasterio
Monday, lunes
money order, giro postal
money, moneda
monopoly, monopolio
month, mes
monthly, mensual
monument, monumento
moon, luna
moonlight, luz de la luna
moral, moral
morality, moralidad
more, más
moreover, además
morning, mañana
mortar, mortero
mortgage, hipoteca
Moslem, musulman
mosque, mezquita
most, muchos
mostly, en su mayor parte
mother, madre
motion, movimiento
motor, motor
motorboat, lancha con motor
motorway, autopista
mold, moho
mountain, montaña
mountaineering, alpinismo
mounted, montado
mounting, subida
mouth, bocas
mouthwash, enjuague
move, movimiento
movement, mecanismo
movie, película
moving, moción
much, mucho
mud, barro
mug, jarro
multiple, múltiple
multitude, multitud
municipal, municipal
murder, asesinato
muscle, músculo

museum, museo
mushroom, champiñones
music, música
musical, musical
mussel, mejillón
must, mosto
mustard, mostaza
mutton, carne de carnero
mutual, mutual
my, mi
myself, yo
mysterious, misterioso
mystery, misterio
myth, mito

N

nail, uña
naked, desnudo
name, nombre
namely, a saber
napkin, servilleta
narrative, narrativo
narrow, estrecho
nation, nación
national, nacional
nationality, sentimiento
    nacional
native, nativo
natural history, historia
natural, natural
nature, naturaleza
naval, naval
navy, armada
near, cercano
nearby, cerca
nearly, de cerca
neat, aseado
necessary, forzoso
necessity, necesidad
neck, cuello
necklace, collar
need, necesidad
needle, aguja
negative, negativo
neglect, abandono
negligible, despreciable
negotiate, negociar

negotiation, negociación
Negro, negro
neighbor, vecino
neighborhood, vecindad
neighboring, vecino
neither, ninguno de los dos
nephew, sobrino
nerve, nervio
nervous, nervudo
nest, nido
net, red
never, nunca
nevertheless, no obstante
new, nuevo
news, noticia
newspaper, diario, periódico
next, próximo
nickel, níquel
niece, sobrina
night, noche
nightmare, pesadilla
nine, nueve
nineteen, diez y nueve
nineteenth, decimonono
ninety, noventa
no, no
nobility, nobleza
noble, noble
nobody, nadie
noise, ruido
noisy, ruidoso
nominal, nominal
nomination, nominación
none, ninguno
nonsense, cosa sin sentido
noodle, tallarín
noon, mediodía
nor, ni
normal, normal
North America, Norteamérica
north, norte
northern, del norte
Norway, Noruega
nose, nariz
nosebleed, hemorragia nasal
not, no
notable, notable
notably, notablemente

note paper, papel de cartas
note, nota
notebook, cuaderno
noted, nombrado
nothing, nada
notice, informe
notify, notificar
notion, idea
notorious, notorio
notwithstanding, no obstante
noun, nombre
novel, nuevo, novela
novelist, novelista
November, noviembre
now, ahora
nowadays, hoy día
nowhere, en ninguna parte
nuclear, nuclear
nucleus, núcleo
nuisance, molestia
number, número
numerous, numerosos
nurse, ama
nursery, cuarto o aposento
    destinado a los niños

O

O.K., conforme
oak, roble
oath, juramento
object, objeto
objection, objeción
objective, objeto
obligation, obligación
oblivious, desmemoriado
obscene, obsceno
obscenity, obscenidad
obscure, oscuro
observation, observación
observe, observar
obsession, obsesión
obstacle, obstáculo
obtain, obtener, sacar
obvious, obvio
occasion, ocasión
occasional, ocasional
occasionally, ocasionalmente

occupation, ocupación
occupy, emplear
occur, hallarse, ocurrir
occurrence, incidente
October, octubre
odd, impar
odds, ventaja
of, de
off, apagar
offense, ofensa
offender, ofensor
offensive, ofensivo
offer, oferta
offering, oblación
office, oficio
officer, persona que tiene cargo
    público
official, oficial
officially, oficialmente
offset, compensación
often, a menudo
oil, aceite
oily, aceitoso
old, viejo
old-fashioned, anticuado
ominous, ominoso
on, en
once, vez
one, uno
one-way, una dirección
onion, cebolla
only, solo
onto, hacia
onward, que se mueve hacia
    adelante
onyx, ónix
open, abierto
opening, apertura
openly, abiertamente
opera house, teatro de la
    ópera
opera, ópera
operate, hacer funcionar,
    operar
operating, operando
operation, operación
operator, operador
operetta, opereta

opinion, opinión
opponent, oponente
opportunity, sazón
oppose, oponer
opposed, opuesto
opposite, frontero
opposition, oposición
optician, óptico
or, o
oral, oral
orange, naranja
orangeade, naranjada
organization, organización
orientation, orientación
origin, origen
original, original
ornithology, ornitología
orthodox, ortodoxo
other, otro
otherwise, otramente
our, nuestro
ourselves, nosotros mismos
out of order, desordenado
out of stock, vendido
out, fuera
outcome, resultado
outdoor, a fuera de casa
outer, exterior
outlaw, bandido
outlet, salida
outline, contorno
outlook, atalaya
output, rendimiento
outset, comienzo
outside, exterior
outstanding, saliente
outward, exterior
oval, oval
oven, horno
over, arriba
overalls, mono, overoll
overcome, vencer
overhead, sobre la cabeza de uno
overheat, acalorar
overnight, pasar la noche, nocturno, de la noche a la mañana

overwhelming, aplastante
owe, deber
own, propio
owner, propietario
ownership, propiedad
oxidation, oxidación
oxide, óxido
oxygen, oxígeno
oyster, ostra

P

pace, paso
pacifier, pacificador
pack, empacar
packet, paquete
packing, empacando
pagan, pagano
page, paje
paid, pagado
pail, cubo
pain, dolor
painful, doloroso
paint, pintura
paintbox, caja de colores o pinturas
painter, pintor
painting, pintura
pair, par
pajamas, pijama
palace, palacio
pale, pálido
palpitation, palpitación
pan, pan
panel, tabla
panic, pánico
panties, bragas
panting, jadeante
pants, pantalones
paper, papel
paperback, libro en rústica
parable, parábola
parade, pompa
paradise, paraíso
paradox, paradoja
paragraph, párrafo
parallel, paralelo
parameter, parámetro

parcel, paquete
pardon, perdón
parent, padre o madre
parental, paternal
parish, parroquia
park, parque
parking, estacionamiento
parliamentary, parlamentario
parsley, perejil
part, parte
partial, parcial
participate, participar
participation, participación
particle, partícula
particular, particular
parting, partida
partly, en parte
partner, socio
partnership, sociedad
partridge, perdiz
party, partido
pass, paso
passage, paso
passenger, pasajero
passing, paso
passion, pasión
passionate, apasionado
passive, pasivo
passport, pasaporte
past, pasado
paste, masa, pasta
pastry shop, pastelería
pastry, pastelería
patch, remiendo
path, camino
pathetic, patético
patience, paciencia
patient, paciente
pattern, modelo
pause, pausa
pavement, pavimento
pay, paga
payable, pagable
paying, pago
payment, pago
pea, guisante
peace, paz
peaceful, pacífico

peach, durazno
peak, pico
peanut, cacahuete
pear, pera
pearl, perla
peasant, campesino, labriego
peculiar, peculiar
pedestrian, peatón, pedestre
peel, piel
peg, clavija
pen, pluma
penalty, pena
pencil sharpener
    sacapuntas
pencil, lápiz
pendant, cosa que cuelga
penicillin, penicilina
penknife, cortaplumas
pension, pensión
pensioner, pensionado
people, pueblo
pepper, pimienta
per cent, por ciento
per, por
percentage, porcentaje
perception, percepción
perch, perca
perfect, perfecto
perform, hacer
performance, ejecución
perfume, perfumar
perhaps, quizás
perhaps, tal vez
period, período
permanent, permanente
permission, permiso
permit, permiso
perpetual, perpetuo
persistent, persistente
person, persona
personal, personal
personality, personalidad
personnel, personal
perspective, perspectiva
persuade, persuadir
pet, mascota
petrol, gasolina
petty, pequeño

pewter, peltre
phase, fase
pheasant, faisán
phenomenon, fenómeno
philosopher, filósofo
philosophy, filosofía
phone, teléfono
photo, fotografía
photocopy, fotocopia
photograph, fotografía
photograph, retrato
photographer, fotógrafo
photography, fotografía
phrase, frase
physical, físico
physics, física
piano, piano
pick up, recoger
pick, pico
picture, pintura
piece, pieza
pier, pilar
pig, cerdo
pigeon, pichón
pile, estaca
pill, píldora
pillar, pilar
pillow, almohada
pilot, piloto
pin, alfiler
pine, pino
pineapple, piña
pink, clavel
pipe, tubo
pistol, pistola
pit, hoyo
pitch, lanzar
pity, piedad
place, lugar
plaice, platija
plain, llano
plan, plano
plane, plano
plant, mata, planta
plantation, plantación
plaster, yeso
plastic, plástico
plate, placa

platform, plataforma
platinum, platino
plausible, plausible
play, juego
player, actor, jugador
playground, patio de recreo
plea, argumento
pleasant, agradable
please, agradar
pleasing, agradable
pleasure, placer
plenty, copia
plot, porción de terreno
plug, tapón
plum, ciruela
plump, regordete
plus, más
pneumonia, neumonía
pocket, bolsillo
poem, poema
poet, poeta
poetry, poesía
point, punta
pointed, puntiagudo
poison, veneno
police, policía
policy, línea de conducta
polite, cortés
politic, sagaz
political, político
politician, político
pond, estanque
pool, piscina
poor, pobre
pop, estallido
popular, popular
popularity, popularidad
population, población
porcelain, porcelana
pork, cerdo
pornographic, pornográfico
pornography, pornografía
port, puerto
portable, portátil
porter, portero
portion, porción
portrait, retrato
Portugal, Portugal

Portuguese, portugués
position, posición
positive, categórico
possess, poseer
possession, dominio de sí
   mismo
possibility, contingencia,
   posibilidad
possible, posible
possibly, posiblemente
post office, correo
post, poste
postage stamp, sello de
   correos
postage, franqueo
pot, marmita
potential, potencial
pottery, alfarería
poultice, cataplasma
poultry, pollería
pound, libra
pour, verter
poverty, pobreza
powder, polvo
power, poder
powerful, poderoso
practicable, practicable
practical, práctico
practically, prácticamente
practice, práctica
practice, practicar
practiced, práctico
practitioner, médico
praise, alabanza
prayer, súplica
precaution, precaución
preceding, precedente
precious, precioso
precise, preciso
precision, precisión
predecessor, predecesor
predominant, predominante
prefer, preferir
preference, preferencia
pregnancy, preñez
pregnant, preñada
prejudice, prejuicio
preliminary, preliminar

premier, primero
premium, galardón, premio
preoccupation, preocupación
preparation, preparación
prepare, preparar
prescribe, prescribir
presence, presencia.
present, presente
present-day, actual
presentation, presentación
presently, dentro de poco
preservation, preservación
preserve, conservar
preserved, en conserva
president, presidente
press, comprimir
pressing, insistir
pressure, presión
prestige, prestigio
pretend, aparentar, pretender
pretty, lindo
prevent, prevenir
prevention, prevention
previous, previo
price, precio
pride, orgullo
priest, sacerdote
primarily, primariamente
primary, primario
prime, primero
primitive, primitivo
prince, príncipe
princess, princesa
principal, principal
principle, principio
print, impresión
printing, impresión
prior, anterior
priority, anterioridad
prison, prisión
prisoner, preso
private, privado
privately, privadamente
privilege, privilegio
prize, premio
probability, probabilidad
probable, probable
probe, sonda, tienta

problem, problema
procedure, proceder
proceed, proseguir
proceeding, procedimiento
process, proceso
procession, cortejo
produce, producto
producer, director
product, producción
production, producción
productivity, productividad
profession, profesión
professional, profesional
professor, profesor
profile, perfil
profit, ganancia, provecho
profitable, provechoso
profound, profundo
program, programa
progress, progreso
progressive, progresivo
prohibit, prohibir
project, proyecto
prominent, prominente
promise, promesa
promising, prometiente
promote, promover
promotion, promoción
pronounced, pronunciado
pronunciation, pronunciación
proof, prueba
prop, sostener
propaganda, propaganda
proper, propio
properly, propiamente
property, finca
proportion, proporción
proposal, proposición
propose, proponer
proposition, proposición
prospect, perspectiva
prosperity, prosperidad
prosperous, próspero
protect, proteger
protection, protección
protective, protector
protest, protesta
Protestant, protestante

proud, orgulloso
prove, probar
provide, proveer
province, provincia, región
provincial, provincial
provision, prevención
provocative, provocativo
prune, ciruela pasa
psychiatrist, psiquiatra
public, público
publication, publicación
publicity, publicidad
publish, publicar
publisher, editor
pull, tirón
pulpit, púlpito
pump, bomba
pumpkin, calabaza
puncture, puntura
punishment, castigo
pupil, discípulo
purchase, compra
pure, puro
purple, purpúreo
purpose, propósito
purse, bolsa
pursue, seguir
pursuit, seguimiento
push, empujón
put through, llevar a cabo
put, poner
pajamas, pijama

Q

qualification, calificación
qualified, calificado
qualify, calificar
qualifying, calificativo
quality, cualidad
quantity, cuantidad
quarrel, riña
quarter, cuarto
quartz, cuarzo
queen, reina
queer, raro
quest, búsqueda
question, pregunta

questioning, interrogar
quick, rápido, veloz
quickly, rapidamente
quiet, quieto
quilt, colcha
quite, completamente
quotation, cita
quote, cita

R

rabbi, rabí
rabbit, conejo
race, raza
racial, racial
racing, carrera
racket, raqueta
radar, radar
radiation, radiación
radiator, radiador
radical, radical
radio, radio
radioactive, radiactivo
radish, rábano
rage, rabia
rail, baranda
railway, ferrocarril
rain, lluvia
raise, aumento
rally, reunión
random, azar
range, alcance
rare, raro
rash, erupción, inconsiderado
raspberry, frambuesa
rat, rata
rate, razón
rather, más bien
rating, clasificación
ratio, relación
ration, ración
rational, racional
raw, crudo
ray, rayo
razor, navaja de afeitar
reach, alcanzar
read, leer
reader, lector

readily, prontamente
readiness, prontitud
reading, lectura
ready, preparado
real, real
realize, comprender, realizar
really, de veras
realm, reino
rear, trasero
reason, razón
reasonable, racional
reasoning, razonamiento
rebel, rebelde
rebellion, rebelión
recall, llamada
receipt, receta
receive, recibir
receiver, receptor
recent, reciente
reception, acogida, recepción
receptionist, recepcionista
recession, retroceso
record, inscripción
recover, recobrar
recovery, recuperación
rectangle, rectángulo
rectangular, rectangular
rector, rector
red, rojo
redemption, redención
reduce, reducir
refer, referir
reference, referencia
reflect, reflejar
reflection, reverberación
reform, reforma
refugee, refugiado
refund, reintegrar
refusal, rechazamiento
refuse, negar
regard, miramiento, respeto
regarding, tocante a
regardless, indiferente
regency, regencia
regime, régimen
regiment, regimiento
region, región
register, registrar

registration, inscripción, registración
regression, regresión
regret, pesar
regular, regular
regulation, regulación
reign, reino
reluctance, repugnancia
reluctant, renuente
rely, contar con
remain, quedar
remainder, resto
remains, reliquias
remark, observación
remarkable, observable
remedy, remedio
remember, recordar
remote, remoto
removal, acción de quitar o llevarse
remove, quitar
render, dar, rendir
rent, renta, alquiler
rental, renta
repair, reparar
repeat, repetir
repetition, repetición
replace, reponer
replacement, reemplazar
reply, responder
report, reportar
reporter, informador
represent, representar
representation, representación
representative, representativo
republic, república
reputation, reputación
request, petición, ruego
require, requerir
requirement, requisito
rescue, liberar, rescatar
research, búsqueda, investigación
resemblance, parecido
resentment, resentimiento
reservation, reservación
reserve, reserva
reserved, reservado

residence, residencia
resident, residente
residential, residencial
residual, residual
resignation, dimisión
resigned, resignado
resin, resina
resist, resistir
resistance, resistencia
resistant, resistente
resolution, resolución
resolved, resuelto
resort, recurso
resource, recurso
respect, respeto
respectable, respetable
respective, respectivo
respiration, respiración
respond, responder
response, respuesta
responsibility, responsabilidad
responsible, responsable
rest, descanso
restaurant, restaurante
restless, inquieto
restore, restaurar
restraint, refrenamiento
restrict, restringir
restriction, limitación
result, resultado
retail, venta
retain, retener
retire, retirarse
retired, retirado
retirement, retiro
retiring, retraído
retreat, retiro
return, retornar
reveal, revelar
revelation, revelación
revenue, renta
reverse, inverso
reversible, reversible
review, revista
revision, revisión
revival, reavivamiento
revolt, revuelta

revolution, revolución
revolutionary, revolucionario
reward, premio
rheumatism, reumatismo
rhythm, ritmo
rib, costilla
ribbon, cinta
rice, arroz
rich, rico
rid, librar
ride, paseo
rider, jinete
ridge, espinazo
ridiculous, ridículo
riding, cabalgata
rifle, rifle
right, recto
rigid, rígido
ring, anillo
ringing, resonante
ripe, maduro
rise, levantamiento
rising, subida
risk, riesgo
ritual, ritual
rival, competidor
rivalry, rivalidad
river, río
roach, escarbacho
road, carretera
roast, asado
rock, roca
rocket, cohete
rocky, rocoso
rod, vara
role, papel
roll, irritar
rolling, rodante
romance, romance
roof, techo
room, cuarto
root, raíz
rope, cuerda
rosary, rosario
rose, rosa
rosemary, romero
rotor, rotor
rough, áspero

roughly, ásperamente
round, redondo
route, ruta
routine, rutina
row, riña
royal, regio
rubber, caucho
rubbish, basura
ruby, rubí
rucksack, mochila
ruin, ruina
rule, regla
ruler, soberano
ruling, gobernante
rum, ron
rumor, rumor
run, corrida
running, carrera
rural, rural
rush, movimiento o avance
    impetuoso
Russia, Rusia
Russian, ruso

S

sack, saco
sacred, sagrado
sacrifice, sacrificio
sad, triste
safe, salvo
safeguard, salvaguardia
safely, seguramente
safety pin, imperdible
safety, seguridad
saffron, azafrán
sage, salvia
sail, buque de vela
sailing, navegación
sailor, marinero
saint, santo
sake, causa
salad, ensalada
salary, sueldo
sale, venta
salmon, salmón
salt, sal
salty, salado

salvage, salvamento
salvation, salvación
same, mismo
sample, muestra
sand, arena
sandwich, emparedado
sandy, arenoso
sapphire, zafir
sardine, sardina
satin, raso
satisfaction, satisfacción
satisfactory, suficiente
satisfy, contentar
Saturday, sábado
sauce, salsa
saucepan, cacerola
saucer, platillo
sausage, salchicha
savage, salvaje
save, salvo
saving, salvar
saw, sierra
say, dicho
saying, dicho
scale, platillo
scallop, venera
scandal, escándalo
scarce, escaso
scarcely, escasamente
scarf, ensamblar a media madera
scarlet, rojo
scene, escena
scenery, paisaje
scent, olfato
schedule, lista
scheme, esquema
scholar, escolar
scholarship, saber
school, escuela
schooling, instrucción
science, ciencia
scissors, tijeras
scooter, patinete
scope, alcance
score, muesca
Scotland, Escocia
Scottish, escocés

scramble, lucha
scrambled eggs, huevos revueltos
scream, chillido
screaming, chillón
screen, pantalla
screw, tornillo
Scripture, Sagrada Escritura
scrutiny, escrutinio
sculptor, escultor
sculpture, escultura
sea, mar
seal, foca
search, busca
searching, escrutador
season, estación
seasoning, sazonamiento
seat, asiento
second, segundo
secondary, secundario
secret, secreto
secretary, secretario
section, sección
sector, sector
secure, seguro
security, protección
see, sede
seed, semilla
seeing, vista
seek, buscar
seem, parecerle a uno
seemingly, aparentemente
seldom, raramente
select, selecto
selection, trozo escogido
self, mismo
selfish, interesado
sell, engaño
senate, senado
senator, senador
send, enviar
senior, mayor
sensation, sensación
sense, sentido
sensible, sensible
sensitive, sensitivo
sensitivity, sensibilidad
sentence, fallo

sentimental, sentimental
separate, separado
separately, por separado
separation, porción
September, septiembre
sequence, sucesión,
    sequencia
sergeant, sargento
serial, de serie
series, serie
serious, serio
seriously, seriamente
serum, suero
servant, sirviente
serve, servicio
service, servicio
session, sesión
set, juego
setting, puesta
settle, banco
settlement, instalación
seven, siete
seventeen, diecisiete
seventeenth, decimoséptimo
seventh, séptimo
seventy, setenta
several, varios
severe, severo
sew, coser
sex, sexo
sexual, sexual
shade, sombra
shadow, sombra
shaft, astil
shake, menear
shall, Con el pres
shallow, bajo
shame, vergüenza
shampoo, lavado
shape, forma
share, parte
sharp, agudo
sharply, grandemente
shave, afeitado
shaving brush, brocha de
    afeitar
she, ella
sheath, vaina

shed, cobertizo
sheep, papanatas
sheer, puro
sheet, hoja
shelf, anaquel
shell, concha
shelter, resguardo
sherry, vino de Jerez
shift, recurso
shilling, chelín
shining, brillante
shiny, brillante
ship, buque
shirt, camisa
shocking, ofensivo
shoe polish, crema o betún
    para los zapatos
shoe, zapato
shoot, pimpollo
shooting, disparar
shop, tienda
shore, orilla
short, corto
shortage, escasez
shortly, brevemente
shorts, pantalones cortos para
    deporte
shot, tornasolado
should, como signo del
    subjuntivo
shoulder, hombro
shout, grito
shouting, aclamación
shovel, pala
show, presentación
shower, chaparrón
shrewd, agudo
shrimp, camarón
shrine, urna
shrink, contracción
shrub, arbusto
shut, cerrado
shutter, cerrador
shy, tímido
sick, enfermo
sickness, enfermedad
side, lado
sideboard, aparador

sideburns, patillas
sideways, dirigido hacia un lado
sigh, suspiro
sight, visión
sightseeing, turismo
sign, signo
signal, señal
signature, firma
significance, significado
significant, significante
silage, forraje conservado en silo
silence, silencio
silent, silencioso
silk, seda
silly, tonto
silver, plata
silverware, objetos de plata
similar, similar
simple, simple
simplicity, simplicidad
sin, pecar, pecado
since, desde
sincere, sincero
sincerity, sinceridad
sing, cantar
singer, cantante
single, soltero, único
singular, singular
sinister, siniestro
sink, lavabo
sir, señor
sister, hermana
sit, sentar
site, sitio
sitting, acción de sentarse o estar sentado
situation, posición, situación
six, seis
sixteen, dieciséis
sixteenth, decimosexto
sixth, sexto
sixty, sesenta
size, medida
skate, patín, patinar
sketch, boceto
ski, esquí

skill, habilidad
skilled, experto, práctico
skin, piel
skipper, saltador
skirt, falda
sky, cielo
slaughter, carnicería
slave, esclavo
sleep, sueño
sleeping bag, saco de dormir
sleeping, durmiente
sleeve, manga
slender, delgado
slice, pedazo, rebanada
slide, deslizamiento
sliding, corredizo
slight, ligero
slim, esbelto
slip, resbalón
slipper, pantufla
slogan, grito de combate
slope, cuesta
slow, lento, despacio
slow down, hacerse más lento, más despacio
slum, barrio miserable
small, pequeño
smart, vivo
smell, olfato
smile, sonrisa
smiling, sonriente
snack, bocadillo, porción
snack bar, bar donde se sirven bocadillos
snail, caracol
snake, culebra
snow, nieve
so, así
so-called, llamado
soap, jabón
social, social
socialism, socialismo
socialist, socialista
society, reunión, sociedad
sock, calcetín
socket, hueco en que encaja algo
soda, soda

sodium, sodio
sofa, sofá
soft, blando, suave
softly, blandamente,
    suavemente
soil, tierra
soldier, soldado
sole, planta
solemn, gravesolemne
solicitor, especie de abogado o
    procurador
solid, sólido
solitary, solitario
solo, solo
soloist, solista
solubility, solubilidad
solution, solución
solve, resolver
some, un
somebody, alguien
somehow, de algún modo
something, algo
sometimes, algunas veces
somewhat, algo
somewhere, en alguna parte
son, hijo
song, canto
soon, luego, pronto
sooner, más pronto
sophisticated, sofisticado
sore throat, mal de garganta
sore, penoso
sorry, afligido
sort, clase
sound, sonido, sund
soup, sopa
sour, ácido
source, fuente
south, sur
southern, del sur
souvenir, recuerdo
sovereign, supremo
space, espacio
spade, espada, laya
Spain, España
span, palmo
Spaniard, español
Spanish, español

spare, de repuesto
spark plug, bujía
sparkling, chispeante
speak, hablar
speaker, el que habla, orador
special delivery, correo
    urgente
special, especial
specialist, especialista
species, especie
specimen, espécimen
spectacle, espectáculo
spectacular, sensacional
spectator, espectador
speculation, especulación
speech, discurso, palabra
speed, rapidez
spell, hechizo
spend, gastar
sphere, globo
spice, especia
spin, giro
spinach, espinaca
spine, espinazo
spinning, hila
spirit, espíritu
spiritual, espiritual
spite, despecho
splendid, espléndido
split, hendedura
spoil, despojo
spoke, rayo
spokesman, vocero
sponge, esponja
spoon, cuchara
sport, deporte
sporting, deportivo
spot, mancha
sprain, torcedura
spray, líquido pulverizado
spread, extendido
spring, primavera
spy, espía
squadron, escuadra, squadron
square, cuadrado
stability, estabilidad
stable, estable
stadium, estadio

staff, personal técnico
stage, escenario
stain, mancha
stair, escalon, grada, peldaño
staircase, escalera
stake, estaca, poste
stamp, estampa
stand, parada, posición
standard, normal
standing, derecho, de pie
standstill, alto, parada
staple, armella, grapa
star, estrella
stare, mirada fija
staring, que mira fijamente
start, sobresalto, comienzo, principio, salida
starter, el que comienza o sale
starting, empezando
startling, sorprendente, alarmante, asombroso
starvation, hambre
state, estado
statement, declaración
static, parásito atmosférico
station, estación
stationary, estacionario, inmovil
statistic, estadística
statistical, estadístico
statue, estatua
status, estado legal
statute, ley
statutory, estatuido
stay, estancia, permanencia
steady, estable, fijo, firme
steak, filete, tajada
steal, hurto, robo
stealing, hurto
steam, vapor
steel, acero
steering, dirección
stem, pie, tallo
step, paso, pidada
stern, duro, severo
stew, estofado, guisado
stewed, estofado
stick, baston, palo

sticking, pegajoso
stiff neck, torticolis
stiff, rigido, tieso
stiffness, rigidez, tiesura
still, quieto
stimulus, estímulo
sting, picadura
stir, movimiento
stitch, puntada
stitch, punto
stock, tronco
stocking, media
stole, estola
stomach ache, dolor de estómago
stomach, estómago
stone, piedra
stop, alto
storage, almacenaje, bodega
store, tienda, almacen
storm, tempestad, tormenta
story, cuento, historia
stout, fuerte, recio
stove, estufa, hornilla
straight, recto
strain, tensión
strained, forzado
strange, extraño, raro
stranger, desconocido
stranger, forastero
straw, paja
strawberry, fresa
stream, corriente
street, calle
streetcar, tranvía
strength, fuerza
strengthen, fortalecer
stress, esfuerzo
stretch, estiron
strict, estricto
strike, huelga
striking, notable
string, cordón, cuerda
strip, tira
strong, fuerte
structural, estructural
structure, estructura
struggle, esfuerzo, lucha, contienda

student, estudiante
studied, estudiado, premeritado
studio, taller, estudio
study, estudio
stuff, materia prima, material
stupid, estúpido
sturdy, robusto, fuerte
style, estilo, moda
subject, sometido
subjective, subjetivo
submarine, submarino
submit, someter
subsection, subdivisión
subsequent, subsecuente
subsidiary, subsidiario
subsidy, subvención
substance, substancia
substantial, substancial
substitute, sustitutivo
substitution, reemplazo
subtle, sutil, fino
subway, tren subterráneo
succeed, tener éxito, triunfar
success, éxito, triunfo
successful, que tiene éxito
succession, seguida
successive, sucesivo
successor, sucesor
such, tal
sudden, súbito
suede, piel de Suecia
suet, saín
suffer, sufrir
suffering, padecimiento
sufficient, suficiente
sugar, azúcar
suggest, sugerir
suggestion, indicación
suicide, suicidio
suit, petición
suitable, apropiado
suitcase, maleta
suite, séquito
sum, suma
summary, sumario
summer, verano
summit, ápice

sun, sol
sunburn, quemadura del sol
Sunday, domingo
sunlight, luz del sol
sunny, soleado
sunshade, quitasol
sunshine, luz o claridad del sol
super, superior, estupendo
superb, soberbio
superficial, superficial
superintendent, superintendente
superior, superior
superiority, superioridad
supernatural, sobrenatural
supper, cena
supplement, suplemento
supply, provisión
support, soporte
supporter, sostenedor
suppose, creer, suponer
supposed, supuesto
suppository, supositorio
supreme, supremo
surcharge, sobrecarga
sure, seguro
surely, ciertamente, seguramente
surface, superficie
surfboard, esquí acuático
surgeon, cirujano
surgery, cirugía
surname, apellido
surplus, sobrante
surprise, sorpresa
surprising, asombroso, soprendente
surrender, rendición
surround, rodear
survey, medición, encuesta
survival, supervivencia
survive, sobrevivir
suspect, sospechoso
suspenders, tirantes
suspension, suspensión
suspicion, sospecha
suspicious, sospechoso
swallow, golondrina

sway, balanceo, oscilación
swear, jurar
sweat, sudor
sweater, suéter
sweep, barrido
sweet, azucarado, dulce
swell, bulto
swelling, hinchazón
swift, veloz
swiftly, velozmente
swim, nadar
swimming pool, piscina
swimming, natación
swing, oscilación
swinging, oscilante
switch, vara flexible
switch, verdasca
switchboard, cuadro de distribución
sword, espada
symbol, símbolo
symmetry, simetría
sympathetic, simpático
sympathy, simpatía
symphony, sinfonía
symptom, síntoma
synagogue, sinagoga
syntax, sintaxis
system, método
system, sistema

T

table, mesa
tablet, tableta
tackle, equipo
tail, cola
take, tomar
taking, tomando
talcum powder, talcos
tale, cuento
talent, talento
talk, conversación
talking, parlante
tall, alto
tampon, tapón
tangerine, tangerino
tank, tanque

tap, grifo
tape recorder, aparato magnetofónico de cinta
tape, cinta
target, blanco
tariff, tarifa
task, tarea
taste, gusto
tax, impuesto
taxation, imposición de tributos
taxi, taxi
taxpayer, contribuyente
tea, té
teach, enseñar
teacher, maestro
teaching, enseñanza
team, equipo, tiro
tear, lágrima
teaspoon, cucharilla
technical, técnico
technique, técnica
teeth, diente
telegram, telegrama
telegraph, telégrafo
telephone, teléfono
telephone directory, guía telefónica
television, televisión
tell, numerar
telling, eficaz
temper, temple
temperament, temperamento
temperature, temperatura
temple, templo
temporary, temporario
temptation, tentación
ten, diez
tenancy, tenencia
tenant, inquilino
tend, cuidar
tendency, propensión, tendencia
tender, tierno
tendon, tendón
tennis court, pista de tenis
tennis, tenis
tense, tenso
tension, tensión

tent, tienda
tenth, décimo
term, término
terminal, terminal
terminus, término
terrace, terraza
terrible, terrible
terribly, terriblemente
terrific, terrífico
territory, región
terror, terror
test, examen
testament, testamento
tested, probado
tetanus, tétano
text, texto
textile, textil
texture, textura
than, que
thank you, gracias
that, ese
the, el
theatre, teatro
theatrical, teatral
thee, te
theft, robo
their, su
them, los
theme, tema
themselves, se
then, entonces
theological, teológico
theology, teología
theorem, teorema
there, allí, allá
thereafter, de allí en adelante
thereby, en relación con esto
therefore, por esto
thereof, de ello
thermal, termal, térmico
thermometer, termómetro
thesis, tesis
they, ellos
thick, espeso
thickness, espesor
thief, ladrón
thigh, muslo
thin, delgado

thing, cosa
think, pensar
thinking, pensamiento
third, tercero
thirdly, en tercer lugar
thirteen, trece
thirty, treinta
this, esta, este
thorough, completo
thoroughly, completamente
those, esos, esas
though, aunque
thought, pensamiento
thousand, mil
thread, hilo
threat, amenaza
three, tres
thrill, temblor
throat, garganta
throne, trono
through, a través
throughout, por todo
throw, lanzamiento
thrust, golpe de punta
thumb, pulgar
thunder, trueno
thunderstorm, tronada
Thursday, jueves
thus, así
thy, tu
thyme, tomillo
ticket office, despacho de billetes o localidades
ticket, billete, boleto
tide, marea
tie, cinta
tight, bien cerrado
till, hasta
timber, madera
time, tiempo
timetable, guía, horario
tin, estaño
tint, tinte
tiny, pequeñito
tip, propina
tire, llanta
tired, cansado
tissue paper, papel de seda

tissue, tisú
title, título
toast, tostada
tobacco, tabaco
today, hoy
toe, dedo del pie
together, junto
toilet, sanitario
toilet paper, papel higiénico
tolerance, tolerancia
tomato, tomate
tomb, sepulcro
ton, tonelada
tone, sonido
tongs, tenazas
tongue, lengua
tonsil, tonsila
too, demasiado
tool, herramienta
tooth, diente
toothache, dolor de muelas
toothbrush, cepillo para los
   dientes
top, parte o superficie superior
topic, asunto, topico
torch, antorcha
tore, roto
torn, roto
total, total
totally, totalmente
touch, toque
touching, tocante a
tough, duro
tour, viaje
tourist, viajero
toward, hacia
towards, hacia
towel, toalla
tower, torre
town hall, casa del
   ayuntamiento
town, población
toy, juguete
trace, huella
track, rastro
tract, región
tractor, tractor
trade, comercio, profesión

trader, comerciante
trading, comercio
tradition, tradición
traditional, tradicional
traffic, tráfico
traffic jam, embotellamiento del
   tráfico
traffic light, semáforo
tragedy, tragedia
trail, cola, rastra
trailer, remolque
trailing, colgando
train, tren
training, adiestramiento
transfer, transferencia
transformer, transformador
transfusion, transfusión
transient, transitorio
transition, transición
translate, traducir
translation, traducción
transmission, transmisión
transport, transporte
trap, trampa
travel, viaje
travelled, que ha viajado
   mucho
traveller, viajero
travelling, que viaja
tray, cubeta
treasure, tesoro
treasury, tesoro
treat, agasajo
treatment, tratamiento
treaty, tratado
treble, triple
tree, árbol
trench, foso
trend, dirección
trial, prueba
tribal, tribal
tribe, tribu
tribunal, tribunal
tribute, tributo
trick, treta
trickle, goteo
tricky, trapacero
tried, probado

trigger, gatillo
trim, bien arreglado
trio, trío
trip, viaje
triumph, triunfo
troop, tropa
trouble, perturbación
trough, comedero, pesebre
trousers, pantalones
trout, trucha
truck, carretilla
true, verdadero
truly, verdaderamente
trunk, tronco
trust, confianza
trustee, fiduciario
truth, verdad
try, prueba
trying, probando
tube, tubo
tuition, enseñanza
tumbler, tambor
tune, aire
tunnel, túnel
turbot, rodaballo
turf, césped
turn, vuelta
turning, giro
turnip, nabo
turnover, doblado o vuelto
    hacia abajo
turquoise, turquesa
tutor, preceptor, tutor
tweezers, pinzas
twelve, doce
twentieth, vigésimo
twenty, veinte
twice, dos veces
twin, gemelo
twist, torsión, torcer
twisting, que se enrosca
two, dos
type, tipo
typewriter, máquina de
    escribir
typical, típico
tyre, tiro

U

ugly, feo
ultimate, último
umbrella, paraguas
unable, incapaz
unaware, desprevenido
uncertain, incierto
uncertainty, incertidumbre
unchanged, inalterado
uncle, tío
uncomfortable, penoso
unconscious, inconsciente
under, blanquear
underdone, poco asado
undergraduate, estudiante que
    aún no tiene ningún grado
    académico
underground, subterráneo
underlying, subyacente
underneath, debajo
undershirt, camiseta
understand, entender
understanding, comprensión
undertake, emprender
undertaking, empresa
underworld, los profundos
uneasy, intranquilo
unemployed, desocupado
unemployment, desocupación
uneven, desigual
unexpected, inesperado
unfair, injusto
unfamiliar, poco familiar
unfortunate, infortunado
unfortunately,
    desgraciadamente
unhappy, infeliz
uniform, uniforme
union, unión
unique, único
unit, unidad
united, unido
United States, Estados
    Unidos
unity, unidad
universal, universal
universe, universo

university, universidad
unknown, desconocido
unless, a menos que
unlike, desemejante
unlikely, improbable
unnecessary, innecesario
unpleasant, desagradable
unpopular, impopular
unreliable, no confiable
unsatisfactory, que no satisface
unsuitable, impropio
until, hasta
unto, y hacia
unusual, extraordinario
up, aguzar los oídos o las orejas
upon, sobre
upper, superior
upright, derecho
upset, volcado
upward, dirigido hacia arriba
Urban, Urbano
urge, impulso
urgency, insistencia
urgent, urgente
urine, orina
us, nos
use, uso
used, usado
useful, útil
useless, inútil
usual, usual
utmost, sumo
utter, absoluto
utterly, completamente

V

vacancy, vacatura
vacant, vacante
vacation, vacación
vaccinate, vacunar
vacuum flask, termos
vacuum, vacío
vague, vago
vain, fútil
valid, válido
validity, validez

valley, valle
valuable, valioso
valuation, valoración
value, valor
van, carromato
vanilla, vainilla
vapor, vapor
variable, variable
variation, variación
varied, vario
various, vario
vary, variar
varying, variante
vast, vasto
vastly, inmensamente
veal, ternera
vegetable, de hortalizas
vegetarian, vegetariano
vegetation, vegetación
vehicle, vehículo
vein, vena
velocity, celeridad
velvet, terciopelo
venture, ventura
verb, verbo
verbal, verbal
verdict, veredicto
vermouth, vermut
verse, verso
version, versión
vertical, vertical
very, mismo
vessel, vasija
vest, chaleco
veteran, veterano
veterinarian, veterinario
via, via
vicar, vicario
vice, vicio
victim, víctima
victory, victoria
view, vista
vigorous, vigoroso
vigor, fuerza
villa, villa
village, lugar
villager, lugareño
vinegar, vinagre

vineyard, viña
vintage, vendimia
violence, violencia
violent, violento
virgin, virgen
virtue, virtudes
visibility, visibilidad
visible, visible
vision, vista
visit, visita
visitor, visitador
visual, visual
vital, vital
vivid, vívido
vocabulary, vocabulario
vocal, vocal
voice, voz
voltage, voltaje
volume, volumen
voluntary, espontáneo
vomit, vómito
vote, voto
voting, votación
voyage, viaje por mar
vulgar, vulgar

W

wagon, furgón
waist, cintura
waistcoat, chaleco
wait, espera
waiter, mozo
wake, estela
Wales, Gales
walk, paso
walking, marcha
wall, pared
wallet, zurrón
walnut, nuez
waltz, vals
want, falta
wanting, falto
war, guerra
ward, guarda
warehouse, depósito
warfare, guerra
warm, caliente

warmth, calor
warning, advertencia
warrant, autorización
wartime, tiempo de guerra
wash, lavatorio
washing, acción de
waste, yermo
watch, reloj de bolsillo
watching, vigilia
water, agua corriente
waterfall, cascada
watermelon, sandía
wave, ola
way, vía
we, nosotros
weak, débil
weakness, debilidad
wealth, riqueza
wealthy, rico
weapon, arma
wear, usar
weary, cansado
weather, tiempo
wed, casarse con
wedding, casamiento
Wednesday, miércoles
week, semana
weekend, fin de semana
weekly, hebdomadario,
    semanalmente
weight, unidad de peso
welcome, bien venido
welfare, bienestar
well, bien, fuente
well-known, conocido
Welsh, galés
west, oeste
western, occidental
wet, mojado
what, qué
whatever, cualquier cosa que
wheat, trigo
wheel, rueda
when, cuando
whence, de donde
whenever, cuando quiera que
where, donde
whereas, considerando que

whereby, con que
wherever, dondequiera que
whether, si
which, ¿qué?
while, mientras, rato
whip, látigo
whisky, whisky
whisper, susurro
whistle, silbato
white, blanco
who, quien
whole, todo
wholesale, al por mayor
wholly, totalmente
whom, quien
whose, cuyo
why, ¿por qué?
wicked, malo, diabolicó
wide, ancho
widely, extensamente
widespread, extenso
widow, viuda
width, anchura
wife, esposa
wig, peluca
wild boar, jabalí
wild, salvaje
wildly, en estado salvaje
will, en las primeras personas
willing, deseoso
willingness, buena gana,
    buena voluntad
win, ganar
wind, viento
window, ventana
windshield, parabrisas
wine, vino
wing, vuelo
winner, ganador
winning, triunfante
winter, invierno
wiper, limpiador
wire, alambre
wisdom, sabiduría
wise, cuerdo
wish, deseo
with, con
withdraw, retirar

withdrawal, retiro
within, dentro de
without, sin
witness, testigo
wolf, lobo
woman, mujer
womb, útero
women, mujer
wonder, asombro
wonderful, maravilloso
wondering, asombrado
wood carving, talla de la
    madera
wood, bosque
wooden, de madera
wool, lana
word, palabra
work, trabajo
worker, obrero
working day, día laborable
working, de trabajo
workshop, obrador, taller
world, mundo
worm, gusano
worn, desgastado
worried, angustiado
worry, cuidado
worse, lo peor
worship, culto
worst, lo peor
worth, valor
worthy, excelente
wound, herida
wounded, herido
wretched, infeliz
wrist, muñeca
write, escribir
writer, escritor
writing, escritura
wrong, injusto
wrought, trabajado

X, Y

X-ray, radiográfico
yacht, yate
yard, yarda
year, año

yellow, amarillo
yes, sí
yesterday, ayer
yet, todavía
yield, producto
you, te
young, joven
younger, más joven
your, tu

yourself, tú
youth, juventud

Z

zero, cero
zip, silbido
zone, zona
zoo, parque zoológico
zoology, zoología

5,000 palabras de cada día
5,000 Everyday Words

A

a bordo, aboard
a la moda, fashionable
a la vez, at once
a largo plazo, long-term
a través, across
a menos que, unless
a menudo, often
a puro, through sheer
a saber, namely
abadía, abbey
abajo, down, beneath, below
abandono, neglect, abandon
abanico, fan
abatimiento, depression
abdominal, abdominal
abertura, breach, opening
abiertamente, openly
abierto, open
abogado, advocate, lawyer
abolición, abolition
abono, manure
abrebotellas, bottle opener
abrelatas, can opener
abreviación, abbreviation
abrigo, housing, shelter,
  overcoat, to wrap
abril, April
absceso, abscess
absolutamente, absolutely
absoluto, utter, absolute
absorbente, absorbent
absorber, to absorb
absorbido, absorbed
absorción, absorption
abstracción, abstraction
abstracto, abstract
absurdo, absurd
abuelos, grandparents

abundante, affluent, abundant
abuso, abuse
acabando, finishing
acabar, to finish
academia, academy
académico, academic
acalorar, overheat
acaso, maybe
acceso, access
accesorios, accessories
accidente, accident
acción, action
aceite, oil
aceitoso, oily
acento, accent
aceptable, acceptable
aceptación, acceptance
acero, steel
acetileno, acetylene
achicoria, chicory
aciago, unlucky
ácido, sour
aclamación, acclamation
acogida, reception
acomodación, accommodation
acomodar, to accommodate
acompañar, to accompany
aconsejable, advisable
aconsejador, adviser
aconsejar, to advise
acontecer, to happen
acorde, in agreement
acostarse, lie down
acostumbrado, accustomed
acre, acre
actitud, attitude
activamente, actively
activo, active
acto, act

actor, actor, player
actriz, actress
actual, present-day
acuerdo, accordance, concert
acumulación, accumulation, collection, gathering
acusado, accused
adaptación, adaptation
adaptador, adapter
adecuado, adequate
además, moreover, furthermore
adhesivo, adhesive, clinging
adicional, additional, further
adiestramiento, training
adiós, good-bye
adjetivo, adjective.
administrador, administrator
administrativo, administrative
admirable, admirable
admiración, admiration
admirar, to admire
admisión, admission
admitir, to admit
adolescencia, adolescence
adoptar, to adopt
adquirir, to acquire
adquisición, acquisition
adulterio, adultery
adulto, adult
advenimiento, advent
advertencia, warning
adyacente, adjacent
aéreo, aerial
aeronave, airship
aeroplano, airplane
aeropuerto, airport
afectado, affected
afecto, affection
afeitado, shave
afición, addiction, hobby
aficionado, fond of
afilalápices, pencil sharpener
afligido, distressed
afortunadamente, luckily
afortunado, fortunate, lucky
Africa, Africa
africano, African
afuera, outdoor

agarro, grasp
agasajo, fine reception
agenda, notebook, pocket calendar
agente, agent
agilidad, agility
agitación, agitation
agonía, agony
agotamiento, exhaustion
agradable, enjoyable, pleasant
agradar, to please
agradecido, grateful
agrandar, enlarge
agregar, add
agrícola, agricultural
agricultura, agriculture
agrietar, to crack, split
agua mineral, mineral water
agua corriente, water
agudo, acute, keen, sharp, shrewd
aguja, needle
aguja indicadora, finger
agujero, hole
aguzar los oídos o las orejas, to prick up one's ears
ahora, now
aire, air, presence, tune
ajedrez, chess, chess set
ajeno, alien
ajo, garlic
ajuar, furniture
al aire libre, outdoor
al lado, aside
al menos, at least
al por mayor, wholesale
al por menor, retail
al instante, instantly
al costado, alongside
alabanza, praise
alambre, wire
alarma, alarm
alba, dawn
albahaca, basil
albaricoque, apricot
alboroto, fuss
alcalde, mayor

alcance, scope
alcanzar, to attain, to reach
alcohólico, alcoholic
alcorza, icing
alcurnia, ancestry, lineage
alegado, alleged
alegre, cheerful, gay, glad, merry
alegremente, gladly
alemán, German
Alemania, Germany
alentador, encouraging
alentar, breathe, encourage
alérgico, allergic
alerta, alert
aleta, fin
alfabeto, alphabet
alfarería, pottery
alfiler, pin
alfombra, carpet
algo, anything, something, somewhat
algodón, cotton, cotton wool
alguien, anybody, anyone, somebody
algunas veces, sometimes
aliado, allied
aliados, allies
alianza, alliance
alimento, feed, feeding, food
aliviar, to relieve
alivio, relief
almacén, department store, warehouse
almacenaje, storage
almeja, clam
almendra, almond
almirantazgo, admiralty, admiral's dues
almohada, pillow
almuerzo, lunch
alojamiento, lodging
alojar, to lodge
alpinismo, mountaineering
alquilar, to rent
alquiler de automóviles, car rent
altamente, highly

alternativo, alternative
alto, aloud, halt, high, standstill, stop, tall
altura, height
aluminium, aluminium
alzamiento, lift
ama, mistress, nurse
amable, lovely
amado, darling
amaneramiento, lit
amante, lover, loving
amar, to love
amargo, bitter
amargor, bitterness
amarillo, yellow
amateur, amateur
ámbar, amber
ambición, ambition
ambicioso, ambitious
ambiente, environment
ambos, both
ambulancia, ambulance
amenaza, menace, threat
América, America
americano, American
amigo, boyfriend, friend
amillarar, assess
amistad, friendship
amistoso, friendly
amo, master, proprietor
amor, love
amplificador, amplifier
amplio, ample
amueblado, furnished
ánade, duck
análisis, analysis
analogía, analogy
análogo, analogous
ananás, pineapple
anaquel, shelf
ancho, broad, wide
anchoa, anchovy
anchura, breadth, width
ángel, angel
anglicano, Anglican
anguila, eel
angular, angular
ángulo, angle, corner

angustiado, worried
anillo, ring
animal, animal
ánimo, encouragement
aniversario, anniversary
anónimo, anonymous
anorac, anorak
anormal, abnormal
ansia, longing, eagerness
ansiedad, anxiety
ansioso, anxious
anterior, foregoing, prior
anterioridad, priority
antiguamente, formerly, long ago
antibiótico, antibiotic
anticoncepcional, contraceptive
anticuado, old-fashioned
antidepresivo, antidepressant
antiguo, ancient, early
antiséptico, antiseptic
anual, annual
anuncio, announcement
añadidura, addition, affix
año, year
año bisiesto, leap year
apacible, mild
aparador, cupboard, sideboard
aparato, apparatus
aparato magnetofónico de cinta, tape recorder
aparcamiento, car park, parking lot
aparecer, appear
aparentar, pretend
aparentemente, seemingly
aparición, appearance
aparte, apart
apasionado, passionate
apelación, appeal
apellido, last name, surname
apéndice, appendix
apendicitis, appendicitis
aperitivo, appetizer
apetito, appetite
ápice, summit
apio, celery

aplastante, overwhelming
aplicable, applicable
aplicación, application
aplicarse, apply
apología, apology
aportación, contribution
aprecio, appreciation
aprender, learn
aprendiz, apprentice
aprobación, approval
aprobar, approve
apropiado, appropriate, meet
aprovechable, available, usable
aprovechar, to make use, to make progress
aproximación, approximation
aproximadamente, approximately
apto, apt
apuesta, bet
apuro, fix
aquí, here
arábigo, Arabic
arándano, blueberry
arándano agrio, cranberry
árbol, tree
arbusto, bush, shrub
arcilla, clay
ardiente, burning
área, area
arena, sand
arenoso, sandy
arenque, herring
argüir, argue
argumentar, to argue
argumento, argument, plot
arma, weapon
armada, navy
armazón, frame
armella, screw-eye
armisticio, armistice
armonía, harmony
arpeo, grappling iron
arqueología, archaeology
arquero, archer
arquitecto, architect
arquitectura, architecture

arrastrar, to drag
arrastre, draw
arreglar, arrange
arreglo, adjustment, disposition, layout
arrendamiento, lease
arriba, over
arrogante, arrogant
arrojadizo, missile
arroyo, gutter
arroz, rice
arruinado, lost
arte, art, craft
arte de cocinar, cookery
arteria, artery
ártico, arctic
articulación, joint
artículo, article
artificial, artificial
artificio, artifice
artista, artist
artístico, artistic
arzobispo, archbishop
asado, roast
asamblea, assembly
aseado, neat
asegurado, insured
asegurar, assure, ensure
asentir, agree
aserto, assertion
asesinato, murder
asesor, advisory
así, so, thus
Asia, Asia
asiático, Asian
asiento, seat
asimiento, grasp
asistencia, assistance, attendance
asistir, assist, attend
asma, asthma
asociación, association, combine
asociado, associate
asombrado, amazed, wondering
asombrar, to amaze
asombro, amazement

asombroso, amazing, surprising
aspecto, aspect
ásperamente, roughly
áspero, harsh, rough
aspirina, aspirin
astil, shaft
asumir, assume
asunción, assumption
asunto, affair, concern, topic
asustado, afraid
atadura, binding, fastening
atalaya, outlook
ataque, attack, fit
atar, to tie
ático, Attic
Atlántico, Atlantic
atmósfera, atmosphere
atómico, atomic
atractivo, attraction
atraer, attract
atrás, ago, back, behind
atrayente, appealing
atrevido, daring, fearless
atroz, awful
auditorio, audience
aumento, increase, raise
aunque, although, though
ausencia, absence
ausente, absent
austríaco, Austrian
autobús, bus
automático, automatic
automóvil, motorboat
autopista, motorway, turnpike
autor, author
autoridad, authority
autorización, warrant
autorizado, authoritative
avalúo, assessment, valuation
avance, advance
avanzado, advanced
ave, bird
avenida, avenue
aventura, adventure
avergonzado, ashamed
averiguación, investigation
aversión, disgust

ávido, eager
avion, aircraft
avíos, kit
avíos de pescar, fishing tackle
avisado, advised
aviso, advertisement
ayer, yesterday
ayuda, aid, help
ayudante, assistant, helper
ayunador, faster
azabache, jet
azafrán, saffron
azar, hazard, random
azúcar, sugar
azúcar cande, candy
azucarado, sweet
azul, blue

B

bacalao, cod, haddock
baile de espectáculo, ballet
baile, dancing
bajamar, low water
bajo, low, mean, shallow
bala, bullet
balsadero, ferry
banco, bench, settle
bandada, flock
bandido, outlaw
banquete, dinner
baño, bath
baño de espuma, bubble bath
bar donde se sirven bocadillos, snack bar
barato, cheap, inexpensive
barba, beard, chin
barbero, barber
barcaza, barge
barco, boat
barra, bar, rail
barrer, to sweep
barrera, barrier
barrido, swept
barrio miserable, slum
barro, mud
base, base

básico, basic
bastante, enough, rather
basura, garbage, trash
bata, bathrobe, dressing gown
batalla, battle
batería, battery
batido, beaten
bautismo, baptism
bayo, bay
beber, to drink
bebida, beverage, drink
beige, beige
belga, Belgian
Bélgica, Belgium
belleza, beauty
bello, beautiful
bendecir, bless
bendición, blessing
beneficio, benefit
berenjena, eggplant
Berlín, Berlin
beso, kiss
bestia, beast
Biblia, Bible
biblioteca, library
bibliotecario, librarian
bicicleta, bicycle
bien perfilado, clear-cut
bien cerrado, tight
bien arreglado, well-dressed
bienes, wealth
bienestar, well-being
bienvenido, welcome
billete, bill, ticket
billón, billion
biografía, biography
biológico, biological
blanco, target, white
blandamente, softly
blando, soft
blanquear, to blanch, to whiten
bloque, block
blusa, blouse, jumper
bocas, mouths
boceto, sketch
bola, ball
boleto, ticket
bolígrafo, ball point pen

bolsa, purse
bolsillo, pocket
bomba, bomb, pump
bombilla, bulb
bondad, goodness, kindness
bondadoso, kindly
boquear, gasp
boquete, gap
bordado, embroidery
borde, border
borracho, drunk
bosque, forest, wood
bota, boot
botánica, botany
botella, bottle
botón, button
botones, bellboy
boxeo, boxing
boza, painter, stopper
bragas, panties
brazo, arm
break, break
breve, brief
brevemente, briefly, shortly
brezo, heath
brigada, brigade
brillante, bright, brilliant,
    shining, shiny
brisa, breeze
británico, British
brocha de afeitar, shaving
    brush
broche, clasp
broma, fun, joke
bronce, bronze
buena gana, willingness
bueno, good, kind
bujía, spark plug
bulto, bulk, swell
buque, ship
buque de vela, sail
burbuja, bubble
busca, quest, search
buscar, to look for, seek,
    search
búsqueda, research
butano, butane gas
buzón, letter box, mailbox

C

cabalgar, to ride
caballero, gentleman, knight
caballo, horse
cabaña, cabin
cabecilla, header, leader
cabello, hair
cabeza, head
cable, cable
cabrito, kid
cacahuete, peanut
cacerola, saucepan
cada, every
cadena, chain
café, cafe, coffee
caída, breakdown, fall
caja, box
caja de colores o
    pinturas, paintbox
cal, lime
calabaza, pumpkin
calambre, cramp
calcetín, sock
calculadora, calculator
cálculo, calculation
calefacción, heating
calendario, calendar
calidad de miembro o socio,
    membership
caliente, hot, warm
calificación, qualification
calificado, qualified
calificar, qualify
calificativo, qualifying
caliza, limestone
calle, street
calleja, alley
calor, heat, warmth
cama, bed
cama de campaña,
    campbed
cámara, chamber, cine camera
camarón, prawn, shrimp
cambio, change, exchange,
    replacement
camino, journey, path
camisa, shirt

camiseta, undershirt
campamento, camp, camping
campana, bell
campeón, champion
campeonato, championship
camping, camp site
campo, field
campo de golf, golf course
Canada, Canada
canadiense, Canadian
canciller, chancellor
candidato, candidate
canela, cinnamon
canguro, kangaroo
cansado, tired, weary, worn
cantante, singer
cantidad, amount, quantity
canto, song
cañón, cannon, pipe, tube
caoba, mahogany
caos, chaos
capa, cape, cloak, cope
capacidad, capacity
capaz, able, capable
capilla, chapel
capital, capital
capitán, captain
capitana, admiral's ship
capítulo, chapter
capturar, to capture
cara, face
caracol, snail
carácter, character
característica, characteristic
carbón, coal
carbón de leña, charcoal
carente, lacking
carga, burden, charge, load,
  loading
carne de carnero, mutton
carne de vaca, beef
carne, flesh, meat
carnicería, butcher's
caro, expensive
carrera, career, racing, running
carretera, road
carretero, carter
carretilla, push cart

carromato, caravan, van
carruaje, carriage
carta de crédito, letter of
  credit
**carta que acompaña a
  otra**, inclusion
carta, letter
cartera, pocketbook, wallet
casa de huéspedes,
  boarding house
casa, establishment, household
casa de moneda, mint
casa del ayuntamiento, town
  hall
casado, married
casamiento, wedding
casar, marry
casarse con, wed
cascada, waterfall
cáscara, hull
casete, cassette
casi, almost
casita, cottage
caso, case, event
casta, breed
castigo, punishment
castillo, castle
catálogo, catalogue
cataplasma, poultice
catedral, cathedral
categoría, category
categórico, positive
católico, catholic
catorce, fourteen
catorceno, fourteenth
caucho, rubber
caución, caution
causa, cause, sake
cautivo, captive
cayente, falling
caza con escopeta, shooting
caza, hunt, hunting
cebolla, onion
ceder, to give way
Ceilán, Ceylon
celda, cell
celebración, celebration
celebrar, to celebrate

célebre, famous
celeridad, velocity
celestial, heavenly
celos, jealousy
celoso, jealous
cementerio, cemetery
cena, supper
cenar, to eat supper
cenicero, ashtray
ceniza, ash
centavo, cent
centeno, rye
centímetro, centimeter
central, central
centro, center, midst
cepillo, brush
cepillo para el pelo,
    hairbrush
cepillo para los dientes,
    toothbrush
cerca, nearby
cerca de, about, beside, by
cerca, close
cercano, near
cerdo, pig, pork
cereal, cereal
cerebro, brain
ceremonia, ceremony
ceremonial, ceremonial
cereza, cherry
cero, zero
cerrado, closed, shut
cerrador, shutter
cerrar, to close
certeza, certainty
certificado, certificate
cervecería, brewery
cerveza, beer
cesación, cease
césped, grass, lawn, turf
cesta, basket
ciclismo, cycling
ciclo, cycle
ciego, blind
cielo, sky
cien, hundred
ciencia, science
**ciencia y práctica
    financiera**, finance

ciertamente, certainly, surely
cigarrillo, cigarette
cincel, chisel
cine, cinema
cínico, cynical
cinta, ribbon, tape, tie
cinto, girdle
cintura, waist
cinturón, belt
cinturón salvavidas, life belt
circuito, circuit
circulación, circulation
circular, circular
círculo, circle
circumstancia, circumstance
ciruela, plum
ciruela pasa, prune
cirugía, surgery
cirujano, surgeon
cita, quotation, quote
ciudad, city
ciudadano, citizen
cívico, civic
civil, civil
civilización, civilisation
claramente, apparently, clearly
claridad, clarity
claro, apparent, clear
clase, class, sort
clásico, classic, classical
clasificación, classification
clavel, pink
clavija, peg
clerical, clerical
clero, clergy
clima, climate
climax, climax
clínico, clinic
cloruro, chloride
club, club
cobertizo, shed
cobre, copper
coche, car, coach
coche de teleférico, cable-car
cocina, cooker, cuisine,
    kitchen
cocinar, to cook
cocinero, cook

coco, coconut
código, code
código postal, area code
codo, elbow
coeficiente, coefficient
coetáneo, contemporary
cogedura, catch
cohete, rocket
cohombro, cucumber
coincidencia, coincidence
col, cabbage
cola, glue, tail, trail
colcha, quilt
colchón, mattress
colega, colleague
colegio, college
cólera, anger
colérico, angry
coles de Bruselas, Brussels sprouts
colgante, hanging, trailing
colgar, to hang
coliflor, cauliflower
colina, hill
collar, necklace
colocación, laying
colocador, layer
color, color
columna, column
combinación, combination
combustible, fuel
comedero, feeding place
comedia, comedy
comentario, commentary
comentar, to comment
comenzar, to begin
comer, to eat
comercial, commercial
comerciante, trader
comercio, business, commerce, trading
comestible, edible, foodstuff
comestibles, groceries
cometer, commit
cómico, comic, funny
comisión, commission
comité, committee
como, as

cómo, how
cómodamente, comfortably
cómodo, convenient
compañerismo, fellowship
compañero, companion, fellow
compañía, company
comparable, comparable
comparación, compare, comparison
comparar, to compare
comparativamente, comparatively
comparativo, comparative
compensación, compensation, offset
competencia, competence
competición, competition
competidor, rival
competir, compete
complejo, complex
complemento, complement
completamente, completely, quite, thoroughly, utterly
completo, thorough
compota, jam
compra, buy, purchase
comprender, realize
comprensión, understanding
comprobar, check up
comprometer, engage
compromiso, embarrassment, engagement
común, common, community
comunicación, communication
comunión, communion
comunismo, communism
comunista, communist
comúnmente, commonly
con, with
con calma, calmly
con que, whereby
conceder, allow
concentrar, concentrate
concepto, concept
concesión, allowance, grant
concha, shell
concluir, to conclude

concreto, concrete
conde, earl
condenado, damned
condenar, to condemn
condestable, constable
condición, condition
conducta, behavior, conduct
conductor, conductor, leader
conejito, bunny
conejo, rabbit
conferencia, conference, lecture
confesar, to confess
confesión, confession
confianza, confidence, dependence, trust
confidencial, confidential
confirmación, confirmation
confirmado, confirmed
confirmar, to confirm
conflicto, conflict
conforme, O.K.
conformidad, conformity
confortable, comfortable
confusión, confusion
confuso, confused
congestión, congestion
congratulación, congratulation
congregación, congregation
congreso, congress
conjetura, guess
conmemorativo, memorial
conmovedor, affecting
conocer, to know
conocido, well-known
conocimiento, acquaintance, awareness, knowledge
consagrado, devoted
consagrar, to devote
consejo, advice
consejo de administración, direction
conservar, to preserve
considerando que, whereas
considerar, to consider
consistir, to consist
constante, constant
constitución, constitution
constitucional, constitutional, limited
constituir, to constitute
construcción, building, construction
constructivo, constructive
constructor, builder
construir, to build, to construct
consuelo, comfort
consultación, consultation
consultar, to consult
consumidor, consumer
consunción, consumption
contacto, contact
contagioso, catching, contagious
contaminación, contamination, infection
contaminar, to contaminate
contar con, rely
contención, contention
contener, contain
contenido, content
contentar, satisfy
contexto, context
contienda, contest
contiguo, adjoining
continente, continent, continental
contingencia, possibility
continuado, continued
continuar, to continue
continuo, continual, continuous
contorno, outline
contra, against
contracción, contraction, shrink
contrario, contrary
contraste, contrast
contratiempro, check
contrato, contract, covenant
contribuir con, contribute
contribuyente, taxpayer
contusión, bruise
convenir, to agree, to become
conversar, to talk
conversación, talk

coñac, brandy, cognac
cooperación, cooperation
cooperar, to cooperate
copia, copy, plenty, store
corazón, heart
corbata de lazo, bow tie
cordero, lamb
cordón, lace, string
coro, chorus
corporación, corporation
correcto, correct
corredizo, sliding
corredor, corridor
correlación, correlation
correo, mail, mail service, post office
correo urgente, special delivery
correspondencia, correspondence
corresponder, to correspond
correspondiente, correspondent, corresponding
correr, to run
corrida, run
corriente, stream
corrosión, corrosion
corrupción, corruption
cortante, cutting
cortaplumas, penknife
cortar, cut off
corte, chop
corte de pelo, haircut
cortejo, procession
cortés, polite
corteza, bark
corto, short
cosa, thing
cosa que cuelga, pendant
cosa sin sentido, nonsense
coser, to sew
costa, coast
coste, cost
costilla, rib
costoso, costly, expensive
creador, creative
crear, to create
crecer, to grow

crecido, grown
creciente, growing
crecimiento, growth
crédito, credit
creencia, belief
creer, to believe, to suppose
crema o betún para los zapatos, shoe polish
crema, cream
creyente, believer, believing
cría, breeding
criar, to breed, to raise, to rear
criatura, creature
criatura, baby
crimen, crime
criminal, criminal
cristal, crystal
cristalería, glassware
cristianidad, Christianity
cristiano, Christian
Cristo, Christ
crucero, cruise
crudo, raw
cruel, cruel
crueldad, cruelty
crujido, crack
cuadrado, square
cuadro de distribución, switchboard
cualidad, quality
cualquier, any
cualquier cosa que, whatever
cuán lejos, how far
cuando, when
cuando quiera que, whenever
cuántos, how many
cuarenta, forty
cuaresma, Lent
cuartel general, headquarters
cuarto o aposento destinado a los niños, nursery
cuarto, apartment, quarter, room; fourth
cuarto de baño, bathroom
cuarzo, quartz
cuatro, four
cubano, Cuban

cubeta, bucket, tray
cubierta, coat, covering, deck
cubo, bucket, cube
cuchara, spoon
cucharilla, teaspoon, small
    spoon
cuchillería, cutlery
cuchillo, knife
cuello, collar, neck
cuenco, bowl
cuenta, account, count
cuento, tale
cuerda, line, rope
cuerdo, wise
cuero, fell, hide, leather
cuerpo, body, figure
cuesta, slope
cueva, cave
cuidado, care, look out
cuidadosamente, carefully
cuidadoso, careful
cuidar, to tend, to take care of
culebra, snake
culpa, blame, guilt
culpable, guilty
culpar, to accuse, to blame
cultivado, cultivated
cultivar, to cultivate
cultivo, culture, farming
culto, worship
cumplido, accomplished
cumplimiento, fulfilment
cumplir, to accomplish, to
    fulfill
cuñado, brother-in-law
cura, healing
curar, to cure, to treat
curva, loop
cuyo, whose

C H

chaleco, vest, waistcoat
chambelán, chamberlain
champán, champagne
chaparrón, shower
chaqueta, jacket
chaqueta de punto,
    cardigan

charco, puddle
charla, chat
charlar, to chatter
cheque, check
chillar, to shriek
chillido, scream
chillón, shrill, whiney
chimenea, chimney
China, China
chino, Chinese
Chipre, Cyprus
chismografía, gossip
chispeante, sparkling
chiste, joke
chocolate, chocolate
chofer, chauffeur
chorrear, to drip
choza, hut

D

dado, die, given
danés, Danish
danza, dance
danzar, to dance
dañar, injure
daño, damage, injury, nuisance
dar fuerza a, enforce
dar, to give, to render
datos, data
de, hence, from
de abajo, downstairs
de algún modo, somehow
de allí en adelante,
    thereafter
de antemano, beforehand
de cara, faced
de cerca, nearly
de competición, competitive
de conformidad, accordingly
de cualquier modo que,
    however
de dirección única, one-way
de eso, thereof
de la clase media, middle-
    class
**de la dirección o
    redacción**, editorial

de la noche a la mañana, overnight
de leche, foster
de madera, wooden
de mediana edad, middle-aged
de nuevo, again
de ojos, eyed
de oro, golden
de parte de, behalf
de primera clase, first-class
de refilón, glancing
de repuesto, spare
de serie, serial
de todos modos, anyway
de veras, really
debajo, underneath
debate, argument, debate
deber, duty, owe
debido, due
débil, weak
debilidad, weakness
década, decade
decaimiento, decay
decente, decent
decidir, decide
décimo, tenth
decimoctavo, eighteenth
decimonoveno, nineteenth
decimoséptimo, seventeenth
decimosexto, sixteenth
decisión, decision, judgment
decisión final, conclusion
decisivo, decisive
declaración, declaration, statement
declarar, to declare
declinación, decline
dedo del pie, toe
defender, to defend, to justify
defendido, guarded
defensa, defense
deficiencia, deficiency
definir, define
del sur, southern
del norte, northern
delantal, apron
delante, ahead, before, forth

delantero, forward
delegación, delegation
delegado, delegate
deleite, delight
deleitoso, delightful
delgado, lean, slender, thin
deliberadamente, deliberately
deliberado, deliberate
delicado, delicate
demanda, demand
demandado, dependent
demasiado, too
demonio, demon, devil
dentadura, denture
dental, dental
dentista, dentist
dentro de, within
dentro de poco, before long, shortly
departamento, compartment
dependiente, dependent, employee
deporte, sport
deportivo, sporting
depósito, deposit, warehouse
depreciación, depreciation
derecho, erect, standing, upright
derivado, derived
derivar, to derive, to elect
derrelicto, derelict
derrota, defeat
derrotar, to defeat
derrumbamiento, collapse
desafío, challenge, defy
desagradable, unpleasant
desayuno, breakfast
descansar, to rest
descanso, rest
descarga, discharge
descendente, downward
descendiente, descendant
desconocer, to ignore, not to know
desconocido, stranger, unknown
describir, to describe

descubrir, detect, discover
descuidado, careless
desde el principio, all along
desde, since
desecho, refuse
desembarco, landing
desemejante, not like, unlike
desenvolver, to develop
desenvolvimiento, development
desear, to wish, to want
deseo, wish
deseoso, willing
desesperado, hopeless
desgraciadamente, unfortunately
desigual, uneven
deslizamiento, slide
deslumbrador, dazzling
desmemoriado, forgetful, oblivious
desnudamente, barely
desnudo, bare, naked, nude
desocupación, unemployment
desocupado, unemployed
desodorante, deodorant
desorden, disorder
desordenado, out of order
despacho de billetes o localidades, ticket office
despacho particular del juez, camera
despecho, spite
despejo, clearance
despertador, alarm clock
despliegue, display
despojo, spoil
despreciable, negligible
desprecio, contempt
desprevenido, unaware
después, afterward
después de, after
destinación, destination
destitución, deposition
destrucción, destruction
destructivo, destructive
destruir, destroy
desvío, deflection, detour

detalle, detail
detective, detective
detención, detention
deterioración, deterioration
determinación, determination
determinado, determined
determinar, determine
detrás, behind
deuda, debt
devoción, devotion
día, day
día de descanso, day off
día laborable, working day
diabético, diabetic
diagrama, diagram
dialecto, dialect
diamante, diamond
diámetro, diameter
diario, daily, diary, everyday, journal, newspaper
diarrea, diarrhea
dibujo, drawing
diccionario, dictionary
dicho, say, saying
diciembre, December
dieciséis, sixteen
diecisiete, seventeen
diente, teeth, tooth
diestro, clever
dieta, diet
diez y nueve, nineteen
diez y ocho, eighteen
diez, ten
diferencia, difference
diferencial, differential
diferente, different
diferir, differ
difícilmente, hardly
digital, digital
dignidad, dignity
dilación, delay
dimisión, resignation
Dinamarca, Denmark
Dios, God
diploma, diploma
diputado, deputy
dirección, administration, leadership, management, steering, trend

directamente, directly
directo, direct
director, director, manager, producer
directorio, directory
dirigido hacia arriba, upward
dirigido hacia un lado, sideways
discernimiento, insight, discrimination
disciplina, discipline
discípulo, pupil
disco, disc
disco compacto, compact disc
discreción, discretion
discurso, address, speech
discutir, to discuss
disertante, lecturer
disfraz, disguise
disposición, disposal
dispuesto, minded
disputa, dispute
distancia, distance
distante, distant
distinción, distinction
distinguido, distinguished
distinguir, distinguish
distinto, distinct
distribución, allocation
distrito electoral, constituency
diversión, diversion
divertido, amusing
divieso, boil
divino, divine
divisa, badge
división, division
divisoria de aguas, divide
divorcio, divorce
do, do
doblado o vuelto hacia abajo, turnover
doble, double
doblez, fold
doblón de oro, pistol
doce, twelve
docena, dozen
doctor, doctor

doctrina, doctrine
documento, document
dólar, dollar
dolor de espalda, backache
dolor, distress, grief, pain
dolor de estómago, stomach ache
dolor de garganta, sore throat
dolor de muelas, toothache
doloroso, painful
doméstico, domestic
dominante, dominant
domingo, Sunday
dominio de sí mismo, self-control
donación, gift
doncella, maid, maiden
donde, where
dondequiera que, wherever
doquiera, anywhere
dormido, asleep
dormitorio, bedroom
dos veces, twice
dos, two
dosis, dose
drama, drama
drástico, drastic
drenar, to drain
droga, drug
dual, dual
duda, doubt, hesitation
dudas, questioning
dudoso, doubtful, dubious
dueño, employer
duque, duke
duquesa, duchess
durable, lasting
duración, duration
durante, during
durmiente, sleeping
duro, hard, hard-boiled, stern, tough

E

eco, echo
economía, economy
económico, economic

ecuación, equation
eczema, eczema
edad, age
editor, publisher
educación, education
educado, educated
educativo, educational
efectivo, actual, real
efecto, effect
eficaz, effective, telling
eficiencia, efficiency
eficiente, efficient
Egipto, Egypt
eje, axis
ejecución, achievement, performance
ejecutivo, executive
ejemplo, instance
ejercicio, exercise
ejército, army
el, the
él, he, him
el/lo, it
él mismo, itself
el universo, creation
elasticidad, give
elástico, elastic
electricidad, electricity
electricista, electrician
electrónico, electronic, electron
elegancia, elegance
elegante, elegant
elemental, elementary
elemento, element
elevador, elevator
eliminar, eliminate
ella, her, she
ellos, they
embajada, embassy
embajador, ambassador
embarcar, embark
embargo, execution
embotado, dull
embotellamiento del tráfico, traffic jam
emergencia, emergency
emerger, emerge
emoción, emotion

emocional, emotional
empalizada, fence
empaque, packing
emparedado, sandwich
empleado, clerk, employee
emplear, occupy, to employ, to use
empleo, employ, job
emprender, undertake
empresa, enterprise, undertaking
empujón, push
en, on
en alguna parte, somewhere
en blanco, blank
en cambio, instead
en conjunto, altogether
en conserva, canned, preserved
en derredor, around
en medio, between
en ninguna parte, nowhere
en o a otra parte, elsewhere
en parte, partly
en relación con esto, thereby
en su mayor parte, mostly
en tercer lugar, thirdly
en tierra, ashore
en, at, in, into
enamorado, lover
encanto, charm
encarcelamiento, imprisonment
encarnado, red
encendedor, lighter
encender, to light
encendido, alight
encía, gum
encuentro, encounter
eneldo, dill
energía, energy
enérgicamente, briskly
enero, January
énfasis, emphasis
enfermedad, disease, illness, sickness
enfermo, ill, sick

engañar, to deceive, to cheat
engaño, sell
engendro, get
enjuagar, to rinse
enjuague, mouthwash
enmienda, amendment, correction
enorme, enormous
ensalada, salad
ensamblar a media madera, scarf
enseñanza, instruction
enseñanza, teaching, tuition
enseñar, teach
ensueño, fantasy
entalladura, carving
entender, understand
enterado, aware
enteramente, entirely
entero, complete, entire
entierro, burial, funeral
entonces, then
entrada, entrance, entry, income
entrar en o por, enter
entre, among, amongst
entretanto, meanwhile
entretener, entertain
entrevista, interview
entusiasmo, enthusiasm
enviar, send
envidiar, envy
envoltura, envelope
envolver, involve
envuelto, involved
episodio, episode
época, epoch
equidad, equity
equilibrio, balance, equilibrium
equipaje, baggage, luggage
equipo, equipment, tackle
equivalente, equivalent
equivocación, mistake
equivocado, mistaken
era, era
erario, exchequer
error, error
esbelto, slim

escalera, staircase
escalera mecánica, escalator
escándalo, scandal
escape, escape, exhaust
escarcha, frost
escasamente, scarcely
escasez, shortage
escaso, scarce
escena, scene
escenario, stage
esclavo, slave
escoger, to choose
escogido, choice, select
escolar, scholar
escolta, escort
escondido, hidden
escribir, to write
escritor, writer
escritorio, bureau
escritura, writing
escrutador, searching
escrutinio, scrutiny
escuadra, squadron
escuchar, to listen
escuela, school
escultor, sculptor
escultura, sculpture
ese, that
esencia, essence
esencial, essential
esfuerzo, effort, endeavor, struggle
eslabón, link
esmalte, enamel
esmeralda, emerald
esos, those
espacio, space
espada, sword
espantoso, appalling, dreadful, fearful
España, Spain
español, Spaniard, Spanish
espárrago, asparagus
especia, spice
especial, special
especialista, specialist
especialmente, especially

especie, species
especie de abogado o procurador, attorney, solicitor
especie de jábega, trawl
especie de lenguado, halibut
espécimen, specimen
especioso, plausible
espectáculo, spectacle
espectador, spectator
especulación, speculation
espejo, mirror
esperanza, hope
esperar, to expect, to hope, to wait
espeso, thick
espesor, thickness
espía, spy
espinaca, spinach
espinazo, ridge, spine
espíritu, ghost, spirit
espiritual, spiritual
espléndido, splendid
esponja, sponge
espontáneo, spontaneous
esposa, wife
espuma, foam
esqueleto, framework, skeleton
esquema, scheme
esquí, ski
esquí acuático, surfboard
esquimal, Eskimo
esta, this
estabilidad, stability
estable, stable
establecer, establish
estaca, stake
estación, season, station
estacionamiento, parking
estacionario, stationary
estadio, stadium
estadístico, statistic, statistical
estado, estate, state
estado legal, status
Estados Unidos, United States

estallido, crash, pop
estampa, stamp
estanque, pond, reservoir
estaño, tin
estatua, statue
estatuido, statutory
estay, stay
este, east
estela, wake
estético, aesthetic
estilo, style
estilográfica, fountain pen
estimación, estimate
estimar, appreciate
estímulo, stimulus
estío, summer
estirar, to stretch
estofado, stew, stewed
estola, stole
estómago, stomach
estorbo, let, prevention
estrecho, narrow
estrella, star
estreno, debut
estreñimiento, constipation
estricto, strict
estructura, build, structure
estudiar, to study
estudiante, student
estudiante que aún no tiene ningún grado académico, undergraduate
estudio, study
estufa, stove
estúpido, stupid
Europa, Europe
europeo, European
evangelio, gospel
eventualmente, eventually
evidencia, evidence
evidente, evident
evitar, avoid
evolución, evolution
exactitud, accuracy
exacto, accurate, exact
examen, examination
examinar, to examine
exceder, exceed

excelencia, excellency
excelente, excellent, worthy
excéntrica, eccentric
excepción, exception
excepcional, exceptional
excepto, except
excesivo, excessive
exceso, excess
excitante, exciting
exclusivo, exclusive
excursión, excursion
excusa, excuse
exhausto, exhausted
exhibición, exhibition
existir, exist
éxito, success
expansión, expansion
expectante, expectant
expedición, expedition
experiencia, experience
experimentado, experienced, expert
experimental, experimental
experimentar, to experience, to experiment
experimento, experiment
expiración, expiration
explicar, explain
explosión, blast, explosion
explosivo, explosive
exportación, export
exposición a la intemperie, exposure
expresamente, expressly
expreso, express
expuesto, exposed, liable
expulsión, expulsion
exquisitez, exquisite
extender, expand, extend
extendido, extended, spread
extensamente, widely
extensión, extension, extent
extensión en acres, acreage
extensivo, extensive
extenso, widespread
exterior, outer, outside, outward
externo, external
extra, extra

extracto, extract, far
extranjero, foreign, foreigner
extraño, strange
extraordinario, extraordinary, unusual
extraviado, missing
extremadamente, extremely
extremo, extreme, tip

F

fábrica, factory
fabril, manufacturing
fácil, easy
factor, factor
factura, invoice
facturar, check in, to invoice
faisán, pheasant
faja, band
falda, lap, skirt
fallo, judgement, sentence
falso, false, pretended
falta, fault, lack, want
faltar, to be lacking, wanting or missing
falto, wanting
fama, fame
familiar, familiar
familiaridad, familiarity
famoso, famous
fantasía, fancy
farmacia, chemist's, drugstore
fase, phase
fatal, fatal
fatigar, fatigue
favor, favor
favorable, favorable
favorecido, favored
favorito, favorite
febrero, February
fecha, date
federación, federation
federal, federal
feliz, happy
femenino, feminine
fenómeno, phenomenon
feo, ugly
ferrocarril, railway

festivo, festival
fiador/ra, guarantee
fiambre, cold meat, delicatessen
fibra, fibre
ficción, fiction
fiduciario, fiduciary, trustee
fiebre del heno, hay fever
fiebre, fever
fielmente, closely, loyalty
fiero, fierce
fiesta, feast, holiday, party
figurado, figured
fijo, certain, fixed
filo, edge
filosofía, philosophy
filósofo, philosopher
filtro, filter
fin, end, ending, finish
final, final
finalmente, finally
financiero, financial
finca, property
finito, finite
firma, signature
firmar, to sign
firme, steady
firme, firm
firmemente, firmly
física, physics
físico, physical
flexibilidad, flexibility
flor, flower
fluctuación, fluctuation
fluido, fluid
flujo, flow
foca, seal
foco, focus, focal point, center
folleto, booklet
fondo, background, bottom, fund
forastero, stranger
forcejear, to struggle
forcejeo, flounder
forma, fashion, form, shape
formación, formation
formal, earnest, formal
formato, format
formidable, formidable

fornicar, wore
forraje conservado en silo, silage
fortalecer, to strengthen, to fortify
fortaleza, fortress
forzado, forced, strained
forzoso, necessary
fósforo, match
foso, trench
fotocopia, photocopy
fotografía, photo, photograph, photography
fotógrafo, photographer
fragmento, fragment
fragmento, fraction
frambuesa, raspberry
Francia, France
franela, flannel
franja, fringe
franqueo, postage
frase, phrase
frecuencia, frequency
frecuente, frequent
freído, fried
freno, brake
frente, forehead, front
fresa, strawberry
fresco, cool, fresh
frío, cold
frontera, frontier
frontero, opposite
frunce, gather, shirr
frustración, frustration
frustrar, frustrate
fruto, fruit
fuego, fire
fuelle, sing
fuente, fountain, source, well
fuera, out
fuera de casa, abroad
fuerte, fast, loud, stout, strong
fuerza, force, strength, stress, vigor
función, function
funciónario/ria, officer
fundación, foundation

fundamental, fundamental
fundamentalmente, basically
fundar, found
fundidor, founder
furgón, wagon
furioso, furious
fusión, melting, fusion
fútbol, football
fútil, vain
futuro, future

G

gabinete, cabinet
galardón, premium
galería, balcony, gallery
Gales, Wales
galés, Welsh
galleta, biscuit, cookie
gallo, cock, fowl
gana, desire, wish
ganado, cattle
ganador, winner
ganancia, gain, profit
ganar, earn, win
gancho, hook
ganso, geese
garaje, garage
garganta, throat
gas, gas
gasa, gauze
gasolina, gasoline, petrol
gastar, to spend
gasto, expenditure, expense
gastritis, gastritis
gatillo, trigger
gato, cat
gema, gem
gemelo, twin
generación, generation
general, general
generalmente, generally
género, commodity, description
género humano, mankind
generoso, generous
genético, genetic
genio, genius

gente, folk
genuino, genuine
geología, geology
geometría, geometry
gigante, giant
gigantesco, gigantic
ginebra, gin
ginecólogo, gynecologist
giro postal, money order
giro, spin, turning
glándula, gland
globo, sphere
gloria, glory, heaven
glorioso, glorious
gobernación, government
gobernador, governor
gobernante, ruling
gobernar, govern
golf, golf
golondrina, swallow
golpe, blow, hit, impact, knock, strike
goma de mascar, chewing gum
gordo, fat
gorra, cap
gota, drop
goteo, trickle
gozar o disfrutar de, enjoy
gozne, hinge
gozo, joy
gracia, grace
gracias, thank you
gracioso, gracious
grado, degree, grade
graduado, gradual
gramática, grammar
Gran Bretaña, Britain
grande, big, grand, great, huge, large
grandemente, sharply
granero, barn
granja, farm, farmhouse
granjero, farmer
grano, corn, grain
grapa, clip
grasiento, greasy
gratitud, gratitude

grave, grave
grave, solemn
gravedad, gravity
Grecia, Greece
gremio, guild, association
griego, Greek
grifo, tap, faucet
gris, gray
grito, cry, crying, faucet, shout
grito de combate, slogan
grito de entusiasmo, cheer
grosellero silvestre,
    gooseberry
grueso, gross
grulla, crane
grupo, group
guante, glove
guarda, keeping, ward
guardabosque, forester
guardarropa, cloakroom
guardia, guard
guardián, guardian
guerra, war, warfare
guía, guide, guidance,
    timetable
guía de turismo, guidebook
guía telefónica, telephone
    directory
guión, continuity, script
guisante, pea
gusano, worm
gusto, taste

H

haba, bean
haber, have
habilidad, ability, skill
habilitar, enable
habitante, inhabitant
hábito, frock, habit
hablar, to speak
hacedor, maker
hacendado, landed
hacer, make up, perform
hacer funcionar, operate
hacerse más lento, slow
    down

hacha, torch
hacia, onto, toward, towards
hacia abajo, downwards
**hacia el centro o en el
    centro de la ciudad**,
    downtown
hado, fate
hálito, breath
hallarse, occur
hallazgo, find, finding
hambre, starvation
hambriento, hungry
harina, flour, meal
hartura, fill
hasta, till, until
hasta aquí, hitherto, so far
havia atrás, backward
hazaña, exploit
hebdomadario, weekly
hebilla, buckle
hechizo, spell
hecho, done, fact, made
hechura, make, making
helado de crema, ice cream
helicóptero, helicopter
hemorragia nasal, nosebleed
hendedura, split, crack
heno, hay
herencia, heritage, inheritance
herida, hurt, wound
herido, wounded
hermana, sister
hermano, brother
hermoso, handsome
héroe, hero
heroico, heroic, heroical
herrada, pail
herramienta, tool
hidráulico, hydraulic
hielo, ice
hierba, grass, herb
hija, daughter
hijo, son
hila, spinning
hilo, thread
hilo de lino, linen
hinchazón, swelling
hindú, Hindu

hinojo, fennel
hipoteca, mortgage
hipótesis, hypothesis
historia, history, natural history,
    story
historiador, historian
hito, landmark
hogar, fireplace, hearth, home
hoja, sheet
hoja de laurel, bay leaf
hoja, blade, leaf
¡hola!, hello
Holanda, Holland
holandés, Dutch
hombre, man, men
hombro, shoulder
honor, honor
honorario, honorary
honorarios, fee
honradez, honesty
honrado, honest
hora, hour
horcón, fork
horizontal, horizontal
horizonte, horizon
hornada, batch
horno, oven
horrible, ghastly
horror, horror
hortaliza, garden vegetable
hospedar, to provide lodge for
hospedero, host
hospital, hospital
hospitalidad, hospitality
hostil, hostile
hostilidad, hostility
hotel, hotel
hoy, today
hoy día, nowadays
hoyo, pit, hole
hueco, hollow
hueco en que encaja algo,
    socket
huella, trace
hueso, bone
huésped, guest
huevo, egg
huevo frito o estrellado,
    fried egg

huevos revueltos,
    scrambled eggs
humanidad, humanity
humano, human
humedad, moisture
húmedo, damp
humilde, humble
humor, humor
hurto, steal, stealing

I

ida, go
idea, idea, notion
ideal, ideal
ido, gone
iglesia, church
ignición, ignition
ignorancia, ignorance
ignorante, ignorant
igual, alike, equal, even, like
igualdad, equality
ilegal, illegal
iluminación, lighting
ilusión, illusion
ilustrado, learned, cultured
ilustrar, illustrate
imagen, image
imaginación, imagination
imaginar, imagine
imaginativo, imaginative
impaciencia, impatience
impaciente, impatient
impar, odd
imperdible, safety pin
imperial, imperial
imperio, empire
impersonal, impersonal
impertinente, irrelevant,
    impertinent
ímpetu, momentum
implicación, implication
implicar, imply
implícito, implied
imponer, impose
impopular, unpopular
importancia, import,
    importance
importante, important

imposible, impossible
imposición de tributos, taxation
impresión, impress, impression, print, printing
impresionante, imposing, impressive
improbable, improbable, unlikely
impropio, unsuitable
impuesto, tax
impulsar, to drive, to impel
impulso, impulse, urge
impureza, alloy
inadecuado, inadequate
inalterado, unchanged
incapaz, unable
incertidumbre, uncertainty
incidente, incident, occurrence
incierto, uncertain
incitativo, incentive
inclinación, bend, bow, inclination, liking
inclinado, inclined
incluir, include
incompleto, incomplete
inconsciente, unconscious
increíble, incredible
indagación, inquiry
indemne, harmless
independencia, independence
independiente, independent
India, India
indicación, hint, suggestion
indicador, indicator
indicar, indicate
indicio, clue, indication
indiferente, indifferent, regardless
indigestión, indigestion
indignación, indignation
indio, Indian
individual, individual
indudable, doubtless
industria, industry
industrial, industrial
inesperado, unexpected
inevitable, inevitable

inexperto, inexperienced
infancia, childhood
infante, infant
infantil, childish
infectar, infect
infeliz, unhappy, wretched
inferior, inferior
infierno, hell
infinito, infinite
inflación, inflation
inflamación, inflammation
influencia, influence
influenciar, to influence
influenza, influenza
influir, to affect
información, information
información o pesquisa judicial con ayuda de un jurado, inquest
informado, informed
informador, informant, reporter
informal, casual, informal
informe, inform, notice
infortunado, unfortunate
ingeniería, engineering
ingeniero, engineer
ingenio, engine, ingenuity
ingenioso, ingenious
inglés, English, Englishman
ingrediente, ingredient
inherente, inherent
inicial, initial
iniciar, to initiate, to commence
iniciativo, initiative
injusticia, injustice
injusto, unfair, wrong
inmediatamente, immediately
inmediato, immediate
inmensamente, vastly
inmenso, immense
inmigración, immigration
inmigrante, immigrant
inmortal, immortal
innecesario, unnecessary
innumerable, innumerable

inocencia, innocence
inocente, innocent
inquieto, restless
inquilino, tenant
inquina, despite
insatisfactorio, unsatisfactory
inscripción, record, registration
insecto, insect
insertar, fill in
insignificante, insignificant
insistencia, urgency
insistente, pressing
insistir, to insist
inspección, inspection
inspector, inspector
inspiración, inspiration
instalación, installation, settlement
instante, instant
instinto, instinct
institución, institution
instituto, institute
instrucción, learning, instruction, schooling
instruido, well-read
instrumental, instrumental
instrumento, appliance, instrument
insuficiente, insufficient
intacto, intact
integrante, integral
intelectual, intellectual
inteligencia, intelligence
inteligente, intelligent, knowing
intención, intention
intensidad, intensity
intenso, intense, intensive
intento, attempt
interés, interest
interesado, selfish
interferencia, radio
interminable, endless
interino, acting, interim
interior, indoor, inland, inner, inside, interior, internal
intermedio, intermediate
interminable, endless

intermitente, intermittent
internacional, international
interponerse, interfere
interposición, interference
interpretación, interpretation
interpretar, interpret
interrupción, interruption
intersección, intersection
intervalo, interval
intervención, intervention
intestinos, bowel
íntimo, intimate
intranquilo, uneasy
intrincado, intricate
introducir, introduce
intuición o impresión de lo que va a suceder anticipation
inundación, flood
inútil, useless
invento, invention
inversión, investment
inverso, reverse
investigar, investigate
investir, invest
invierno, winter
invisible, invisible
invitación, invitation
invitar, invite
inyección, injection
Irlanda, Ireland
irlandés, Irish
irreflexivo, rash, inconsiderate
irregular, irregular
irrigación, irrigation
irritar, to irritate
irse, go away
isla, island, isle
Israel, Israel
Italia, Italy
italiano, Italian
item, item
izquierdo, left

J

jabalí, wild boar
jabón, soap
jade, jade

jadeante, panting
jalea, jelly
Japón, Japan
japonés, Japanese
jaqueca, headache
jardín, garden
jarra, jar
jarro, jug, mug
jaula, cage
jazz, jazz
jefe, commander
jefe de cocina, chef
jengibre, ginger
Jersey, Jersey
Jesús, Jesus
jinete, rider
jockey, jockey
joven, young
judaico, Jewish
judaísmo, Judaism
judicial, judicial
judío, Jew
juego, game, play, set
jueves, Thursday
juez, judge
juguete, toy
julio, July
junio, June
junípero, juniper
junto, together
juramento, oath
justicia, justice
justificación, justification
justo, just
juventud, youth

K

keroseno, kerosene
kilo, kilo
kilogramo, kilogram
kilómetro, kilometer

L

la Gran Bretaña, Great Britain
la tarde, afternoon
labio, lip
labriego, peasant
ladeo, leaning
lado, side
ladrillo, brick
ladrón, thief
lago, lake, loch
lágrima, tear
laico, lay
lámina, cut
lámpara, lamp
lana, wool
langosta, lobster
lanzamiento, launch, throw
lápiz, pencil
lápiz para los labios, lipstick
largo, long
latente, latent
latido, beat
látigo, whip
latino, Latin
latón, brass
lavabo, sink
lavadero, washing place
lavado, shampoo, wash
lavar, to wash
lavatorio, wash
laxativo, laxative
laya, spade
leal, loyal
lealtad, loyalty
lebrel, hound
lección, lesson
leche, milk
lechería, dairy
lecho, bed
lector, reader
lectura, reading
legal, legal
legislación, legislation
legislativo, legislative
legítimo, legitimate
lejía, bleach
lejos, away, off
lengua, tongue
lenguaje, language
lente, lens
lenteja, lentil
lento, leisurely, slow

león, lion
letra, letter
letrado, lawyer
levantar, to rise
levantarse, get up
ley, law, statute
leyenda, legend
liberación, delivery, rescue
liberal, liberal
libertad, freedom, liberty
libertar, to liberate
libra, pound
librar, rid
libre, free
libremente, freely
librería, bookshop
libro, book
libro en rústica, paperback
licencia, license
licitación, bid
licor, liquor
liebre, hare
liga, league
ligeramente, lightly
ligero, slight
lima, file
limitación, limitation, restriction
límite, limit
limón, lemon
limonada, lemonade
limpiador, wiper
limpieza, cleaning
limpio, clean
linde, boundary
lindo, pretty
línea, range
línea aérea, airline
lineal, linear
linterna, lantern
linterna eléctrica, flashlight
lío, pack
líquido para frenos, brake fluid
líquido pulverizado, spray
lista, list, schedule
lista de platos, menu
literario, literary

literatura, literature
litro, liter
llama, flame
llamada, call, recall
llamado, so-called
llamarada, flash
llano, level, plain
llanta, tire
llave, key
llegar, arrive
llegarda, arrival
lleno, full
lleno de color, colorful
llevar a cabo, put through
lluvia, rain
lo peor, worse, worst
lo arrastrado, drift
lo mismo, likewise
lobo, wolf
local, local
loción facial, after-shave
loco, mad
locura, madness
lógica, logic
lógico, logical
lograr, to achieve
lomo de caballo, horseback
lona, canvas
longitud, length
longitud o recorrido en millas, mileage
loro, parrot
los, them
lucha, scramble
luego, soon
lugar donde se aloja, house
lugar, place
lugar, village
lugareño, villager
lujo, luxury
luna de miel, honeymoon
luna, moon
lunes, Monday
luz de la luna, moonlight
luz del día, daylight

M

macho, male
macizo, massive
madera, timber
madre, mother
madurez, maturity
maduro, mature, ripe
maestro, teacher
magia, magic
magistrado, magistrate
magnético, magnetic
magnífico, magnificent
majestad, majesty
mal, harm
maldición, damn
maleta, suitcase
malla, mail
malo, bad, wicked
mamá, mom
manada, drove
mancha, spot, stain
mandar, to command
mando, control
manejar, manage
manera, manner
manga, sleeve
manicura, manicure
manifestación pública, demonstration
manojo, bunch
mansamente, gently
manta, blanket
mantener, maintain
mantequilla, butter
manual, manual
manufactura, manufacture
manuscrito, manuscript
manzana, apple
mañana, morning
mapa, map
máquina, machine
máquina de escribir, typewriter
maquinaria, machinery
mar, sea
maravillosamente, beautifully
maravilloso, wonderful

marbete, label
marca, brand
marcado, marked
marcha, departure, hike, walking
Marcos, Mark
marea, tide
marfil, ivory
margen, margin
marido, husband
marinero, sailor
mariscal, marshal
marítimo, marine
marjal, marsh
marmita, pot
martillo, hammer
marxista, Marxist
marzo, March
más, else, more, plus
más alto, higher
más bajo, lower
más joven, younger
más largo, longer
más lejos, farther
más pronto, sooner
más reciente, latter
masa, mass, paste
mata, plant
matemáticas, mathematics
materia prima, stuff
materia, matter
material, material
matrimonio, marriage
matriz, matrix
mayor, elder, elderly, greater, major, senior
mayordomo, butler
mayoría, majority
me, me
mecánico, mechanic, mechanical
mecanismo, mechanism, movement
mechero, burner, cigarette lighter
medalla, medal
media, stocking
medianoche, midnight

medicina, medicine
medición, measurement, survey
médico, medical, practitioner, doctor
medida, gauge, measure, size
medido, measured
medidor, meter
medieval, medieval
medio, medium, middle
mediodía, noon
medir, to measure
Mediterránea, Mediterranean
mejilla, cheek
mejillón, mussel
mejor, best, better
mejorar, improve
mejoría, mend
melancolía, melancholy
melodía, melody
melón, melon
memoria, memoir, memory
mención, mention
meneo, shake
menor, junior, lesser, minor
menos, fewer, less
mensaje, message
mensual, monthly
mental, mental
mente, mind
mentir, to lie
mentira, lie
mentiroso, lying
menudo, minute
meramente, merely
mercader, merchant
mercado, market
mercancías, goods
merecer, deserve
mérito, desert, merit
mermelada, marmalade
mero, mere
mes, month
mesa, table
meta, goal
metal, metal
método, method, system
metro, meter

metropolitano, metropolitan
mezcla, blend
mezcla, mix, mixture
mezclado, mixed
mezclar, to mix, to blend
mezquita, mosque
mi, my
miedo, fear
miel, honey
miembro, member
mientras, while
miércoles, Wednesday
migración, migration
mil, thousand
milagro, miracle
militar, military
milla, mile
millón, million
mineral, mineral
minería, mining
minero, miner
miniatura, miniature
mínimo, least
ministerio, department, ministry
ministro, minister
minoridad, minority
mío, mine
mirada, glance, look
mirada fija, gaze, stare
miramiento, regard
misceláneo, miscellaneous
miserable, miserable
miseria, misery
misericordia, mercy
misión, mission
mismo, same, self, very
misterio, mystery
misterioso, mysterious
mitad, half
mito, myth
mochila, knapsack, backpack
moción, moving
modelo, model, pattern
moderación, moderation
moderno, modern
modificación, alteration, modification

modificar, alter
modo, mode
moho, mold
mojado, wet
molino, mill
momento, moment
monarca, monarch
monarquía, monarchy
monasterio, monastery
moneda, coin, currency, money
mono, overalls
monopolio, monopoly
montar, to mount
montado, mounted
montaña, mountain
montón, heap, pile
monumento, monument
morada, dwelling, mansion
moral, moral
moralidad, morality
mordaza, gag
moreno, brown
moribundo, dying
mortal, deadly, lethal
mortero, mortar
mosca, fly
mostaza, mustard
mosto, must
motor, motor
mover, to move
movilidad, mobility
movimiento o avance impetuoso, rush
movimiento, motion, move, stir
mozo, waiter
muchacha, girl
muchacho, boy
mucho, much
muchos, many, most
mudo, dumb, mute
muerte, death, exit, kill, killing, slaughter
muerto, dead
muesca, score
muestra, sample
mujer, woman, wife
múltiple, multiple

multitud, crowd, multitude, press
mundo, world
municipal, municipal
muñeca, doll; wrist
músculo, muscle
museo de pintura, art gallery
museo, museum
música popular, folk music
música, music
musical, musical
muslo, thigh
musulmán, Moslem
mutual, mutual
muy, greatly, very

N

nabo, turnip
nacer, to be born
nacido, born
nacimiento, birth
nación, commonwealth, nation
nacional, national
nada, nothing
nadar, to swim
nadie, nobody
naranja, orange
naranjada, orangeade
nariz, nose
narrativo, narrative
natación, swimming
natalicio, birthday
nativo, native
natural, natural
naturaleza, nature
navaja de afeitar, razor
naval, naval
navegación, sailing, navigation
navegar, to sail, to navigate
Navidad, Christmas
necesidad, need, necessity
necio, fool
negar, deny
negativo, negative
negociar, negotiate
negocio, trade, business

negro, black, Negro
nervio, nerve
nervudo, sinewy, wiry
neumonía, pneumonia
ni, nor
nido, nest
niebla, fog, mist
nieve, snow
ninguno, none
ninguno de los dos, neither
niña, girl
niño, boy, child, children
níquel, nickel
Niza, Nice
no, not
no, no
no confiable, unreliable
no obstante, nevertheless,
    notwithstanding
noble, noble
nobleza, nobility
noche, night
nombrado, noted
nombre, name, noun
nombre de pila, first name
nominación, nomination
nominal, nominal
norma, standard
normal, normal
normas de conducta, policy
norte, north
Norteamérica, North
    America
Noruega, Norway
nosotros, us, we
nosotros mismos, ourselves
nota, note
notable, notable, striking
notablemente, notably
noticia, news
notificar, to notify
notorio, notorious
novelista, novelist
noventa, ninety
novia, bride
noviembre, November
nube, cloud
nuclear, nuclear

núcleo, nucleus
nuestro, our
nueve, nine
nuevo, new, novel
nuez, walnut
numerar, to tell
número, number
numerosos, numerous
nunca, never

O

o, or
obispo, bishop
objeción, objection
objeto, exhibit, object, objective
objetos de plata, silverware
objetos de plomo, leading
oblación, offering
obligación, obligation
obligado, bound, essential
obligatorio, compulsory
obra, work, piece of work
obrador, workshop
obrar, to work, to perform
obrero, worker
obscenidad, obscenity
obsceno, obscene
obsequios, attention, present,
    gift
observable, remarkable,
    noticeable
observación, observation,
    remark
observar, to observe
obsesión, obsession
obstáculo, difficulty, obstacle
obtener, to obtain
obvio, obvious
ocasión, occasion
ocasional, occasional
ocasionalmente,
    occasionally
occidental, western
ochenta, eighty
ocho, eight
ocio, leisure
octubre, October

ocultar, to hide
ocupación, employment, occupation
ocupado, busy
odio, hate, hatred
oeste, west
ofensa, offense
ofender, to offend, to insult
ofensivo, offensive, shocking
ofensor, offender
oferta, offer
oficial, official
oficialmente, officially
oficio, office
oído, hearing
oír, to hear
ojo, eye
ola, wave
olfato, scent, smell
olvidar, to forget
ominoso, ominous
once, eleven
ónix, onyx
ópera, opera
operación, operation
operador, operator
opereta, operetta
opinión, opinion
oponente, opponent
oponer, oppose
oposición, opposition
óptico, optician
opuesto, opposed
oración breve, clause
orador, speaker
oral, oral
orden, command
ordenador, computer
ordenamiento, ordinance
ordeñar, to milk
oreja, ear
organización, organization
orgullo, pride
orgulloso, proud
orientación, orientation
oriental, eastern
origen, origin
original, original

orilla, shore
orina, urine
ornamentación, decoration
ornitología, ornithology
oro, gold
ortodoxo, orthodox
oscilar, to oscillate
oscuridad, darkness
oscuro, dark, dusk, gloomy, obscure
oso, bear
ostra, oyster
otalgia, earache
otoño, autumn
otramente, otherwise
otro, another, other
oval, oval
oxidación, oxidation
óxido, oxide, rust
oxígeno, oxygen

P

paciencia, patience
paciente, patient
pacificador, pacifier
pacífico, peaceful
pacto, agreement, compact
padecer, to suffer
padre, father
paga, pay
pagable, payable
pagar, to pay
pagano, pagan
pagar y marcharse, check out
pago, payment
país, country
paisaje, landscape, scenery
paisano, civilian, one from the same area
paja, straw
paje, page, bellboy
pala, shovel
palabra, speech, word
palacio, palace
pálido, pale
paliza, beating
palma, palm tree

palmo, span, measure of length
palo, stick
palpar, to feel, to touch
palpitación, palpitation
pan, bread, pan
panadería, baker's
panadero, baker
pañal, diaper
pánico, panic
pantalla, screen
pantalones, pants, trousers
pantalones cortos para deporte, shorts
pañal, diaper
paño, cloth, washcloth
pantufla, slipper
papanatas, ninny, simpleton
papel de seda, tissue paper
papel de cartas, note paper
papel, paper, role
papel higiénico, toilet paper
paquete, packet, parcel
par, couple, pair
parábola, parable
parabrisas, windshield
paradojo, paradox
paraguas, umbrella
paraíso, paradise
paralelo, parallel
paramento, facing
parámetro, parameter
parásito, parasite
parcial, partial
parecerle a uno, to seem
parecido, resemblance
pared, wall
parentesco, kinship
parientes, kin
parlante, talking
parque de atracciones, amusement park
parque zoológico, zoo
parque, park
párrafo, paragraph
parrilla, grill
parroquia, parish
parte, part, share

parte o superficie superior, top
participación, participation
participar, to participate
partícula, particle
particular, particular
partida, departure
partido, district, party
pasado, former, past
pasajero, fare, passenger
pasaporte, passport
pasar el fin de semana, week-end
pasar la noche, overnight
Pascua de Resurrección o florida, Easter
paseo, walk
paseo en coche, drive
paseo o viaje a caballo, ride
pasión, passion
pasivo, passive
paso, footstep, going, pace, pass, passage, passing, step, walk
pastel, cake, crayon
pastelería, cake shop, pastry, pastry shop
patatas fritas, chips
paternal, parental
patético, pathetic
patillas, sideburns
patín, skate
patínar, to skate
patinete, scooter
patio de recreo, playground
pausa, pause
pavimento, pavement
paz, peace
pecar, to sin
pecho, breast, chest
peculiar, peculiar
pedestre, pedestrian
pedir, to ask
pedrería, jewellery
pegajoso, sticky
peine, comb
peldaño, step
película, color film, film, movie

peligro, danger
peligroso, dangerous
pelo, hair
pelotón, gang
peltre, pewter
peluca, wig
peludo, hairy
peluquero, hairdresser
pena, penalty
pender, to hang, to dangle
pendiente, pending
penicilina, penicillin
penoso, sore, uncomfortable
pensamiento, thought
pensar, to think
pensión, pension
pensionado, pensioner
pepinillo, gherkin
pequeñito, tiny
pequeño, little, petty, small
pera, pear
perca, perch
percepción, perception
perder, to lose
pérdida, loss
perdiz, partridge
perdón, pardon
perdonar, to forgive
perejil, parsley
perezoso, lazy
perfeccionamiento,
    improvement
perfecto, perfect
perfil, profile
perfumar, perfume
perico, parrot
período, period
perla, pearl
permanente, permanent
permiso, permission, permit
pernil, ham
perpetuo, perpetual
perro, dog
persecución, persecution
pérsico, peach
persistente, persistent
persona, person
personal, personal, personnel

personalidad, personality
perspectiva, perspective,
    prospect
persuadir, persuade
pertenecer, to belong
perturbación, disturbance,
    trouble
pesadamente, heavily
pesadilla, nightmare
pesado, heavy
pesar, to weigh, to grieve
pesca, fish
pescar, to fish
pesebre, manger, stall, trough
petición, suit
petróleo, oil
pez, fish, pitch
pez de agua dulce,
    freshwater fish
piano, piano
picadura, sting
pichón, pigeon
pico, bill, peak, pick
pie, foot
piedad, pity, mercy
piedra, stone
piel, fur, peel, skin
piel de suecia, suede
pierna, leg
pies, feet
pieza, piece
pijama, pajamas
pilar, pier, pillar
píldora, pill
piloto, pilot
pimienta, pepper
pimpollo, shoot, sprout
pino, pine
pintura, paint, painting, picture
pinza, clothespin, pliers
pinzas, tweezers, forceps
piscina, swimming pool
pista de tenis, tennis court
placa, plate, plaque
placer, pleasure
plano, flat, plan, plane
planta, sole
plantación, plantation

plástico, plastic
plata, silver
plataforma, platform
plátano, bánana
platija, plaice
platillo, saucer, scale
platino, platinum
plato, dish
playa, beach
pleamar, high tide
plenamente, fully
plomo, lead
pluma, feather, pen
plus, bonus
población, population, town
pobre, poor
pobreza, poverty
poco asado, underdone
poco familiar, unfamiliar
pocos, few
poder, power
poderío, might
poderoso, mighty, powerful
poema, poem
poesía, poetry
poeta, poet
polaco, Polish
policía, police
político, political, politician
pollería, poultry shop
pollo, chicken
polvo, dust, powder
polvoriento, dusty
pomelo, grapefruit
pompa, parade, show
poner, to put
popular, popular
popularidad, popularity
por, for, per, through
por ciento, per cent
por esto, therefore
por o en todas partes, everywhere
¿por qué?, why
por separado, separately
por todo, throughout
porcelana, porcelain
porcentaje, percentage

porción, lot, portion
porción de terreno, plot
pornografía, pornography
pornográfico, pornographic
porque, because
portarse, behave
portátil, portable
porte, transport, freight
porteador, carrier
portero, porter
portillo, gap
Portugal, Portugal
portugués, Portuguese
posada, inn
posadera, host, hostess
poseer, to possess
posible, possible
posiblemente, possibly
posición, position, situation, stand
poste, post
postre, dessert
potencial, potential
práctica, practice
practicable, practicable
prácticamente, practically
practicar, to practice
práctico, practical, practice, skilled
prado, meadow
precaución, precaution
precedente, preceding
preceptor, tutor
precio, price
precioso, precious
precipitado, hurried
precisión, definition, precision
preciso, definite, precise
predecesor, predecessor
predominante, predominant
preferencia, preference
preferir, to prefer
pregunta, question
preguntar, to ask
prejuicio, prejudice
preliminar, preliminary
premio, prize, reward
premura, hurry

preñada, pregnant
preñez, pregnancy
preocupación, bother, care, preoccupation
preparación, preparation
preparado, ready
preparar, to prepare
presa, arrested, capture, morsel
présbita, far-sighted
prescribir, to prescribe
presentación, presentation, show
presente, present
preservación, preservation
presidente, chairman, president
presión, pressure
presión arterial, blood pressure
preso, prisoner
prestado, borrowed
préstamo, loan
prestar, lend
prestigio, prestige
presupuesto, budget
prevención, provision
prevenir, prevent
previo, previous
primario, primary
primavera, May, spring
primero, first, firstly, main, premier, prime
primitivo, primitive
primogénito, eldest
princesa, princess
principal, chief, principal
principalmente, chiefly, mainly
príncipe, prince
principiante, beginner
principio, principle, starting
prisa, haste
prisión, prison
privadamente, privately
privado, private
privilegio, privilege
probabilidad, probability

probable, likely, probable
probado, tested, tried
probar, to prove, to test, to try
problema, problem
proceder, to proceed
procedimiento, procedure
proceso, process
proclama, proclamation
pródigo, extravagant
producción, product, production
producir, to produce
productividad, productivity
producto, produce, yield
profesión, profession, trade
profesional, professional
profesor, professor
profundidad, depth
profundo, profound
progenitor, ancestor
programa, program
progresivo, onward, progressive
progreso, progress
prohibido, forbidden
prohibir, forbid, prohibit
promedio, average
promesa, promise
prometiente, promising
prominente, prominent
promoción, promotion
promover, to promote
pronóstico, forecast
prontamente, readily, quickly
prontitud, readiness
pronunciación, pronunciation
pronunciado, pronounced
pronunciar, to pronounce
propaganda, propaganda
propensión, tendency
propiamente, properly
propiedad, ownership
propietario, landlord, owner
propio, fitting, own, proper, suitable
proponer, to propose
proporción, proportion
proposición, proposal, proposition

propósito, purpose
propuesto, proposed, proposal
proseguir, proceed
prosperidad, prosperity
prosperidad rápida y creciente, boom
próspero, prosperous
protección, security, protection
protector, protective
proteger, to protect
protesta, protest
protestante, Protestant
protocolo, protocol, formality
protuberancia redondeada, knob
provecho, profit
provechoso, profitable, helpful
proveer, provide
provincial, provincial
provisión, supply
provocativo, provocative
proximidad, proximity
próximo, nearest, next
proyecto, project
prueba, proof, trial, try
psiquiatra, psychiatrist
publicación, publication
publicar, publish
publicidad, advertising, publicity
público, public
pueblo, people
puente, bridge
puerro, leek
puerta, door, doorway, gate
puerto, harbor, port
puesta, setting
pulga, flea
pulgada, inch
pulgar, thumb
pulmón, lung
púlpito, pulpit
pulsera, bracelet
punta, point
puntada, stitch
puntal, prop

puntapié, kick
puntería, aim
puntiagudo, pointed
punto, stitch
punto de unión o de encuentro, join
puntura, puncture
puño, fist
puro, cigar, pure, sheer
purpúreo, purple

Q

que, than
qué, what
¿qué?, which
que sienta, becoming
que tiene éxito, successful
que viaja, travelling
quedar, to remain
queja, complaint
quejar, to complain
quemadura, burn
quemadura del sol, sunburn
querido, beloved, dear, pet
queso, cheese
quien, who, whom
quieto, quiet, still
quijada, jaw
químca, chemistry
químico, chemical
quincena, fortnight
quitar, to remove, to take off
quitasol, sunshade, parasol
quizás, perhaps

R

rábano, radish
rábano picante, horseradish
rabí, rabbi
rabia, rage
racial, racial
ración, ration, helping
racional, rational, reasonable
radar, radar
radiación, radiation
radiactivo, radioactive
radiador, radiator

radical, radical
radio-despertador, clock radio
radiográfia, X-ray
raíz, root
rama, branch
rana, frog
rapidez, speed
raqueta, racket
raramente, seldom
raro, queer, rare
rasgo, feature
raso, open, flat
raspador, eraser, grater
rastrar, to drag
rastro, track
rata, rat
rato, bout, while
rayo, ray, spoke
raza, race
razón, rate, reason
razonamiento, reasoning
razonar, to reason
real, effective, real
realmente, actually, indeed
reavivamiento, revival
rebanada, slice
rebaño, herd
rebelde, rebel
rebelión, rebellion
recatado, modest
recepción, reception
recepcionista, receptionist
receptor, receiver
receta, receipt
rechazamiento, refusal
rechazar, to reject
recibir, to receive
reciente, recent
recipiente, container
reclamación, claim
recobrar, to recover
recoger, to pick up
recomendar, to commend, to recommend
recordar, to remember
rectangular, rectangular
rectángulo, rectangle

rector, rector, right, straight
recuerdo, souvenir
recuperación, recovery
recurso, resort, resource, shift
red, net
redactor, editor, writer
redención, redemption
redondo, round
reducir, reduce
reemplazo, substitution, replacement
referencia, reference
referir, to refer
reflejar, to reflect
reforma, reform
refrenamiento, restraint
refugiado, refugee
regencia, regency
régimen, regime
regimiento, regiment
regio, royal
región, province, region, territory, tract
regla, rule
regordete, plump
regresión, regression
regulación, regulation
regular, regular
reina, queen
reino, kingdom, realm, reign
reintegro, refund
rejilla, grid
relación, ratio, relation
relámpago, lightning
reliquias, remains
relleno, filling
reloj, clock
reloj de bolsillo, watch
reloj de cuco, cuckoo clock
reloj de sol, sundial
remedio, remedy
remiendo, patch
remolque, trailer
remoto, remote
rendición, surrender
rendido, blown, exhausted
rendimiento, output
renta, rent, rental, revenue

renuente, reluctant
reparación, repair
reparto, allotment
repetición, repeat, repetition
repetir, to repeat
reponer, to replace
representación, representation
representar, to represent
representativo, representative
república, republic
repugnancia, repugnance
reputación, reputation
requerir, to require
requisito, requirement
resbalón, slip
resentimiento, resentment
reserva, reserve, resist
reservación, reservation
reservado, reserved
resguardo, shelter, protection
residencia, residence
residencial, residential
residente, resident
residual, residual
resignado, resigned
resina, resin
resistencia, resistance
resistente, resistant
resolución, resolution
resolver, solve
resonante, resonant
respectivo, respective
respetable, respectable
respeto, respect
respiración, breathing, respiration
resplandor, glow
resplandor fugaz, glimpse
responder, to reply, to respond
responsable, responsible
respuesta, answer, response
restaurante, restaurant
restaurar, to restore
resto, remainder
restringir, restrict
resuelto, resolved

resultado, outcome, result
retener, to retain
retirado, retired
retirar, to withdraw, to retire
retiro, retirement, retreat, withdrawal
reto, dare
retraído, retiring, shy
retrato, portrait
retrato, photograph
retroceso, recession, backing up
reumatismo, rheumatism
reunión, meeting
reunir, to collect, together
revelación, revelation
revelar, to reveal
reventón, burst, explosion
reverberación, reverberation
reversible, reversible
revisión, revision
revista, review, magazine
revolución, revolution
revolucionario, revolutionary
revuelta, revolt, riot
rey, king
ribazo, sharp slope, embankment
rico, wealthy, rich, tasty
ridículo, ridiculous
riesgo, risk, liability
rifle, rifle
rígido, rigid
riña, quarrel, row
riñón, kidney
río, river
riqueza, wealth
risa, laugh, laughter
risco, cliff
risa, laughter
risueño, laughing
ritmo, rhythm
ritual, ritual
rivalidad, rivalry
rizo, curly
roble, oak
robar, to rob
robo, theft

robusto, sturdy
roca, rock
rocoso, rocky
rodaballo, turbot
rodante, rolling
rodear, to go around, to surround
rodilla, knee
rojo, red
romance, romance
romero, rosemary
ron, rum
ropa, clothes
rosa, rose
rosario, rosary
roto, torn
rotor, rotor
rozamiento, rubbing, friction
rubí, ruby
rubio, blond
rudo, gruff
rueda, wheel
ruego, request
ruibarbo, rhubarb
ruido, clash, noise
ruidoso, noisy
ruina, ruin
rumor, rumor
rural, rural
ruta, route
rutina, routine

S

sábado, Saturday
saber, scholarship, to know
sabiduría, wisdom
sabor, flavor
sacacorchos, corkscrew
sacar, to get, to obtain, to draw out
sacerdote, priest
saco, suit coat, bag, sack
saco de dormir, sleeping bag
saco, sack
sacrificio, sacrifice
sagaz, politic
sagrado, sacred

saín, suet
sal, salt
salado, salty
salchicha, sausage
saledizo, outstanding
salida, issue, outlet, exit
salida de auxilio, emergency exit
salir, to go out
salir a campaña, to campaign
salmón, salmon
salón de belleza, beauty salon
salsa, gravy, sauce
saltador, hopper, skipper
salto, jump, leap
salud, health
saludo, greeting
salvación, salvation
salvador, saving, saviour
salvaguardia, safeguard
salvaje, savage, wild
salvamento, salvage
salvia, sage
salvo, beyond, safe, save
salvoconducto, protection
sandía, watermelon
sangrar, to bleed
sangre, blood
sangriento, bloody
sano, healthy
santo, holy, saint
sardina, sardine
sargento, sergeant
satisfacción, satisfaction
sazón, seasoning, ripeness
sazónar, to season, to ripen
se, themselves, himself, herself, yourself, yourselves, oneself, itself
secar, to dry
secar con secador, blow dry
sección, section
seco, dried, dry
secretario, secretary
secreto, secret

sector, sector
secundario, secondary
seda, silk
sede, see
seguido/da, successive
seguidor, disciple
seguimiento, pursuit
seguir, to follow, to pursue
segundo, second
seguramente, definitely
seguridad, assurance, safety
seguro, assured, confident,
    insurance, secure, sure, safe
seis, six
selecto, select
sello de correos, postage
    stamp
selva virgen, jungle
semáforo, traffic light
semana, week
sembrado a vuelo,
    broadcast
semilla, seed
senado, senate
senador, senator
senda, footpath, lane
sensación, sensation
sensacional, spectacular
sensibilidad, sensibility
sensible, sensitive
sentar, to sit
sentencia, verdict
sentido, sense
sentimental, sentimental
señal, signal
señalamiento, appointment
señor, lord, mister, sir
señora, lady, madam, Mrs.
señoría, lordship
señorío, gentry
señorita, Miss
separado, separate
septiembre, September
séptimo, seventh
sepulcro, tomb
séquito, suite
ser, to be
seriamente, seriously

serie, series
serio, serious
servicial, helpful
servicio o casa de correo,
    post office
servicio, service
servida, helping
servilleta, napkin
sesenta, sixty
sesgo, bias
sesión, session
seta, mushroom
setenta, seventy
seto vivo, hedge
severo, severe
sexo, sex
sexto, sixth
sexual, sexual
si, if, whether, yes
sidra, cider
siempre, always, ever, forever
sierra, saw
siete, seven
siglo, century
significación, meaning
significado, significance
significante, meaningful,
    significant
signo, sign
siguiente, following
silbato, whistle
silbido, whistle, hiss, hoot
silencio, silence
silencioso, silent
silla, chair
silla plegable o de tijera,
    folding chair
símbolo, symbol
simetría, symmetry
similar, similar
simpatía, sympathy
simpático, sympathetic,
    pleasant
simple, simple
simplicidad, simplicity
sin, without
sin hijos, childless
sinagoga, synagogue

sinceramente, sincerely
sinceridad, sincerity
sincero, sincere
sinfonía, symphony
singular, singular
siniestro, sinister
sino, destiny, but, except
sintaxis, syntax
síntoma, symptom
sirviente, servant
sistema, system
sitio, site
situación, locality, situation
soberano, ruler
soberbio, superb
sobrante, surplus
sobre, above, upon
sobre la cabeza de uno, overhead
sobrecarga, surcharge
sobrenatural, supernatural
sobresatar, to startle, to show up clearly
sobrevivir, survive
sobrina, niece
sobrino, nephew
social, social
socialismo, socialism
socialista, socialist
sociedad, partnership, society
socio, partner
soda, soda
sodio, sodium
sofá, sofa
sofisticado, sophisticated
sol, sun, sunlight, sunshine
solaz, amusement, solace
soldado, soldier
soleado, sunny
soledad, isolation, loneliness
sólido, solid
solista, soloist
solitario, solitary
solo, alone, himself, lonely, only, solo
soltero, bachelor
solubilidad, solubility
solución, solution

solvencia, solvency, reliability
sombra, shade, shadow
sombrero, hat
someter, submit
sometido, subject to
sonido, sound
sonreir, to smile
sonrisa, smile
sopa, soup
soportar, to endure, to support
soporte, support, bracket
soporte colgante, hanger
sorprendente, startling
sorpresa, surprise
sospecha, suspicion
sospechoso, suspect, suspicious
sostén, bra, maintenance
sostenedor, supporter
sostenimiento, maintenance
soviet, soviet
su, its, their
suavemente, mildly
subdivisión, subsection
subida, mounting, rising
subir, to arise, to go up
súbito, sudden
subjetivo, subjective
submarino, submarine
subsecuente, subsequent
subsidiario, subsidiary
substancia, substance
substancial, substantial
subterráneo, underground
subvención, subsidy
subyacente, underlying
suceder, to succeed, to follow
sucesión, sequence
sucesivo, successive
suceso, happening
sucesor, successor
sudar, to sweat
sudor, sweat
suegro, father-in-law
sueldo, salary
suelo, floor
suelto, loose

sueño, dream, sleep
suero, serum
suerte, fortune, luck
suficiente, satisfactory, sufficient
sufrir, to suffer
sugerir, to suggest
suicidio, suicide
suma, sum
sumario, summary
sumidero, sink, drain
sumo, utmost
superficial, superficial
superficie, surface
superintendente, superintendent
superior, super, superior, upper
superioridad, superiority
supervivencia, survival
suplemento, supplement
súplica, prayer, petition, request
supositorio, suppository
supremo, sovereign, supreme
supuesto, assumed, supposed
sur, south
suspensión, suspension
suspiro, sigh
sustituto, substitute
susurro, whisper
sutil, subtle

T

tabaco, tobacco
tabla, board, panel, tablet
tablazón, boards, decking
tacto, touch, sense of touch
tajada, slice, cut
tal, such
talco, powder, talcum
tal vez, perhaps
taladro, bore, drill
talento, talent
talla de la madera, wood carving
tallarín, noodle

taller, studio, workshop
tallo, stem
talón, heel
talón de equipaje, baggage check
talonario, checkbook
tamaño largo, king-size
también, also
tangerino, Tangerine
tanque, tank
tapa, cover
tapón, plug, tampon
tarde, evening, late
tarea, task, homework
tarifa, tariff
tarjeta de crédito, credit card
taxi, taxi
taxímetro, taxicab
taza, cup
te, thee, you
té, tea
teatralidad, theatrical
teatro, theatre
teatro de la ópera, opera house
techo, roof
técnica, technique
técnico, technical, technician, technique
tejido, fabric
teléfono, phone, telephone
telégrafo, telegraph
telegrama, telegram
televisión, television
tema, theme
temblor, trembling, earth tremor
temperamento, temperament
temperatura, temperature
tempestad, storm
templado, moderate
temple, temper
templo, temple
temporario, temporary
tenaza, tongs
tendón, tendon
tenencia, holding, tenancy

tener afición a, affect
tener la intención de, to intend
tenis, tennis, sneakers
tensión, strain, tension
tenso, tense
tentación, temptation
tentativo/a, tentative, attempt
teología, theology
teológico, theological
teorema, theorem
teorización, ideology
tercero, third
terciopelo, velvet
termal, thermal
terminación, completion
terminal, terminal
término, term, terminus
termómetro, thermometer
termo, thermos
ternera, veal
ternero, calf, calves
terraza, terrace
terrible, terrible
terriblemente, terribly
terrífico, terrific
terror, terror
tesis, thesis
tesoro, treasure, treasury
testamento, testament
testigo, witness
teta, breast
tétano, tetanus
textil, textile
texto, text
textura, texture
tía, aunt
tiempo, time, weather
tiempo de guerra, wartime
tienda, shop, tent
tienta, probe
tierno, tender
tierra, earth, ground, land, soil
tieso, stiff
tiesura, stiffness
tijeras, scissors
tímido, shy
tinta, ink

tinte, tint
tintura, dye, tincture
tío, uncle
típico, typical
tipo, type
tipo del cambio, exchange rate
tira, strip
tirantes, suspenders, straps
tirita, band-aid
tiro, team
tirón, pull
tisú, tissue
titulare, headline, official
título, heading, inscription, title
tiznar, to stain, to smudge
toalla, towel
toalla de baño, bath towel
tobillo, ankle
tocante a, regarding, touching
tocino, bacon
todavía, yet
todo, all, each, everything, whole
todos, everybody, everyone
tolerancia, tolerance
toma, take, taking
tomar, to take, to have, to get
tomar o pedir prestado, borrow
tomate, tomato
tomillo, thyme
tonelada, ton
tontería, folly
tonto, foolish, silly
toque, touch
torcedura, sprain
torcer, to bend or twist
torcido, bent, twisted
tornasolado, shot
tornillo, screw
toro, tore
torpe, awkward
torre, tower
torsión, twist
tortícolis, stiff neck
torvo, grim
toser, cough

tostada, toast
total, total
totalmente, totally, wholly
trabajado, elaborate, wrought
trabajar, to work
trabajo, labor, work
trabajoso, difficult
tractor, tractor
tradición, tradition
tradicional, traditional
traducción, translation
traducir, translate
traer, bring
tráfico, traffic
tragedia, tragedy
traje de baño, bathing suit
traje, costume
traje de noche, evening
    dress
trampa, trap
trancazo, flu
tranquilo, calm
transferencia, transfer
transformador, transformer
transfusión, blood transfusion,
    transfusion
transición, transition
transitorio, transient
transmisión, transmission
transportar, to transport
transporte, transport
transporte en hombros,
    carry
tranvía, streetcar, tram
trapacero, tricky
trasero, back, rear
traslado, displacement,
    remove
tratado, treaty
tratamiento, treatment
trato, bargain
trece, thirteen
treinta, thirty
tren, train
tren subterráneo, subway
tren suburbano, local train
trepa, climb
trepar, to climb

tres, three
treta, trick
tribal, tribal
tribu, tribe
tribunal, court, tribunal
tributar, to pay (as tribute or
    tax)
tributo, tribute
trigo, wheat
trío, trio
triple, treble, triple
triste, dreary, sad
triunfante, winning
triunfar, to triumph
triunfo, triumph
tronada, thunderstorm
tronco, stock, trunk
trono, throne
tropa, troop
trozo, bit, lump
trozo escogido, selection
trucha, trout
trueno, thunder
tu, thy, your
tú, yourself
tubo, pipe, tube
túnel, tunnel
turbar, disturb
turismo, sightseeing
turquesa, turquoise
TV en colores, color
    television

U

últimamente, lately
último, last, ultimate
un, a, an, some
único, single, unique
unidad, unit, unity
unidad de peso, weight
unido, united
uniforme, uniform
unión, merger, rally, union
universal, universal
universidad, university
universo, universe
uno, one

uno y otro, either
uña, nail
urbano, urban
urgente, urgent
urna, shrine
usado, used
usar, to use, to wear
uso, enjoyment, use, wear
usual, usual
usurpación, invasion
útero, womb
útil, useful, helpful
uva, grape

V

vaca, cow
vacación, vacation
vacante, vacant
vacilar, hesitate
vacío, empty, vacuum
vacunar, vaccinate
vago, vague
vaina, sheath
vainilla, vanilla
validez, validity
válido, valid
valiente, bold, brave
valioso, valuable
valle, valley
valor, courage, value, worth
valoración, valuation
vals, waltz
valuación, rating
valuar, to value, appraise, estimate
vapor, steam, vapor
vaporización, evaporation
vara, rod
variable, variable
variación, variation
variante, varying
variar, vary
vario, varied, various
varios, several
vasija, vessel
vaso, tumbler, glass
vasto, vast

vecindad, neighborhood
vecino, neighbor, neighboring
vegetación, vegetation
vegetariano, vegetarian
vehículo, vehicle
veinte, twenty
vejiga, bladder
vela, candle
veloz, swift
velozmente, swiftly
vena, vein
vencer, to overcome
venda, bandage
vendido, out of stock
vender, to sell
vendimia, vintage
veneno, poison
venidero, forthcoming
venir, to come
venta, sale
ventaja, advantage, odds
ventana, window
ventura, chance, happiness, venture
verbal, verbal
verbo, verb
verdad, truth
verdaderamente, truly
verdadero, true
verde, green
veredicto, verdict
vergüenza, shame
vermut, vermouth
versión, version
verso, verse
verter, to pour
vertical, vertical
vertiginoso, dizzy
vestíbulo, hall
vestido, dress, garment, gear
vestir, to dress
veterano, veteran
veterinario, veterinarian
vez, once
via, via
vía, way
viajar, to travel
viaje, tour, travel, trip

viaje de negocios, business trip
viaje por mar, voyage
viajero, tourist, traveller
vicario, vicar
vicio, vice
vicioso, abandoned
víctima, victim
victoria, victory
victoriano, Victorian
vida, life, lifetime, lives
vidrio, glass
viejo, aged, aging, old
viento, wind
viernes, Friday
viga, beam
vigésimo, twentieth
vigilante, awake
vigilar, to watch, keep guard
vigilia, watching
vigoroso, vigorous
villa, borough, villa
vinagre, vinegar
vino, wine
vino de Jerez, sherry
viña, vineyard
violencia, violence
violento, violent
virgen, virgin
virtudes, virtue
visibilidad, visibility
visible, visible
visión, sight
visita, visit
visitador, visitor
vista, vision
vista, seeing, view
visual, visual
vital, vital
viuda, widow
vivamente, quickly
vívido, vivid
viviente, living, alive
vivir, to live, to be alive

vivo, alive, live, lively, quick, smart
vocabulario, vocabulary
vocal, vocal
vocero, spokesman
volar, to fly, to fly away
volcado, upset
volcar, to upset, to overturn, to dump
voltaje, voltage
volumen, volume
vómito, vomit
votación, voting
votar, to vote
voto, vote
voz, report, voice
vuelo, flying, wing
vuelta, return, turn
vulgar, vulgar

W

whisky, whisky

Y

y, and
y hacia, unto
ya, already
yarda, yard
yate, yacht
yermo, waste
yeso, plaster
yo, I, myself

Z

zafir, sapphire
zanahoria, carrot
zapato, shoe
zarzamora, blackberry
zona, zone
zoología, zoology
zumo, juice
zurrón, wallet